PERFORMANCE DEGREE ZERO:
ROLAND BARTHES AND THEATRE

Throughout his career, famed critical theorist Roland Barthes (1915–1980) had a complex and often uneasy relationship with theatre and performance. From his early theatre criticism, through his abrupt and enigmatic silence on theatre, to the theoretical 'stagings' of his thought in the 1970s, Barthes committed several stunning reversals with his opinions on theatrical performance.

In *Performance Degree Zero*, Timothy Scheie argues that Barthes's body of work must be considered a lifelong engagement with theatre. Exploring his changing critical methodologies, Scheie provides a new understanding of the rapid shifts in critical modes Barthes traverses, from a Sartrean Marxism in the 1950s, through semiology, to French post-structuralism and the mournful introspection of his later years. The theatrical figure illuminates Barthes's accounts of the sign, the text, the body, homosexuality, love, the voice, photography, and other important and contested terms of his thought.

Performance Degree Zero offers the first comprehensive account of Barthes's enduring fascination with theatre and performance and fills a significant gap in Barthes criticism. It is essential reading for all Barthes scholars, theatre historians, and performance theorists.

TIMOTHY SCHEIE is an associate professor in the Eastman School of Music at the University of Rochester.

TIMOTHY SCHEIE

Performance Degree Zero

Roland Barthes and Theatre

UNIVERSITY OF TORONTO PRESS
Toronto Buffalo London

© University of Toronto Press 2006
Toronto Buffalo London
utorontopress.com

ISBN 978-0-8020-9071-3 (cloth)
ISBN 978-0-8020-9387-5 (paper)

Library and Archives Canada Cataloguing in Publication

Scheie, Timothy
    Performance degree zero : Roland Barthes and theatre / Timothy Scheie.

    Includes bibliographical references and index.
    ISBN-13: 978-0-8020-9071-3 (bound)
    ISBN-13: 978-8020-9387-5 (pbk.)
    ISBN-10: 0-8020-9071-0 (bound)
    ISBN-10: 0-8020-9387-6 (pbk.)

    1. Barthes, Roland – Criticism and interpretation.   2. Theater.   I. Title.

    PN1708.B37S34 2006   791   C2006-903789-2

University of Toronto Press acknowledges the financial assistance to
its publishing program of the Canada Council for the Arts and the
Ontario Arts Council.

University of Toronto Press acknowledges the financial support for
its publishing activities of the Government of Canada through the
Book Publishing Industry Development Program (BPIDP).

For Craig

Contents

Acknowledgments

I have been fascinated with theatre for as long as I can remember, and more than twenty years have passed since I first began exploring Barthes's work. These interests came together to inform part of my doctoral dissertation, and a few years ago they converged again as I began work on the present study. The long history of this book makes it impossible for me to thank individually all the friends, colleagues, students, professors, and others who showed me kindness, care, and support over the years; my gratitude is none the less heartfelt.

There are individuals and institutions whose support has been decisive. At the University of Wisconsin-Madison I had the privilege to work with some truly remarkable professors: Elaine Marks and Mary Lydon, both of whom are sorely missed; Peter Schofer; Jill Dolan; and especially Judy Miller, whose unfailing generosity as a mentor remains an inspiration to me. The Eastman School of Music, of the University of Rochester, has generously supported my research for this book, and I thank Dean Jim Undercofler for his interest in this project. I wrote much of the third chapter at Princeton University as a National Endowment for the Humanities Summer Fellow; I thank the NEH, seminar director Carolyn Abbate, and the participants for their helpful comments. I would like to recognize the support of the Susan B. Anthony Institute for Gender and Women's Studies for my research on sexuality in Barthes's writings. I thank the University of Toronto Press and my editor, Jill McConkey, with whom it has been a delight to work.

It would be impossible adequately to express my gratitude to my parents, Mary and Carl Scheie, for all they have done for me, but I would like to thank them here specifically for the time at their cabin near Rhinelander, Wisconsin, where I both began and finished this study. I also thank Jim Vesper and Gray Brown for the winter writing retreats in Provincetown, Massachusetts. Without these weeks of sustained work I would likely still be writing this book.

I would like to thank the Humanities Department at the Eastman School of Music for a harmonious and supportive environment in which to work; one could not ask for better colleagues. I am also grateful for the exceptional cohort of friends with whom I have weathered the trials of graduate school and the profession. Elise, Nancy, Cheryl, Loren, Dolly, Sarah, Rebecca, Kathy – what would I have done without you?

Finally, I thank Craig Sellers for his sharp editorial eye, and for the patience and love that sustain me in this and all my endeavours.

Abbreviations and Note on Translations

Throughout his writings Roland Barthes deploys terms with precise, idiosyncratic, ambiguous, and poetic usage that defies translation. Barthes's writings will therefore be cited in both French and English followed by a parenthetical reference to both sources. The first reference will be to the *Œuvres complètes*, vols. 1–3, ed. Eric Marty (Paris: Seuil, 1993–5), indicating the volume in Roman numerals followed by a page number. The second will refer to the published English translation using the abbreviations listed below. 'III 230; *RB* 177' therefore directs the reader to page 230 in the third volume of the *Œuvres complètes*, and to *Roland Barthes*, trans. Richard Howard (New York: Hill & Wang, 1977), page 177. Where a translation is not available I have provided my own, followed by a single reference to the *Œuvres complètes* edition.

CE	*Critical Essays*
CL	*Camera Lucida*
EmS	*Elements of Semiology*
EpS	*The Empire of Signs*
FS	*The Fashion System*
GV	*The Grain of the Voice*
IMT	*Image, Music, Text*
In	*Incidents*
L	*Inaugural Lecture* (in *A Barthes Reader*, 457–78)
LD	*A Lover's Discourse: Fragments*
M	*Mythologies*
OR	*On Racine*
PT	*The Pleasure of the Text*

PTA   'Pouvoirs de la tragédie antique' (in *Œuvres complètes* I, 216–23)
RB   *Roland Barthes by Roland Barthes*
RL   *The Rustle of Language*
SFL   *Sade, Fourier, Loyola*
SZ   *S/Z*
WDZ   *Writing Degree Zero*

PERFORMANCE DEGREE ZERO:
ROLAND BARTHES AND THEATRE

Introduction

Twenty-five years after his death, Roland Barthes's stature as a pre-eminent intellectual of our time remains indisputable. Barthes's critical eye, eloquent pen, and singular knack for stirring controversy have inspired generations of critics of literature, popular culture, music, and the visual arts. His succession of critical 'hits' continues to impress readers, his pithy aphorisms are still widely quoted, and recent reconsiderations of his life and work attest to his enduring appeal to a broad public.[1] Many of his writings have attained canonical status in their fields and continue to spark discussion and pointed response.[2]

Barthes is also a critic of theatre, but unlike the imposing profile he cuts in other disciplines, he is not generally known as an important theorist of theater and performance. Barthes's lifelong interest in Brecht frequently draws critical attention, but the greater part of his theatre criticism, written largely between 1953 and 1960, often remains little more than a *fait divers* in accounts of his life and work.[3] Barthes himself fuels the trend to overlook these writings. His brief tenure as a theatre critic ends abruptly and unceremoniously, and by the time the structuralist quarrel propels him to international intellectual stardom in the early 1960s he has already ceased to write about French theatre. He rarely mentions a specific moment of live performance again, and with the exception of a handful of remarks neglects to draw out the implications of his widely disseminated structuralist and post-structuralist thought for theatre practice in his contemporary France.[4]

The paucity of consideration given to Barthes's role as a theatre critic belies the extent to which theatre preoccupies him in his early career. Though only a select few of his articles on theatre appear in the 1964 anthology *Critical Essays*, in the years immediately following the 1953 publication of *Writing Degree Zero* Barthes's reviews and commentaries on theatre outnumber the short texts that eventually comprise the well-known *Mythologies*.[5] When read alongside *Writing Degree Zero* and *Mythologies*, Barthes's articles and reviews on theatre flesh out the profile of an ambitious and impassioned younger critic stridently staking out positions in a public forum. The early Barthes considers the stage a necessary and powerful force in French society that bourgeois taste and money have tamed to a flaccid ritual of classist self-congratulation. He emerges as an activist advocate of Jean Vilar's revived Théâtre National Populaire and as Brecht's most staunch defender against sceptical French critics. Barthes's criticism is bold, polemic, and at least for a few years deeply committed to realizing a new theatre in France.

Barthes's abrupt desertion of his theatre criticism in 1960 remains an enigma of his life and writings. He offers no explanation for his change of purview, and retrospectively puzzles over it himself.[6] The sudden silence on theatre practice per se is even more surprising when one considers the wealth of figurative theatres and performing bodies that proliferate throughout Barthes's subsequent writings. The later Barthes articulates his thoughts on texts, images, music, and other modes of representation through richly threaded theatrical and corporeal metaphors. Stunning theatre scenes illustrate his writing as it veers through its successive phases, and while considering his career with hindsight in 1975 he writes: 'Au carrefour de toute l'œuvre, peut-être le Théâtre: il n'y a aucun de ses textes, en fait, qui ne traite d'un certain théâtre' ('At the crossroads of the entire *œuvre*, perhaps the Theater: there is not a single one of his texts, in fact, which fails to deal with a certain theater') (III 230; *RB* 177). *Le corps*, the body, becomes an even more ubiquitous figure in his writing, and he eventually dubs it his 'mana' word: 'un mot dont la signification ardente, multiforme, insaisissable et comme sacrée, donne l'illusion que par ce mot on peut répondre à tout' ('a word whose ardent, complex, ineffable, and somehow sacred signification gives the illusion that by this word one might answer for everything') (III 194; *RB* 129).

If the theatrical and corporeal figures thrive throughout Barthes's writings, however, live performance practice clearly does not. Barthes's theatres and the performing bodies that inhabit them remain for the most part metaphorical after 1960. On the rare occasions when the later Barthes invokes a literal moment of theatre practice, he generally castigates it as a hopelessly 'ill' mode of signification, often defined in opposition to theoretical ideals he nonetheless articulates through the theatrical trope: the structural system, the text, love, and other cherished figures. *Le corps* likewise does not return as a live performing body. The 'charmed' figure of an author's body, a lover's body, his mother's body in *Camera Lucida,* even his own body as he invokes it in *Roland Barthes by Roland Barthes,* are inexorably absent bodies, written or photographed traces that inspire both pleasure and melancholy loss through their deferral in time and space.

For a consideration of Barthes as a theorist of theatre and performance, an interrogation of the evacuation of live performance practice from the theatres and bodies invoked throughout his writings promises to yield far more than a study of his early theatre criticism alone. Barthes consistently envisions corporealities from which he excludes the live performing body, and a specifically live performance repeatedly disappoints the theatricality he so often deploys as a privileged theoretical figure. Live performance practice is excessive in Barthes's later work, abstracted but not accounted for, relegated beyond the horizon of the inanimate, figurative, and textual theatres in which he casts his theoretical ideals. Performance, specifically the live performing body, acts as the repressed of Barthes's thought, shaping the critical terms of his successive 'phases' even as it is excluded from the theatrical figures through which he articulates them.

If the displacement of performance is a revealing interpretant of Barthes's entire *œuvre,* his writings, through their uneasy relation to performance, in turn raise a question of performance theory that takes on ever greater urgency in the age of technological reproduction, mediation, and the ascendancy of the virtual: what, if anything, distinguishes a live performance, specifically the live performing body, as a distinct mode of representation? Barthes's abstraction of live performance both participates in and illuminates, with singularly telling ambivalence, a pervasive reluctance – one might even say failure – of performance theory to resolve what is arguably its most fundamental question: the problem of the live performer's *presence.*

The Anxieties of Presence

It is often said that a performer has 'presence.' When asked what it means exactly, those who pay or receive this compliment might answer that presence is an aura-like magnetism that draws the spectator's attention and keeps it riveted to the body on stage. Others might describe the vivid sensation that *somebody's there,* live and immediate, threatening and vulnerable, standing before the spectator. Most, however, would be hard-pressed to say more precisely what constitutes this elusive quality, and they are not alone. Merely to recognize the phenomenon of presence is to wander into a thorny tangle of questions that theorists of performance have pondered for centuries. Is the performer's presence something 'real' that exists independently of the performance, or is it an effect of the performance itself? Does it well up from the depths of an interior self, psychology, or soul, or is it projected onto the body by external pressures, ideology, a historical/material situation, or an epistemological regime? Can more obviously mediated modes of representation also have presence, or is it the proper sphere of a specifically live performance? The question of presence raises practical considerations for theatre as well. How does the performing body's presence, even if only an illusion, aid or interfere with the aims of a performance? Should the performer seek to dispel or to exploit this presence?

In his 1810 essay on puppet theatre, Heinrich von Kleist frames the question of presence in a manner that continues to shape discussions nearly two hundred years later. The narrator's interlocutor, a well-known dancer, proposes the advantages the marionette holds over the live human body. Where the puppet skims the ground in an uninterrupted stream of motion, the human body must, after executing a movement, land in a moment of recovery or rest. Furthermore, the puppet's limbs obey only the laws of gravity, moving in pure geometric arcs free of the affect resulting from human consciousness: 'an admirable quality looked for in vain among the greater part of our dancers.'[7] The dancer also recounts an incident in which a young man innocently strikes a pose of classic beauty, but who upon acquiring an awareness of this insouciant grace can only offer comically degraded attempts to reproduce the pose whose beauty and naturalness thereafter elude him. Kleist's dancer effectively reverses the commonsensical notion that the puppet copies the human body when he concludes instead that the living body is the corrupt imitation of the marionette. The live performing body is inferior both physically, subject to the cumbersome laws of gravity, and also metaphysically as the material marker of a soul or interior subject that, having eaten of the tree of knowledge, visibly taints the ideal innocence with, in Kleist's words, the 'disorders of consciousness.' The performer's body is *animate* with all the etymological weight of the term, and bears the indelible stain of a *somebody* that a flesh-and-blood performer might strive to minimize but can never intentionally remove.

Kleist suffers from an exemplary case of *presence anxiety.* He is neither the first to endure this affliction – at least since Plato the performing body elicits suspicion and unease – nor is he the last. This condition, endemic among performance theorists, expresses itself in the symptomatic desire either to cleanse the performing body of the 'disorders of consciousness' or else to mute, conceal, deconstruct, or eliminate a living body altogether, even in an ostensible investigation of live performance itself. 'On the Marionette Theater' traces two well-trodden trajectories towards a cure for the anxieties of presence that many have followed: either towards a purified performing body unadulterated by cultural, linguistic, technological, and subjective mediation, or toward an ideal body *as* representation that in extreme cases entails the disappearance of all that distinguishes a live and present performer from an inanimate simulacrum.

Antonin Artaud is undoubtedly the emblematic champion of the performing body's pure and immediate 'life itself,' stripped of the rational subject's adulterating taint. Artaud's influence is incalculable, and he inspires celebrations of performance's raw *hic et nunc* that challenge mimetic theatre of the Aristotelian tradition and its suspect investment in normative logic and reason. However, it is the other path traced by Kleist that proves the most travelled in the last century, certainly in its closing decades. Artaud's contemporaries already indict appeals to pure presence as inadequate and naïve insofar as they perpetuate the myth of an unmediated 'real' body or interior state of being that obscures its implication in the contingencies of a historical moment (Brecht) or a signifying system (Prague School theatre semiotics). The advent of the corpus of theory and criticism commonly known as 'poststructuralist' intensifies the unease that treads on the heels of an invocation of performance's immediacy in the here and now. Difference, deferral, and lack become the buzzwords of the day, while presence draws incisive scrutiny as the figment of a moribund Western metaphysics. Deconstruction, notably Derrida's readings of Artaud in *Writing and Difference,* marks a decisive break that leaves in its wake enduring suspicion towards a 'real' body or a 'present' subject, both in performance and elsewhere.[8] To promote presence after deconstruction is to draw charges of being naïve, benighted, untheoretical, or even dangerous. Presence is decried as the mechanism by which an oppressive epistemology of the subject becomes naturalized and perpetuates its authority as the arbiter of identity. These worries inform, and are informed by, the rise of a performance art that interrogates the live performer's presence, and the urgent drive to situate both the performer's subject and body in a historical regime of power and signification is one of the defining tasks of this art form as it comes to prominence as an important cultural force.[9]

Two recent accounts of the 'live' vividly attest to the enduring usefulness of the opposing tacks traced in 'On the Marionette Theater' for mapping efforts to palliate the anxieties of presence. In *Unmarked: The Politics of Performance* Peggy Phelan examines works of photography, film, dramatic literature, and performance in which bodies resist the signs of gender and racial (among other) identity that circulate in the compromised signifying economy of the knowable, the sayable, and the visible.[10] Invoking Lacanian psychoanalysis and theorists such as Julia Kristeva, who posit a powerful if unattainable 'outside' and 'before' to the subject's symbolic representation, Phelan subtly theorizes an excessive 'unmarked' corporeality that unhinges the body from stigmatized categories of identity and reveals subjectivity as an ongoing process. In the words of Janelle Reinelt, the failure of representation fully to seize the living body leads 'to a radical skepticism about the presence or truth of any metaphysical claim within performance.'[11] Phelan locates a singular oppositional potential in live performance specifically: 'Performance implicates the real through the presence of living bodies.'[12] The task at hand is to discredit the meanings and subjectivities that circulate in a representational economy by making the 'unmarked' remainder palpable through a gesture of performance that copies no model and leaves no trace: a body that is not exhausted by a visible and familiar somebody, in Phelan's terms a 'representation without reproduction' that redeems some measure of corporeality from an oppressive epistemology of the subject.[13]

Following the opposing trajectory, Philip Auslander maintains that mediatized reproduction always already claims the performing body.[14] Invoking a Baudrillardian simulation that implodes the difference between an original and its copy, Auslander contends that performance is embedded in a representational economy so dominated by mass reproduction that the ontological specificity of the live as something outside the mediated collapses. Auslander cites performances that strip 'liveness' of primacy to reveal a deconstructed live/mediated binary: the live is a function of mediation (he suggests the very notion of the live emerges with the dawn of technological mediation) and the purportedly live and present body a simulacrum no more original than a reproduced image. Auslander sanctions no supplement, no 'unmarked' gesture of performance to which mediation has not laid hold, and he refutes Phelan's claims for performance's unique resistance to a signifying economy: 'the qualities performance theorists frequently cite to demonstrate that live performance forms are ontologically different from mediatized forms turn out, upon close examination, to provide little basis for convincing distinctions.'[15] Where Phelan identifies the live and present body's stubborn resistance to signification, subjugation, repetition, and commodification as the ontology of performance itself, Auslander divests the performing body's 'liveness' of such privilege; the live performance's purportedly unique presence persists as little more than a profitable myth for the entertainment industry.

Phelan and Auslander forge rare languages for acknowledging and discussing the fraught notions of presence and its index, the body's liveness. Their arguments complement each other and could be considered two sides of a single medallion, struck by Kleist, when they participate in a common drive to separate an uniterable body, purified of the meanings that lay hold of it, from a circulating and mediated body-assign; one champions the former, the other the latter. However, neither theorist is immune to the anxieties of presence that troubled Kleist. Like their predecessor, both recognize that the separation they are attempting to enforce is far from secure, at least in the present, and both envision or at least provide for a distinctly Kleistian evacuation of the live performing body itself as they articulate their theoretical ideals. Phelan privileges live performance, but she dilutes the favour she bestows on it when she more often locates the power of the unmarked in photography, video, and other distinctly 'unlive' media. Moreover, she explicitly valorizes the disappearance of the performer herself as a resistant strategy. The representations of women she cites – Cindy Sherman's prostheses, Lorna Simpson's faceless photograph, Adrian Piper's distanced and disembodied face on a video monitor, performance artist Angelika Festa's wrapped and blindfolded body – obscure the body as much as they reveal its startling irreproducibility, and arguably tend more towards the body's retreat into artifice and mediation than a manifestation of the live and present performer's 'distinctive oppositional edge.'[16] As Sue-Ellen Case observes, Phelan's 'evacuation of the body as figuring "natural" or metaphysical presence could be seen as preparing the way for the virtual, where the body itself would no longer exist and the relation between subject and body would be divided by virtue of the medium.'[17] From this perspective, the 'unmarked' is not as opposed to Auslander's hyperreal simulacrum as it might appear.[18] For his part, Auslander more directly challenges 'live performance' as an ontologically privileged mode of representation, even as a distinct mode at all, but like Phelan he, too, expresses a familiar symptom of presence anxiety when he cites performances that incorporate elaborate technological mediation – rock concerts, baseball games with large-screen simulcasts, Laurie Anderson's manipulation of voice amplification and recording devices – and that arguably less enact the deconstruction of liveness than displace it to an 'unmarked' blind field in his own theoretical discourse. He leaves room for one to doubt, for example, to what extent the implosion of the live/mediated distinction he observes in *MTV Unplugged* characterizes an evening of live music in an intimate cabaret, or if the experience of watching a game or concert from the upper deck of a stadium, where the attributes of performers' and players' bodies are all but indistinguishable without the aid of the screen, is at all commensurate with a technologically bare performance in a small theatre. Responding to this vein of critique, Auslander explains that mediatization does not impact all performances 'in the same way or to the same degree,' a rebuttal whose telling ambiguity both affirms the far reach of mediating technologies and concedes differences of manner and scale that, despite forceful arguments to the contrary, would continue to distinguish live performance among modes of representation.[19]

The chronic failure of the live performing body to exhaust itself in a theoretical ideal and the subsequent efforts to obscure, displace, or disclaim it are evinced more broadly in the tensions that arise between specifically theatrical acts and a more general understanding of performance that emerges as a fluid notion of wide interdisciplinary appeal. An explosion of thought and scholarship on performance, performative acts, and 'performativity' has brought theatrical imagery to the study of anthropology, sociology, linguistics, and cultural studies (among other disciplines). Marvin Carlson observes: 'with performance as a kind of critical wedge, the metaphor of theatricality has moved out of the arts and into almost every aspect of modern attempts to understand our condition and activities, and into almost every branch of the human sciences.'[20] However, when the reach of performance extends so wide that it encompasses nearly all aspects of human behaviour and interaction, it is often difficult to locate specifically theatrical acts under its broad umbrella and the status of non-metaphorical theatres is unsure. Phelan and Auslander maintain ties to a certain theatricality by addressing the relation between a performer and a spectator. Many accounts of performance do not bear so directly on theatrical acts, and others overtly discredit and even disavow acts of a more theatrical nature. In some cases performance appears to be defined in opposition to acts recognizable as theatrical, which are paradoxically marginalized under the broad empire of this term.

Consider, for example, one of the most influential invocations of performance in recent years. In her theorization of performativity and performative acts of identity's constitution, Judith Butler contends that identity such as gender is neither natural nor wilful, but develops through a sedimentation in the body of 'a stylized repetition of acts.'[21] This does not mean that one is free to perform otherwise. A watchful and oppressive epistemological regime enforces 'correct' behaviour and punishes aberrant performances, and Butler provides for no subjective agent who exists before or outside the stylized acts, no 'doer behind the deed' or performer before the performance itself. The powerful appeal of the performative lies precisely in its uprooting of identity from any authoritative alibi of interiority, nature, or inevitability, and in the potential for disruption that follows from the inexorable difference of every repetition, which no matter how obedient always holds the potential of going awry. The repeat performances that generate identity also attest to the failure of this same identity's claim to stability, and each new act participates in an ongoing trial of the subject whose outcome is never definitive.

Butler deploys a wealth of theatrical imagery to articulate the performativity of identity, but she is less welcoming of theatrical or dramatic performance as practice: 'In the theatre, one can say "this is just an act," and de-realize the act, make acting into something that is quite distinct from what is real. Because of this distinction, one can maintain one's sense of reality in the face of temporary challenge to our existing ontological assumptions about gender arrangements; the various conventions which announce that "this is only a play" allow strict lines to be drawn between the performance and life.'[22] A theatrical performance in which a performer plays a dramatic role does not accurately illustrate the more radical reach of Butler's performative identity, for the theatrical act safeguards a space and a performing subject (the actor) beyond the drama, outside the theatre, that are not clearly implicated in the gesture of performance. Butler's oft-cited remark that 'drag implicitly reveals the imitative structure of gender itself – as well as its contingency'[23] has sparked hopeful claims by some theorists and practitioners of theatre who fail to heed Butler's caveat about theatrical acts, prompting Butler explicitly to refute the facile assertion that cross-dressing 'deconstructs' gender and to reiterate her suspicion of dramatic performance as a promising site of subversive acts.[24] Butler aligns anxieties over the 'disorders of consciousness' with a suspect theatrical performance that fails as a performative gesture, and one can observe an 'almost phobic disinterest in theatre history and dramatic art' in her thought.[25] Though articulated through theatrical figures, Butler's performativity does not embrace non-metaphorical theatre practice.

A recent reconsideration of the meaning of 'theatricality' in the age of performance's ubiquity would justify the misgivings towards live theatre practice of Kleist, Butler, and many other theorists, including, as we shall see, Roland Barthes. Josette Féral defines theatricality as a process, not an attribute, and one that demands a conscious act of circumscription by the spectator, the performer, or in many cases both. The theatrical act results from the 'affirmed theatrical intention' of an actor who must 'consciously occupy the here-and-now of a space different from the quotidian,' while a spectator similarly 'selects' theatrical acts and 'of his own initiative transforms the other into a spectacular object.'[26] In this assessment, the disorders of consciousness Kleist observes therefore not only adulterate the body engaged in a theatrical act; they constitute it. Féral fuels the suspicions of those who find it desirable, some would argue necessary, to locate performance in a post-presence, post-live, or post-theatrical ideal.

A startling paradox subtends the drive to abate the worries that attend a specifically live performing body: when the ideal performance demands the live and present body's purification or disappearance as a meaningful or recognizable entity, when a theoretical performance must abstract a specifically live performing body, it is where the ideal fails and unresolved tensions teem that the singularity of live performance resides. Kleist already observes this conundrum. Although he traces two well-travelled paths towards the elimination of the anxieties of presence on which one might plot the arguments of many who follow, he also concedes that for a performer prelapsarian innocence is no more attainable than inanimate grace; pure presence and pure absence both remain out of live theatre's reach. The dancer's ideals inexorably fail as ontologies of live performance practice, a failure that in Kleist's case represents nothing less than the tragedy of human existence. The readers of 'On the Marionette Theatre' who seek an account of the live performing body must consequently avert their eyes from the dancer's ideals to consider instead their failure in practice. If there is an 'essence' of live performance it lies not in any theoretical redemption from the anxieties of presence, but in their persistence as a question and a tension that defy resolution.

One must ask, therefore, if it is the performing body that falls short of the theoretical ideal, or if it is the ideal that fails to account for something (or some body) that lends live performance its power both to unsettle and to appeal. Surveying the limits of theoretical accounts of performance, Jill Dolan, a critic with unimpeachable credentials as a demystifier of naturalized readings of the performing body, wonders if live performance opens a breach in theory where both worries and desire churn.[27] Dolan most often ponders the dangers of presence and reveals its ideological investments, but shadowing her arguments is the palpable realization that something eludes a too tidy deconstruction, something fraught and neglected that demands to be revisited. She avows her complicity in the drive to tame 'presence' with a theory that denies live performance its most disquieting and seductive property: 'This painful, pleasurable, and mostly unarticulated desire came to be replaced over the years in my writing about theatre by a passionate theorizing that fed me instead.'[28] Such theorizing cleanses performance not only of the suspect alibis that demand critical vigilance, but of a powerful excess as well, 'physically, materially embodied circumstances' that outstrip post-structuralist metaphors of performance and performativity.[29]

In the study that follows I explore what is lost in the drive to tame, harness, or explain away the tensions that attend a specifically live performance. Roland Barthes's lifelong ambivalence towards theatre and performance practice provides a singularly rich and subtle site for approaching the live performing body as a conundrum whose interest lies not in any future theoretical resolution, but in its stubborn, anxious, and fascinating persistence in the present. Barthes's writings illuminate, with an uneasy and oblique light, the live and present body's paradoxical status as both the bête noire and raison d'être of performance, both its most anxious question and its specificity among systems of representation, a question so fundamental for performance theory and practice that its resolution entails the disappearance of live performance itself. To be clear, the performer's presence remains a *problem*, and the worries of Barthes and other critics, past and present, amply reveal all that is at stake in the discussion. This investigation draws urgency from the concerns of those who condemn presence as the index of a mythic subjective autonomy, a selfhood that lays claim to stability outside the contingencies of performance in the naturalized truths of a patriarchal, racist, homophobic, and otherwise oppressive epistemological regime. However, in responding to these concerns I do not venture a new account that more neatly eliminates or explains away the troubling presence of performance in a theoretical ideal, nor do I seek to clear the tensions by illuminating the phenomenon with the knowing beam of, for example, fresh philosophical or psychoanalytical terms. Instead I propose to examine the performer's presence as a restless provocation, as a question, not a reassuring answer. The goal of this enquiry is to divine the contours of this problem and raise the questions that seethe within, in all their vexed contradictions, without imagining a future where these knotted questions neatly untangle. The live performer's presence lies in the inexorable failure of an ideal, which in Barthes's case is the failure of theoretical discourse, and it thereby remains a fundamentally, even constitutively unresolved question for performance theory and practice.

The project undertaken in this study, like Barthes's own engagement with performance, is therefore an uneasy endeavour. Herbert Blau describes the nature of the discomfort such an approach will need to tolerate:

> Something is there that can't be formed, or remain unmediated. Whatever we have our actors do nowadays, there is always the memory of the actor's playing a character. Then we remember that there is somebody playing the actor playing the character, and we are caught up in that cycle of performance, or the awareness of it, where the character is really the actor playing that character; and as you reflect further upon the process the concept of character is parsed into concepts of person actor role being and presence (only the words identifying the nuances) playing off each other in various degrees and inflections as in a tonal system, behavior returning to its source, the ubiquitous and slippery thing itself.[30]

To allow the 'slippery thing' into one's analysis, even only as a problem, is to concede that here, on the near side of a perhaps not very imminent epistemological break, the pursuit of a theoretical account of live performance remains an unsettled project, tragic even, and doomed to fail. However, this theoretical failure sparks fascination and desire alongside acute anxieties. Through an unwillingness – or a failure – to accommodate performance within a theoretical discourse, Barthes offers the compelling suggestion that it is in blind fields and unanswered questions, more than in any ideal, safe, or tidily elegant account, that we might find the most vivid reflection on the intricate powers, dangers, discomfort, worries and pleasures of the live performing body.

On Barthesology

Writing on Roland Barthes with regard to any topic is a fraught endeavour. Barthes's oeuvre is a mosaic of terms, thoughts, and figures, often borrowed from his interlocutors of a given moment, that when considered in its entirety produces neither a clear profile of the man who produced it nor the shape of his thought. An unstable theoretical terrain and a willingness to tolerate competing and even contradictory discourses are perhaps the hallmarks of Barthes's writing, and it is while overlapping discourses intertwine that he arguably produces his most provocative essays on literature, culture, art, as well as theatre and performance. His books often seem less works of criticism than virtuoso performances of a writer weaving a text, and his idiosyncratic methods appear to exhaust themselves in the studies they generate. Who would wish to read, let alone write, another round of *Mythologies*, parse another text as in *S/Z*, or write another fragmented biography following the model of *Roland Barthes by Roland Barthes*? Certainly not Barthes himself: by the time one of his texts appears in print he himself has usually veered in a new theoretical direction on the zigzag trajectory of his career.[31] Even those who deeply admire his work wonder if there is such a thing as a Barthesian approach, Barthesian theory, or a Barthes school of criticism. Exactly what constitutes Barthes's legacy and whether it is commensurate with the star status he enjoyed during his lifetime remain open for debate.[32]

When invoking 'Barthesian' writing, thought, or theory on any topic, circumspect critics must identify of which Barthes they are speaking, and there are many. The name Barthes evokes both the committed defender of Sartre and Brecht and an irreverent pleasure seeker who 'shows his derrière' to the political father, both a rigorous semiologist who subordinates all representation to the written word and an influential theorist of photography as that which exceeds language, both the murderer of the author and an introspective autobiographer who restitutes the individual as an important figure. One can imagine a 'vulgar' Barthes criticism that fetishizes one of these voices to distil a theory, science, method, or political stance where Barthes carefully avoids such totalizing gestures. Another methodological pitfall would be to produce reverent pastiches that do little justice to Barthes's elegant and idiosyncratic style, which like his thought evolves markedly throughout his career. In both cases, an imaginary Barthes emerges who is more consistent than his oeuvre would warrant.

By his own account, Barthes, at least in his later years, would have been pleased with the predicament he presents to those who ponder his legacy. A studied predilection for fragmentation is one of the rare consistencies in his writing, and even in his earlier book-length works, already for the most part composed of short anthologized essays, it is not clear that the text coalesces into a discrete and consistent whole.[33] The later Barthes embraces a more radical fragmentation as his preferred mode of writing, and deliberately cultivates an impression of himself, and of his work, that eludes the 'monster of totality.' In 1971 he expresses his wishes for posthumous criticism:

> si j'étais écrivain, et mort, comme j'aimerais que ma vie se réduisît, par les soins d'un biographe amical et désinvolte, à quelques détails, à quelques goûts, à quelques inflexions, disons: des 'biographèmes,' dont la distinction et la mobilité pourraient voyager hors de tout destin et venir toucher, à la façon des atomes épicuriens, quelque corps futur, promis à la même dispersion.

> (were I a writer, and dead, how I would love it if my life, through the pains of some friendly and detached biographer, were to reduce itself to a few details, a few preferences, a few inflections, let us say: to 'biographemes' whose distinction and mobility might go beyond any fate and come to touch, like Epicurean atoms, some future body, destined to the same dispersion.) (II 1045; *SFL* 9)

He writes this biography himself a few years later, and the shattered text of *Roland Barthes by Roland Barthes* resists the imaginary unity of 'Roland Barthes' as either text or author.

Barthes considers his refusal to produce a static or clear image of himself or his thought neither a negative nor a sterile gesture, but a generative one. In a critique of his own notion of an ideal 'zero degree,' he writes in 1973: 'certains veulent un texte (un art, une peinture) sans ombre, coupé de l'"idéologie dominante"; mais c'est vouloir un texte sans fécondité, sans productivité, un texte stérile' ('there are those who want a text (an art, a painting) without a shadow, without the "dominant ideology"; but that is to want a text without fecundity, without productivity, a sterile text') (II 1510; *PT* 32). The ample commentary on Barthes that issues from scholarly journals and university presses leaves little doubt that Barthes's texts, and Barthes himself as a text, cast a long and productive shadow. It is the shape of this shadow, and what it obscures from knowing illumination, that fuels debate and poses the most difficult question for Barthes criticism today.

Barthes often invokes Vico's spiral to conceptualize the trajectory of his career: it comes around to the same place time and again, but always differently, resituated in the preoccupations and intertexts of another theoretical plane. The spiral provides a useful figure for understanding the departure and return of theatres and bodies in Barthes's work, from his earliest published writings until his death in 1980. The chapters that follow are organized according to crucial theoretical episodes, or turns of the spiral. The length of these returns varies considerably, from more than a decade to little more than a year. There is some overlap, but the order will follow generally the chronology of Barthes's career.

Only in his earliest published writings, the first turn of the spiral, does Barthes address at any length theatre as a social practice and an institution, and *le corps* as a living, present performer standing before a spectator. The first chapter of the present study, 'Tragic Utopia: Barthes's Theatre Criticism, 1953–1960,' includes a detailed account of Barthes's career as theatre reviewer and critic, an episode unfamiliar to many readers and whose terms are crucial for an investigation of Barthes as a theorist of performance. Barthes's early activism, his Marxist and Sartrean rhetoric, his advocacy of Jean Vilar and a popular theatre, his epiphanic discovery of Brecht, and the rise of Saussurean semiology culminate in the abrupt and enigmatic end of his theatre criticism. As I survey the course of Barthes's theatre criticism, I critically revise the prevalent assumptions about Barthes's sudden silence on theatre, observing that figurative theatres and rich tropes of theatricality continue to proliferate throughout his later writings. The body, *le corps*, similarly re-emerges as a key figure in his later thought. It is neither theatre nor the body, but live performance practice, specifically a live performing body, that Barthes banishes from his writing after 1960.

In each of the remaining chapters I examine how the withdrawal of the live and present performing body leaves its imprint on Barthes's later thought, shaping it, inflecting it, and tracing the boundaries of other exclusions and silences enforced in his writings. In chapter 2, 'Performance and Its Double: The "Live" and the Structuralist Abstraction,' I articulate the relation between Barthes's unease with the performing body's presence and theatre's abrupt disappearance as he enters the 'scientific delirium' of structuralism and semiology that draws him international fame. In Barthes's many discussions of performing bodies in the 1950s, I identify and track the neatly intelligible body's fascinating double, whose 'secret,' 'tender,' and 'lovable' shadow haunts the more prevalent theorization of signification in *Writing Degree Zero*, in *Mythologies*, and most assiduously in his writings on theatre. The apparent tension between the legacies of Artaud and theatre semiotics, an opposition that begs deconstructive pressure, serves as a useful lens for considering the cohabitation of these two seemingly incompatible corporealities. The rise of Barthes's subscription to a linguistics-based semiology lowers his tolerance for the disruptive apparitions of the body's elusive 'double.' As Barthes embarks on his 'high structuralist' project of the early 1960s, the 'tender and lovable' body and its privileged precinct, live theatre, quickly disappear, along with overt political commitment and the individual subject's agency. I propose that Barthes's structuralist project demands the disappearance of the live performing body, but the gesture that banishes this figure of anxiety and fascination from the bodiless abstractions of *On Racine*, *Elements of Semiology*, and *The Fashion System* cuts in two directions: the displacement of live performance practice from Barthes's theatrical figures preserves a realm of excess and desire beyond his theoretical discourse that will eventually defeat the totalizing and impersonal imperatives of structural analysis.

In chapter 3, 'Staging Theory: Theatricality and the Displacement of Desire,' the imbrication of Barthes's tacit homosexuality and his renewed invocation of theatre illuminates a critical moment of transition in his thought between 1969 and 1971. Competing readings of Artaud by two of Barthes's interlocutors, Jacques Derrida and Julia Kristeva, reveal the unsettled parameters of the theatre that reclaims a place of importance in stunning theoretical 'stagings,' including the performance of the castrato in *S/Z* and Japanese Bunraku in *Empire of Signs*. The ideal theoretical theatre nonetheless continues to demand the displacement of the live performing body and its attendant anxieties. In these same works, Barthes also begins to articulate an eroticized textuality that 'cruises' the reader. Desirable and desiring bodies, either figured in the text or the reader's own body, emerge as the motors of textual pleasure. The account of textual pleasure also emerges through the abstraction of a body, this time Barthes's own, along with the desires he notoriously shelters from the reader's prying eyes. After surveying both favourable and sharply critical accounts of Barthes's discreet homosexuality, I examine how Barthes safeguards his perquisite of discretion by deftly dodging the performing body and its inexorable claim on the spectator's desire, a claim Barthes observes in other spectators but from which he exempts himself by refusing to take a seat in a theatre that has not first been cleansed of the performing body's unsettling presence. Again, however, the displacement of a live and present body fills a salutary function as well: Barthes's silence also traces the limits of the stereotype, the name, and the 'violence' of language and knowledge that otherwise would exhaustively seize his own sexuality with oppressive and pleasureless terms.

In the final years of his life, Barthes more openly reflects on the body's presence and absence, its life and death, in terms of resistance to language, signification, and his own theorizing gestures. In chapter 4, 'Mourning Presence: Performance at the Crossroads,' I consider Barthes's yearning in *Roland Barthes by Roland Barthes, A Lover's Discourse: Fragments,* and *Camera Lucida* for a live and present corporeality that defeats the closure of representation. Sexuality, love, and most importantly photography, again articulated through metaphors of theatricality, enable Barthes to apprehend a certain 'presence' in his later years, though it is far from the collective 'celebration of the human body' he calls for as a theatre critic in the 1950s. At times he appears to find his ideal body: the transport of fulfilled love in the presence of the beloved, for example, or the unexpected apprehension of his mother's unique being in a photograph. However, these moments are exceptional, and Barthes cannot forget that a stultified language inexorably steals away the live and present body, leaving him awash in longing and grief. I locate the body, specifically a live and present body, at the heart of his profound ambivalence. In his final years the body's elusive double that shadows his earlier work takes a spectral shape, neither living nor dead, neither present nor past, whose apparitions testify to the inability of language and representation – and theory – to account for it other than from the bereft shore of its absence.

As both the utopia and tragedy of representation, as the site of both fascination and anxiety, performance constitutes a theoretical impasse for Barthes. Barthes's failure to reconcile live performance with theoretical discourse potentially dampens the optimistic claims of theorists who invoke an unmarked 'presence' to resist the oppressive strictures of representation, as well as those who too neatly dismiss this notion in a deconstructive gesture. Barthes neither champions presence, nor does he liberate his reader from this thorny conundrum. The richness of Barthes's articulation of this impasse throughout his entire career nonetheless forbids us to dismiss it as a failure. Its prize lies in a euphoric, more often vexed, sometimes moving, and singularly complex exploration of a specifically live performing body that neither disappears nor deconstructs, but persists *in the present* as a constitutive question of performance theory.

1 Tragic Utopia: Barthes's Theatre Criticism, 1953–1960

In the opening pages of *Roland Barthes by Roland Barthes*, a photograph shows the author as a university student, masked and playing in a Greek tragedy in the courtyard of the Sorbonne. The caption reads:

> Darios, que je jouais toujours avec le plus grand trac, avait deux longues tirades dans lesquelles je risquais sans cesse de m'embrouiller: j'étais fasciné par la tentation de *penser à autre chose*. Par les petits trous du masque, je ne pouvais rien voir, sinon très loin, très haut: pendant que je débitais les prophètes du roi mort, mon regard se posait sur des objets inertes et libres, une fenêtre, un encorbellement, un coin du ciel: eux, au moins, n'avaient pas peur. Je m'en voulais de m'être laissé prendre dans ce piège inconfortable – tandis que ma voix continuait son débit égal, rétive aux *expressions* que j'aurais dû lui donner.

> (Darius, a part that had always given me terrible stage fright, had two long declamations in which I was likely to forget my lines: I was fascinated by the temptation of *thinking about something else*. Through the tiny holes of the mask, I could see only very high up, and very far away; while I delivered the dead king's prophecies, my eyes came to rest on inert – free – objects and books, a window, a cornice, a piece of the sky: they, at least, weren't afraid. I excoriated myself for getting caught in this uncomfortable trap – while my voice continued its smooth delivery, resisting the *expressions* I should have given it.) (III 117; *RB* 33)

As the distracted young actor teeters on the brink of disrupting the performance, the viability of the character, the drama's narrative, and theatrical illusion hangs in the balance. More broadly, literature, the 'great' Western cultural tradition, subjectivity, language, and meaning itself all have a stake in his ability to execute his role. The prospect of abdicating such weighty responsibility terrifies and fascinates the young Barthes, who both longs to reject his assigned role and worries over the consequences of this transgressive gesture. The latter appears to be the stronger impulse as the reluctant performer ultimately upholds the mask and utters the scripted speech, yet he does not perform well and his voice fails adequately to convey the character's interior thoughts and emotions. Barthes both resists and is complicit in a performance he finds oppressive. He chafes in this ambivalent role, caught in the anxious 'trap' of theatre.

It is not difficult to imagine why this photograph figures among the images in the prefatory section of Barthes's idiosyncratic and fragmented autobiography. Readers familiar with Barthes will recognize familiar topoi to which he returns time and again, not only in *Roland Barthes by Roland Barthes* but throughout his long and prolific career: a reluctant subject constrained to 'be' in a particular way; a desiring body palpable beneath an ideological mask; language and voice severed from their expressive function; and, finally, a utopian dream of liberation from this predicament forever deferred by the inability – or unwillingness – to remove the imposed masks of meaning and subjectivity, usually figurative but in the Sorbonne performance very literal.[1]

The Darius image raises many of the most urgent questions of performance theory and practice, and invites a reconsideration of *Roland Barthes by Roland Barthes* specifically in terms of theatre and performance. What are the ideological and historical constraints that shape a performance? To what extent can one distinguish between performer, performed identity, and the gesture of performance itself? How does the live, desiring body of the performer inflect the performance? What freedom does one have to perform differently, within the traditions of theatre or without, and what is the punitive price of such a gesture? When is a performance a liberating gesture and when is it a 'trap'? Is one necessarily a victim of this trap, or can one negotiate it in strategic ways? The enticing suggestion of a resistant performance practice that reveals and possibly subverts the exigencies of the prevailing system resonates strongly with the goals of many theorists and performers, past and present. If the compulsory masks or roles so precariously upheld are those of race, gender, nationality, or class, for example, a performer who wilfully performs a role poorly and makes the strategically flawed nature of the performance palpable to the spectator, even while submitting to the strictures of an 'obedient' performance, stakes out a promising site for cultural critique.

Barthes's later writings will disappoint a hopeful reader who seeks a sustained discussion of theatre and performance, let alone the blueprint for a resistant performance practice. The Darius photograph might contribute to the autobiographical element in *Roland Barthes* by reminding the reader of Barthes's own involvement in the theatre as a co-organizer and actor in the Groupe de Théâtre Antique de la Sorbonne, and later as a vocal theatre critic in the 1950s, but it also marks one of only a handful of references to a specific moment of performance practice in his later years. After the advent of what he dubs the structuralist 'delirium' of the early 1960s, Barthes turns away from theatre to examine literary texts, photography, music, painting, fashion – seemingly anything but live performance. Despite its potential to provoke thought on the nature of performance, the most remarkable aspect of the Darius photograph is arguably that at this point in his career Barthes is addressing performance practice at all.

Barthes's theatre criticism in the 1950s, prolific and strident, stands as an exception to the ambivalent and most often absent discussion of performance practice in the rest of his work. These numerous articles constitute the only commentary on live performance he sustains at any length, and they betray an activist tone that might surprise those more familiar with the later Barthes, who generally eschews militancy as 'hysterical.' The zeal quickly fades, however, and his career as a theatre critic ends abruptly and unceremoniously, with no explanation, after a brief period of seven years. The few commentaries and criticism of his early work that venture explanations for his sudden distaste for theatre yield more questions than answers, and Barthes himself offers only a few inconclusive retrospective comments. It is illuminating, and perhaps necessary, to open a consideration of Barthes and performance with a critical survey of the writings in which he addresses theatre explicitly, to situate these alongside his other projects of the moment, and to ask why, after seven years of passionate and public advocacy for a new French theatre, he abandons the French stage.

The Zero Degree of Performance

Many of Barthes's earliest published writings are collected in *Writing Degree Zero*, a slim volume of essays written between 1947 and 1953, before he becomes an active theatre critic. Very broadly, these essays offer a subtle investigation of the place of both writer and literature in a specific historical moment, namely, post-war France, and map the possibilities, or lack thereof, that writing affords for political commitment. Despite their brevity, the abstract language and fragmented presentation of these short articles thwart a concise summary of their arguments. Even at this early stage Barthes is something of a theoretical tinkerer, pulling notions from different bodies of work and weaving them into his text. The desire to distil a tidy thesis is further confounded by the ambivalence that suffuses Barthes's negotiation of Marxist and existentialist rhetoric in texts that already betray a keen fascination with how things signify, often at the expense of what is signified. An exhaustive examination of Barthes's discriminating and often idiosyncratic appropriation of different strains of thought in *Writing Degree Zero*, Marxist or otherwise – the sometimes explicit, often faint resonances with or against Trotsky, Lukàcs, Benjamin, Bataille, Merleau-Ponty, Blanchot, Saussure, and (inescapable in 1950s France) Sartre, among others – would be lengthy and in many instances speculative.[2] Barthes rarely acknowledges the critical writings he selectively and incompletely digests, and he shows a surprising tolerance for competing and even contradictory discourses in his writing. The following overview of his first book is intended only as a brief propaedeutic to situate the place of theatre in this early moment of his career.

Writing Degree Zero establishes the relation of literary writing to the rise of capitalism and the ascendancy of the bourgeoisie, and its scope is limited to the modern period. For Barthes as for many others, the revolutionary events that rocked Europe in 1848 mark a watershed, a rupture that not only discredits the self-evidence of capitalism but throws the innocence of literature itself into question as well. This new self-consciousness is absent in the earlier Balzac, whose seemingly untroubled deployment of an accepted literary language remains viable only as long as the bourgeois class dominates the social, political, and cultural realms – including the literary – so completely as to be invisible. For Barthes's Balzac, the bourgeois discourse of literature is not a choice but a necessity, an apparently 'natural' order of language. Such insouciance distinguishes Balzac from the 'pangs of conscience' Barthes senses in the later Flaubert, who finds no apparently neutral mode of writing within the French language. After 1848, bourgeois literary language is no longer self-evident and other modes of writing compete with it. Conscious of the plurality of modes of writing, or *écriture*, and of the literary itself as a uniquely privileged and compromised mode of writing, Flaubert inaugurates the modernist experiment, an ongoing trial of literature that persists to the present day and, one might add, paradoxically enriches and further enshrines the mythic institution of the literary even while revealing its ideological investment. The only escape Barthes proposes is to destroy literature altogether, to pare the conventions of the literary down to their zero degree, to strip away the signs of literature to reach the pure *literality* of a 'white writing' with no literary shadow. Barthes counts Albert Camus, Jean Cayrol, and a few years later Alain Robbe-Grillet among the few authors who flirt with this ideal, but even then he cautions that the zero degree remains a utopia, a virtually unattainable horizon that, as with all horizons, will forever recede into the distance: 'Malheureusement rien n'est plus infidèle qu'une écriture blanche' ('Unfortunately, nothing is more fickle than a colourless writing') (I 180; *WDZ* 78). Camus's neutral language, for example, quickly becomes a set of conventions in its own right, and Barthes accurately foresees the recuperation of *The Outsider*, an apparent example of anti-literature, as a work that will soon prominently figure in the canon of twentieth-century literary masterpieces.

Writing Degree Zero betrays Barthes's uneasy relationship with both Marxist and existentialist approaches to literature, even as he names both Marx and Sartre key influences on his early writings. When Barthes examines literary writing in terms of the material relations of a society, a gesture typical of Marxist critiques, he integrates these concerns into a critical consideration of literary form that challenges the French Communist Party's line on artistic creation. More orthodox communist writers and critics of the 1950s frown on a preoccupation with literary language at the expense of what it represents, denouncing it as an apology for bellettristic aestheticism, formalism, or the justification of a 'decadent' avant-garde. The French Communist Party of the 1950s endorses writers who embrace a conventional realist narrative, clear, familiar, and readable, to depict a society riven by class conflict. Barthes, on the other hand, historicizes all literary convention, not only experimental or avant-garde writing but also a realism that lends writing the appearance of neutrality and clarity. The recurring butt of Barthes's critique is precisely French socialist realism, which lacks a self-conscious implication of its mode of writing in material history and therefore draws a particularly barbed commentary: 'Aussi les écrivains communistes sont-ils les seuls à soutenir imperturbablement une écriture bourgeoise que les écrivains bourgeois, eux, ont condamnée depuis longtemps' ('communist writers are the only ones who go on imperturbably keeping alive a bourgeois writing which bourgeois writers have themselves condemned long ago') (I 177; *WDZ* 73). Barthes prefers a modernist novelist who knowingly 'puts on' a mode of writing that will permit certain kinds of expression and preclude others, though he is quick to caution that all modernist literature, whether prose or poetry, no matter what the content or the radical nature of the chosen *écriture*, is in the present at least to some extent complicit in a bourgeois notion of the quasi-sacred literary.

What room remains for political commitment if the material relations of a historical moment compromise the writer's freedom of expression and imminent recuperation awaits a writer's efforts? In limiting the author's responsibility and agency, Barthes issues a corrective to a thesis of Sartre's *What Is Literature?* (1947). Sartre maintains faith in the writer's freedom to communicate a position, and therefore to intervene in the political arena. Whereas poetic language's preoccupation with form thwarts communication and therefore does not offer the writer a viable site for commitment, Sartre favours a prose whose clarity and transparence dismiss worry over implication in bourgeois ideology or impotent formalism: prose is a tool for communicating a message, and it will be only as good or as bad, as radical or reactionary as the person who wields it. Barthes, however, situates any alleged clarity in the history of literary language itself and reveals the apparent transparence of all writing, with no disclaimer for Sartre's prose, to be yet another set of conventions and characteristics.[3] Even the most lucid prose can never escape the grip of the literary: 'un instrument décoratif et compromettant, une écriture que [l'auteur] a héritée d'une histoire antérieure et différente, dont il n'est pas responsable, et qui est pourtant la seule dont il puisse user' ('a decorative and compromising instrument, a writing inherited from a previous and different History, for which he [the author] is not responsible and yet which is the only one he can use') (I 185; *WDZ* 86). All writing, even at it most clear, casts an ideological shadow. Writing is, in short, *tragic*: 'l'écrivain conscient doit désormais se débattre contre les signes ancestraux et tout-puissants qui, du fond d'un passé étranger, lui imposent la Littérature comme un rituel, et non comme une réconciliation' ('the conscious writer must henceforth fight against ancestral and all-powerful signs which, from the depths of a past foreign to him, impose Literature on him like some ritual, not like a reconciliation') (I 185; *WDZ* 86). One might read this appeal to the tragic as an implicit response to Sartre's *The Flies*, the revisionist tragedy in which Orestes defies the gods to assert his freedom to act in a given situation without regret. Barthes grants the writer-hero no comparable freedom from the gods of language, and in the place of a triumphant and remorseless Orestes he invokes Orpheus's doom as the emblematic situation of a writer who envisions an impossible ideal, but who in the gesture of making it visible destroys it.

Despite strict limits on the writer's agency, *Writing Degree Zero* nonetheless remains more a nuanced revision of Sartre than an outright rejection. Barthes insists on freedom, choice, and responsibility, and reserves a narrow space for *engagement* that rescues his modernist author from the choice between uncritical complicity in the bourgeois regime and frustrated, impotent silence. Writers cannot definitively overthrow the sacrosanct myth of literature, but they can acknowledge their chosen *écriture* as a function of material, historical conditions, namely, the division of social classes. It is by marrying history and literary form, material conditions and writing, that Barthes introduces an ethics and a choice that maintain a measure of commitment. Without guaranteeing the freedom enjoyed by Sartre's Orestes, or that Sartre claims for himself, Barthes nonetheless allows a writer to grasp the meaning of a chosen mode of writing and to reveal this gesture of choice to the reader.[4] The room for incisive social and political criticism is very narrow, perhaps too narrow to navigate, and definitive escape from the impasse remains a utopian dream.[5] Revolution is impossible; revelation remains the only good-faith gesture for a contemporary writer.

There is no discussion of theatre or performance in *Writing Degree Zero*, but a rich theatrical metaphor threads its way throughout. The privileged figure of writing is the performer's mask: '[l'écriture] a pour charge de placer le masque et en même temps de le signaler' ('[writing's] task is to put the mask in place and at the same time to point it out') (I 157; *WDZ* 34). Barthes adopts the Cartesian device *larvatus prodeo*, 'I come forward masked,' as the motto of *écriture*. Like Descartes, Barthes radically discredits the insidious 'masks' of common sense, convention, and generally accepted knowledge that pass unquestioned as real, natural, or true. Literature remains his primary target, and Barthes indicts the use of the preterite (*le passé simple*), the hallmark of a purportedly realist narrative, as the emblem of literary discourse: 'rien d'autre que ce geste fatal par lequel l'écrivain montre du doigt le masque qu'il porte. Toute la Littérature peut dire: "*larvatus prodeo*," je m'avance en désignant mon masque du doigt' ('nothing but the fateful gesture with which the writer draws attention to the mask he is wearing. The whole of Literature can declare *larvatus prodeo*, as I walk forward, I point out my mask') (I 159; *WDZ* 40). In the contemporary alienated and divided society there is no neutral writing. One inescapably wears a mask, and all the *engagé* writer wields is the possibility, and therefore the responsibility, of acknowledging this figurative mask for what it is. In extreme cases the mask of the literary might become so thin it approaches transparence, but in the present zero-degree writing remains the unattainable utopia of literature. The fate of a Flaubert, who knowingly wears the mask and signals it to the reader, better characterizes the tragic, though in Barthes's eyes not altogether powerless, situation of the contemporary writer.

A theatre director must negotiate the same divided society as the writer, and Barthes's earliest writings on theatre, which begin to appear the same year as *Writing Degree Zero*, resonate with similar language and concerns. 'Pouvoirs de la tragédie antique' (Powers of ancient tragedy), a lengthy article published in 1953 and one of his first on theatre, amplifies the scorn of Barthes's rhetoric as he castigates the contemporary French stage. 'Bourgeois' realism is again the target, and Barthes lashes out at the boulevard drama served up by private theatres in terms similar to his critique of literature. Focused on individual emotions, interior psychology, and the isolated and apparently autonomous enclave of the home and family, all portrayed through stale nineteenth-century conventions, this theatre rehashes ad nauseum 'byzantine' questions of cuckoldry (I 217) and imparts no greater understanding of the social, political, economic, and religious systems that shape the action on the stage. The theatrical 'writing' of these performances is as hackneyed and insidiously imbued with reactionary values as the overtrained prose of Balzac's twentieth-century imitators. Barthes does not reserve his impatience for the boulevard. With its fossilized conventions, star system, bloated budgets squandered on needlessly opulent décor and costumes, and most notably the let-the-text-speak-for-itself lack of meaningful stage direction, the Comédie Française fares no better in Barthes's criticism despite its state funding.

As with literature, Barthes envisions a utopian theatre, although instead of looking to a future horizon of neutral 'Adamic' language he invokes an ancient past. Barthes's interest in Greek theatre dates from his student years at the Sorbonne, where he writes his undergraduate thesis on incantation in Greek tragedy. In 'Culture et tragédie,' a short contribution to the student journal of the sanitarium where he spends the greater part of the wartime occupation and his first published article, Barthes already hails the 'âme collective' (collective soul) of ancient Greek audiences as a necessity for tragedy and condemns contemporary drama for corrupting the masses with a 'fausse culture' (false culture) (I 19). 'Pouvoirs de la tragédie antique' crystallizes these thoughts. Barthes extols Greek tragedy for bringing the whole of society together in a collective encounter with a dynamic historical situation. When the *Oresteia* or *Antigone* provoke tears, Barthes's imagined Greek spectators do not mourn individually out of identification with a single character's suffering, but weep collectively in shared understanding of the circumstances that necessitate the tragic acts. The spectators' tears assume a social dimension when they are shed less for the tribulations of an individual – a personal affair – than for a deeper understanding of a human condition that is neither eternal essence nor a psychology or soul burning within the hero, but the issue of a given political or religious system in crisis. Barthes again admires the mask as both the figurative emblem of this exteriority of character and situation – *larvatus prodeo* – and the very literal staging device that guarantees this exteriorization.

Were theatre content merely to indicate its masks for the spectator it would act similarly to Flaubert's self-conscious writing. However, 'Pouvoirs de la tragédie antique' houses a vision of a utopian performance that not only signals the mask but at moments removes it to reveal a less alienated expression underneath. Barthes reserves his most enthusiastic praise for the chorus, which gives the collective 'city' a voice on the stage. While the division between gods, royalty, warriors, and the lower classes continues within the action of the tragedy, the chorus serves as the finger that points to these masks and signals their implication in a system of social relations. In Barthes's view, the chorus's voice brings the populace, the entire 'people' of the city, together in a single expression and a deeper understanding of the represented crisis:

Le chœur est la *parole maîtresse* qui explique, qui dénoue l'ambiguïté des apparences, et fait entrer le gestuaire des acteurs dans un ordre causal intelligible. On peut dire que c'est le chœur qui donne au spectacle sa dimension tragique, car c'est lui, et lui seul, qui est toute parole humaine, il est le Commentaire par excellence.

(The chorus is the *master word* that explains, that clears up the ambiguity of appearances, and makes the actors' gestures enter into an intelligible causality. One could say that the chorus gives the spectacle its tragic dimension, for it, and it alone, is all human speech, it is the Commentary par excellence.) (I 222, emphasis added)

The chorus's voice represents the *people*, not only the lower classes, not a dominant *écriture* that passes as natural in a divided society, not just another mask, but the 'master word' that mends and transcends the division of languages. The reader of *Writing Degree Zero* will recognize in the chorus's insightful and universal voice the pure, Adamic, and truly popular language that lurks out of reach as literature's elusive zero degree.

'Pouvoirs de la tragédie antique' offers a glimpse of an ideal performance practice that responds to the inadequacies of an alienated and compromised present. It remains unclear, however, whether the zero degree of performance represents a viable model for a contemporary theatre or, as with literature, an ever-receding theoretical horizon that merely puts into relief the lamentable state of the present situation. Does it follow from Barthes's pessimistic assessment of literature that a similar threat or even inevitability of failure will attend live performance, or does his enthusiasm for the chorus and the literal manifestation of the *larvatus prodeo* figure confer on theatrical performance a privilege he does not find in writing, past or present? Barthes does not answer this question, at least not initially. The consequent irresolution subtends Barthes's advocacy of a new theatre as he embarks on his career as an active performance critic, generating a tension that initially fosters optimism but also foretokens future frustrations that will in time contribute to despair over the endemic inadequacies of theatre in his contemporary France.

Towards a 'Popular' Theatre

In the 1950s, decolonization, a new French republic, a new Europe divided by the Iron Curtain, and rapid modernization bring about abrupt change in French society. The availability of the automobile, the washing machine, and other conveniences radically alters concepts of space, work, and time, while the role of France on the international stage, as well as internal demographics newly reshaped by an influx of immigrants from the former colonies, change the profile of the new post-war nation.[6] The class markers of the industrial age, so vividly depicted in Proust's salons and Zola's explorations of society's grim underside, are quickly disappearing. Other lines of exclusion and inequality – those drawn along racial and ethnic lines, for example – are not yet clear, and the prospect that the rapid change will bring about a more equitable society incites high hopes among many French intellectuals. When the dust of modernization has settled, what will this nascent society look like? What will be the place of the writer and intellectual? In the pages of *Les temps modernes*, *Esprit*, *Les lettres nouvelles*, *La nouvelle revue française*, *Combat*, and other journals, editors and contributors spar, forge new alliances, renounce old ones, and foster a lively public debate over the direction political commitment and literary production should follow in the new social climate.

The emerging society will demand a new theatre as well. After two world wars have all but decimated the French film industry and at a moment when television remains in its infancy, theatre, as it had for centuries in France, still retains its status as a national public forum of cultural and political importance.[7] Critics, directors, and intellectuals of the 1950s frequently deliberate on the role of theatre in the new postwar France. Many on the left call for a 'popular' French theatre, a tradition that dates from the efforts of fin-de-siècle dramatists and directors Romain Rolland, Firmin Gémier, and Maurice Pottécher, among others. Already in these earlier experiments, however, there is little consensus over exactly who are 'the people' who constitute the audience of this new theatre, or what kind of dramaturgy best serves their interests. Does 'popular' imply a theatre for the working classes or a theatre that brings together the whole of society, the whole of the nation? What kind of play will reach this popular audience?[8] These same questions continue to frame a lively debate in the 1950s. However, even while exchanging heated words over appropriate repertoire or who the ideal spectator should be, advocates of a new theatre in postwar France stand together in calling for an alternative to 'bourgeois' drama, the expensive and conventional divertissement that caters to the sensibilities and pocketbooks of a single class.[9]

In 1953 Barthes, too, believes in theatre as a uniquely powerful and privileged forum, and his initially sanguine assessment of theatre's cultural force sets it apart from literature in his early thought. *Writing Degree Zero* ends on an ambivalent note: though a few authors flirt with the zero degree, in the present the critic and writer can only 'indicate the mask' and the zero-degree literature remains a utopian dream. Lofty and abstract, *Writing Degree Zero* offers little in the way of a program for contemporary writers to follow. With theatre a greater ambition suffuses Barthes's remarks. Although he issues a familiar continuo of laments over the sorry state of the French stage and frequent assertions that theatre, like literature, can only 'indicate its mask' in the present divided society, for a brief period Barthes's stated task as theatre critic is not only to demystify the fossilized conventions of boulevard drama or the museum theatre of the Comédie Française, but also to advocate a new theatre, a popular theatre, with a clear social mission in the emergent society of post-war France.

In an unsigned 1954 editorial published in *Théâtre populaire* that appears just months after 'Powers of Ancient Tragedy,' Barthes again invokes the Greek ideal as a challenge to contemporary French theatre. He begins by rehearsing a familiar condemnation of the institution of commercial theatre: one goes there to watch complacently in luxurious surroundings of velvet and gilt the tribulations of adulterers and broken families, all clothed in the latest fashions and circulating in elegantly appointed salons. The spectator leaves the theatre unflustered, confident that the price of the ticket was worth both the measure of culture received and, perhaps more importantly, the spectacle of lavish costumes, sumptuous decor, and arduous overacting, all in the name of realism: 'Ce théâtre de l'Argent a un nom, c'est le théâtre bourgeois' (This theatre of Money has a name, it is bourgeois theatre) (I 382). Barthes then articulates the mission of the journal and of his own enterprise as a theatre critic: to advocate a theatre that will cease to pander to bourgeois money and taste, and that will foster a collective encounter with a dynamic historical situation. He calls for a more authentic popular theatre, 'purifié des structures bourgeoises, désaliéné de l'argent et de ses masques' (purified of bourgeois structures, disalienated of money and its masks) (I 382). Unlike Sartre and others, by 'popular' Barthes does not suggest a strictly working-class audience or a *Proletkult*, which would create yet another class-specific theatre in a divided society, but rather a theatre that, as in his idealized Greece, will bring together all of society, all of the *city*, in a collective ritual encounter. The task will not be easy, and he moderates his ambition by conceding that this theatre and the society that can produce it do not yet exist. Despite the efforts of numerous 'bons avocats,' the constituents of this new theatre, the people, have yet to be liberated from the class divisions and stultifying bourgeois aesthetic norms that in a society still divided inexorably dominate cultural production. In the present Barthes can only charge theatre once again with the task of wielding the critical finger that reveals the insidious masks of a dissatisfying status quo: 'au triomphe des mythes, ne peut répondre qu'un effort de démystification' (only an effort to demystify can respond to the triumph of myth) (I 383). The authentic and pure theatre appears to remain as unattainable as the zero degree of literature.

However, if bourgeois culture is moribund and a new society is truly at hand, the unalienated theatre Barthes envisions is potentially more than a utopian dream. Echoing the manifesto of the Fédération nationale des amis du théâtre populaire, a grassroots organization in support of the popular theatre movement in which he plays an active role, Barthes reiterates the three fundamental tenets that advocates of a popular theatre propose to remedy the current situation: a 'mass' audience, a repertoire of 'high culture,' and an avant-garde dramaturgy. Barthes recognizes that none of these is entirely radical in itself, and optimistically names instances where each criterion has already been met in 1950s France.[10]

The first tenet is sociological and bears on the audience: the new theatre must bring together the whole of society, not a single class, in the collective encounter he so admires in ancient tragedy. In 'Pouvoirs de la tragédie antique' as well as in 'The World of Wrestling' and 'The Tour de France,' two of the *petites mythologies* that he begins to write in 1953, Barthes suggests his model audience already exists in the modern sporting event. The fans' cheering, waiting, surprise, and disappointment manifest themselves collectively in active response to the athlete's execution of the game in the arena as it unfolds, much like the tears and cries of despair of the ancient spectators watching the hero negotiate a tragic plight – a stark contrast to the spectators of bourgeois theatre, who remain in their plush expensive seats neatly segregated from those who can only afford less expensive tickets, and who watch a play silently as if drugged by the illusion that something is happening on the stage. Barthes believes that the sporting event appeals to a broad swath of spectators that cuts across an otherwise divided society, and therefore brings the entire 'city' together in recognition, appreciation, and understanding of the struggle on the field or in the arena.

Popular appeal nothwithstanding, the sporting event lacks the power of ancient tragedy. As entertainment a football match represents more an escape from the historical moment than a confrontation with it, and violates Barthes's second tenet of the new theatre: it must program a 'répertoire de haute culture' (repertory of high culture) that does not sell the new popular audience short with mere distraction or inferior dramaturgy.[11] Alongside the touchstone Aeschylus, Barthes cites Molière, Shakespeare, Kleist, Corneille, and Büchner as suitable playwrights insofar as they live up to the 'imperious laws of dramatic art.'[12] Other playwrights do not fare so well. The romantic drama of Victor Hugo and the nineteenth-century realism of Dumas, for example, devolve into melodrama and bear too close a resemblance to conventional realism. Claudel also fails to qualify; Barthes reads *Le Soulier de satin* as a long study of adultery, the most bourgeois of dramatic pretexts. At this point he also forswears Racine's plays, which despite their tragic trappings represent a psychological theatre obsessed with the family and adultery, and therefore are forerunners of boulevard drama as well as the heirs of ancient tragedy.[13]

The third principle of the new theatre concerns the art of theatre practitioners. In 'Pouvoirs de la tragédie antique' Barthes hails the sporting event a second time as a close cousin of tragedy, though the choice of *le catch* ('professional' or 'all-in' wrestling) as his example, much more a theatrical spectacle than a competitive demonstration of strength and athletic prowess, tempers a rapprochement to most sporting events. In his *petite mythologie* on the same topic Barthes concedes that 'le catch n'est pas un sport, c'est un spectacle' ('wrestling is not a sport, it's a spectacle') (I 569; M 15), and he explicitly opposes *le catch* to boxing and other sports while encouraging speculation on its relation to theatre. Barthes relishes the stylized wrestlers:

les combattants affichent leur état d'âme (douleur, joie, rage, vengeance, régularité), toutes leurs expressions sont choisies pour présenter au public populaire une lecture immédiate et comme exhaustive de leurs mobiles.

(The combatants exhibit the state of their soul [pain, joy, rage, vengeance, regularity], all their expressions are chosen to present to the popular public an immediate and seemingly exhaustive reading of their motives.) (I 219)

The wrestlers' gestures, which the audience immediately understands as a deliberate choice and not the outward symptom of some interior psychology or emotional state, or even of physical pain, literally realize in performance practice the *larvatus prodeo* device, Barthes's motto for the modernist writer:

à côté de la face douloureuse du catcheur plié, vaincu et présentant à son public circulaire la tête allégorique de l'humiliation ravageuse, mettez le masque antique ... le soleil athénien ou les réflecteurs de la 'Mutualité' ont cette même fonction chirurgicale qui consiste à amener dans les plis significatifs du visage une intériorité qui, cachée, ne serait d'aucune utilité dramatique.

(next to the pained face of the yielding wrestler, vanquished and present-ing to the surrounding public the allegorical face of ravaging humiliation, place the mask of antiquity ... the Athenian sun or the spotlights at the 'Mutualité' have the same surgical function that consists of bringing to the signifying folds of the face an interiority that, hidden, would have no dramatic use.) (I 219)

The theatrical gesture creates meaning, imposes it, reveals it. Action is exteriorized. The struggle between the characters, their identity and their situation, can be read on the face without recourse to a psychologi-cal or emotional state that purportedly churns under, behind, inside, or otherwise pre-positioned outside of the extreme situation represented in the ring or on the stage.

In short, the performer is a *sign*. Barthes's three principles for a new theatre might echo the concerns of other critics, but even in his earliest articles he is adding a semiological spin all his own. Wearing its attitudes on the surface, *le catch*, like tragedy, does not offer a real struggle on stage nor even strive to appear to do so; it *signifies* the confrontation for the spectators, who, caring little if it is a faithful re-creation of a real struggle, take an active role in reading and understanding the situation unfolding on the stage. *Semiosis*, the consideration of all that is on stage as a readable and at least somewhat arbitrary sign, effectively supplants Aristotelian *mimesis*, the idea of theatre as imitation, as its guiding principle. For tragedy, wrestling, and Barthes's new theatre, bourgeois realism is once again the antithesis of the ideal theatre: 'l'extériorité des signes rend dérisoire le réalisme' (the exteriority of signs makes realism laughable) (I 219). Barthes cites a provincial performance in which a misguided performer takes naturalist acting to its absurd extreme by slaughtering a live chicken on the stage with messy and ineffectual consequences. A more intelligible (not to mention intelligent) theatre would simply sig-nify this act with clearly readable gestures. The violent gesture would then be understood as part of a story or a situation: a spectator might wonder, for example, why the woman is killing the chicken in the first place, rather than being aghast at the spectacle of the poor beast's gruesome suffering. Here again, wrestling stands as the ideal:

Il y a là une manière d'intensité qui *charge* le combat sportif ou le spectacle tragique d'une véritable jubilation de l'intelligence, parvenue à une saisie immédiate des rapports, et non des choses, ce qui est la définition même de la culture.

(There is a sort of intensity that *loads* the sporting event or the tragic spectacle with a veritable jubilation of intelligence, arriving at an immediate grasp of the relationships, and not of things, which is the definition of culture itself.) (I 220)

In a gesture that betrays an incipient structuralism, Barthes privileges an underlying system of relationships that lends meaning to the mask over value located in the 'thing itself.' A theatre of signification consequently derives greater power for cultural critique than one that slavishly strives to imitate, not to mention actually to execute, an action on the stage.

Barthes's tragedians and wrestlers announce the future influence of two theorists who will soon inform his thought and remain ubiquitous points of reference in his work long after he abandons his theatre criticism. First, the call for demystification, the abhorrence of realism, and Barthes's insistence on situating the represented event in the material conditions of a historical moment all bear marked affinities to the dramaturgy of Bertolt Brecht.[14] The compatibility of Barthes's idealized tragedy and wrestling with Brecht's epic theatre prepares the way for the incendiary discovery that will soon transfigure his theatre criticism. More clearly evident, perhaps, is a nascent interest in the study of signs and signification. As with Brecht, in 1953 Barthes does not yet name the Swiss linguist Ferdinand de Saussure, the founder of structural linguistics, nor does he specifically invoke semiology by name. However, we know Barthes was familiar with at least some principles of structural linguistics and semiology via the Danish linguist Viggo Brøndal, from whom he culled the notion of a zero degree. The tragedian and the wrestler both transform body, self, mind, and soul into legible surfaces, intelligible and exterior signs circulating within a system of relations, and from Barthes's earliest remarks a distinctly semiological lens colours his discussions of theatre and performance.

In fact, Barthes's earliest, 'pre-Brecht' theatre criticism (roughly March 1953 through July 1954) lays the theoretical framework for a broader semiotics of performance that embraces far more than the written dramatic text or the actor's interpretation of it. Barthes does not limit his remarks in 'Pouvoirs de la tragédie antique' to the performer's body, and he includes a semiological analysis of music as well: 'conjointement au masque, la tragédie antique disposait d'un autre *signe* puissant: la musique' (along with the mask, classical tragedy had another powerful *sign* at its disposal: music) (I 220, emphasis in original). Barthes rejects the romantic notion of music as a privileged mode of expression for a composer's or performer's thoughts and feelings. He prefers that music be intelligible, that it signify, that in revealing a situation, as does the mask, it draw less on *pathos* than on *ethos*, less on emotional impact and the expression of an interior state than on a morally responsible choice of musical modes that align the composer's task with the committed writer's choice of an *écriture*.

Music is only one signifying register in a rich complex of signs that Barthes names theatricality: *théâtralité*. In a 1954 preface to an edition of Baudelaire's complete works Barthes defines this notion:

> Qu'est-ce que la théâtralité? c'est le théâtre moins le texte, c'est une épaisseur de signes et de sensations qui s'édifie sur la scène à partir de l'argument écrit, c'est cette sorte de perception œcuménique des artifices sensuels, gestes, tons, distances, substances, lumières, qui submerge le texte sous la plénitude de son langage extérieur.

> (What is theatricality? It is theater-minus-text, it is a density of signs and sensations built up on stage starting from the written argument; it is that ecumenical perception of sensuous artifice – gesture, tone, distance, substance, light – which submerges the text beneath the profusion of its external language.) (I 1194; *CE* 26)

Barthes proposes a semiology of theatre in which all aspects of a theatrical production contribute to the intelligibility of the spectacle; those that do not are branded 'parasitic' and obscure the play's deeper significance. Along with the performers and the playwright, Barthes charges designers, technicians, musicians, and most importantly the director with the responsibility for creating a mise en scène that does not decorate or merely flesh out a dramatic text, but that reveals it with a rich texture, a 'density' of intelligible signs. Each element must constitute an argument, the result of a clear gesture of choice whose significance the spectators can grasp: 'il nous faut [...] lier telle forme de théâtralité à telle mentalité historique [et] préciser les rapports d'une esthétique et d'une idéologie' (We must link a form of theatricality to a historical mentality, and state clearly the relation of an aesthetic to an ideology) (I 388). The task of designers and directors is therefore analogous to that of writers and literary critics: to situate theatricality in a historic moment that demands responsible choices.

Barthes's earliest remarks on theatre echo his other important critical project of the mid-1950s. Bourgeois theatre constitutes a consummate and particularly galling myth, as Barthes defines this term pejoratively: a cultural artefact whose sheer familiarity or banality constitutes a false 'nature,' a commonsensical and therefore unquestioned alibi of inevitability that insidiously obscures its ideological investment and its implication in the present historical moment. The first meditations on popular culture, many of which eventually are collected in *Mythologies*, begin to appear in *Esprit* and *Les lettres nouvelles* at approximately the same moment as Barthes's debut as a theatre critic. These short articles follow a course already set in *Writing Degree Zero*, which brings to light the obscured implication of the literary in both a historical situation and a system of signification, or more accurately, how writing reveals a historical situation that *is* a system of representation. In the preface to *Mythologies* Barthes invites his reader to consider *Writing Degree Zero* a proto-mythology, a single, long demystification of literature. Many of the articles also target the myth of literature ('The Writer on Holiday,' 'Racine Is Racine,' 'Neither-Nor Criticism,' 'The *Nautilus* and the Drunken Boat,' 'Literature According to Minou Drouet'). Theatre, too, figures prominently in the anthology, and the short articles echo thoughts expressed elsewhere: the condemnation of bourgeois theatre ('Two Myths of the Young Theater,' 'The Lady of the Camellias') or a favourable recognition of the tragic element surprisingly expressed by wrestlers and vaudeville acrobats ('The World of Wrestling,' 'The Music-Hall').

A notable difference, however, distinguishes most of *Mythologies* from Barthes's early theatre criticism. In *Mythologies* he does not lay out the blueprint for, nor does he attempt to represent, a new, more authentic world underneath the mythic masks of meaning; he instead tries to make them intelligible to the reader: 'Introduire l'explication dans le mythe, c'est pour l'intellectuel la seule façon efficace de militer' (Introduce explanation into the myth, that is for the intellectual the only effective way to militate) (I 211). To remove the mask altogether again appears possible only in a distant past or an unimaginable future, not in the chronically alienated present, and in most of these articles the tone remains trenchantly critical. The exemplary performances of the professional wrestlers make 'The World of Wrestling' an anomaly among the *mythologies*. Barthes clearly delights in 'professional' wrestling, which constitutes less a myth begging demystification than an ideal mode of representation, and the biting sarcasm of the other *mythologies* is notably tempered in his account. The petit-bourgeois spectator might in the end read into wrestling some suspect connotation – a reassuring affirmation of the self-evidence of good and evil in the world – but Barthes considers *le catch* a pleasurable performance of purified signifiers that along with the idealized ancient tragedy sets a standard against which most French productions compare unfavourably. At the confluence of theatre and myth, wrestling nonetheless does not entirely elide a tension that will later trouble both Barthes's advocacy of a new theatre and his work as a mythologist: it is unclear what distinguishes the 'popular' audience Barthes applauds at the wrestling match and equates with the unalienated community of ancient Athens from the petit-bourgeois spectatorship he reviles. The subsequent, far less sanguine *mythologies* concede the virtual hegemony of petit-bourgeois sensibility in mass culture and gauge the height of its ascendency in incisive detail.

In 1953, however, Barthes still imagines the spectators of sporting events as the representatives of the new French nation emerging from decades of war and more than a century of capitalist exploitation. The three requisite elements of the new theatre for a new age therefore appear to be at hand: sporting events confirm the existence of a popular audience, a rich choice of classic texts awaits the stage director, and Barthes articulates the principles of new dramaturgy founded on a semiologically informed consideration of all aspects of a *mise en scène*. It remains to be seen if any director can seize this propitious moment, bring these elements together, and realize Barthes's envisioned theatre, or if this ideal will continue to hover out of reach, relegated to a mythic past of ancient Greece or, as with the zero degree of writing, to the utopian future of a post-revolution, classless society.

Jean Vilar's Good Intentions

In his first theatre review, written before he joins the editorial team at *Théâtre populaire*, Barthes equivocates over whether a new and truly popular theatre is possible in post-war France. The play in question is a 1953 production of Heinrich von Kleist's *The Prince of Homburg* at the Théâtre National Populaire (TNP), directed by the theatre's guiding force, Jean Vilar. In the early 1950s the TNP is still something of an experiment, struggling to establish itself as an alternative to both boulevard drama and the museum theatre of the Comédie Française. Vilar assumes directorship of the TNP in 1951, and begins to implement the vision for a new French theatre he already began to realize at the Avignon festival four years earlier. Vilar's efforts clearly inform Barthes's vision for a new theatre. The TNP reaches out to working-class audiences by offering inexpensive tickets, coordinates with unions and other labor groups to organize performances in the suburbs near the factories where these spectators work and live, and eliminates the division of the audience maintained by gradated ticket prices and traditional theatre architecture. Finding contemporary playwrights generally inadequate (with some notable exceptions), Vilar most often turns to the classics when choosing his repertoire. He also insists on an aesthetic of *dé-pouillement*, of stripping bare, that cuts through conventions and gratuitous spectacle to bring out what he believes to be the bare essentials of the text and its interpretation on the stage.[15]

Vilar strives to realize the three criteria for a new theatre Barthes endorses, and the review of *The Prince of Homburg* is duly enthusiastic. Outreach to working-class audiences meets Barthes's wish for a more balanced audience, at least in intent, and Kleist's play constitutes suitable repertoire. It is the elegant mise en scène, however, that most impresses Barthes. Vilar strips the vast playing area of his Palais de Chaillot theatre of realist accoutrements and superfluous design to recreate indoors the barren courtyard of the papal palace where he stages his plays in Avignon. Barthes enumerates the successful production choices regarding all aspects of the production: first the use of space, then mise en scène, then décor, props, acting, and finally the costumes, on which he dwells at some length. An appreciation of *semiosis* and the responsibility of theatre practitioners who create this 'density of signs' suffuses Barthes's remarks. Consider, for example, Barthes's language regarding the set design: 'le décor ne participe pas à l'espace; il est un argument [...] un signe intellectuel projeté par la situation, c'est un accessoire didactique, non magique' (the set does not participate in the space; it is an argument [...] an intellectual sign projected by the situation, a didactic accessory, not a magic one) (I 205); or on theatre properties: 'Lorsque [Vilar] utilise quelque objet, un arbre, un toit, une épée, c'est avec un pur désir d'intelligibilité, c'est parce que cet objet doit rendre une signification' (When [Vilar] uses some object, a tree, a roof, a sword, it is with a pure desire of intelligibility, it is because this object must render a meaning) (I 205). Vilar's textured polyphony of intelligible signs demonstrates the keen sense of the theatricality Barthes will define in the Baudelaire preface a few months later.

Barthes enthusiastically hails *The Prince of Homburg* as a great stride towards a new theatre, and throughout the review he invokes his ideal popular theatres of pure intelligibility, ancient tragedy, and the sporting events 'in the ring,' to justify Vilar's production choices. The discussion of costumes, for example, suggests that an ideal zero degree of performance has been attained: '[la sobriété des costumes] institue un état neutre du vêtement, elle libère la scène de toutes ses valeurs parasites' ([the sobriety of the costumes] institutes a neutral state of the clothing, it liberates the stage of all its parasitic values) (I 207). 'Neutre' is a charged word in Barthes's vocabulary. Years later it will represent the elusive third term in the binary, the fold between positive and negative poles, an impossible utopian excess that upsets the strictures of signification. Already in 1953 its usage to describe Vilar's costumes is noteworthy. Barthes proposes that the costumes do more than signal the ideological 'mask' of meaning deplored in *Writing Degree Zero* or *Mythologies*. It is not merely an *écriture* that signals itself as such, the Flaubertian gesture that Barthes names the intellectual's or artist's sole possibility for *engagement*. The clothing achieves neutrality as a pure sign uncompromised by parasitic connotations of, for example, historical accuracy or haute couture: a costume degree zero.

The rhapsodic praise of Vilar's costumes proves nonetheless parenthetical, and to conclude a less optimistic Barthes reins in his zeal. Vilar's theatre is popular more by its intentions, admirable as they are, than by its sociology. The divisions that still cut through a capitalist society inflect the production, which as an avant-garde artistic practice draws the 'éléments évolués' (evolved elements) of the middle class and the less snobbish bourgeois spectator (I 208). Only a few years later Barthes will indict the 'avant-garde' as a valuable currency in the bourgeois economy of taste.[16] Vilar's *théâtralité*, like *écriture*, carries the burden of being embedded in the present historical moment. It can only signal the masks and not, as the idealized Greek chorus, step out from behind them to speak in an unalienated voice.

Reservations notwithstanding, Vilar's brush with an ideal theatricality holds hope that a new and truly popular theatre is at hand. Barthes's enthusiasm for the costumes of *The Prince of Homburg* is not an isolated instance of a utopian strain woven through his assessments of Vilar's theatre. In the months preceding his discovery of Brecht, the tenor of Barthes's praise suggests a belief that the TNP will soon realize the popular theatre he envisions. Vilar's 1953 staging of Molière's *Dom Juan* generates two enthusiastic reviews in which Barthes's praises a *théâtralité* that exceeds even that of the *Prince of Hombourg*. The stark mise en scène, little more than pools of light, costumes, and the performers' bodies, are a revelation for those familiar with the conventionally gimmicky stagings (pyrotechnics, trapdoors, broad slapstick) of this text.

Barthes's language becomes absolute and superlative: 'A cette plénitude de la signification, tous les éléments de la théâtralité concourent: on croyait la pièce faite pour les démonstrations de machinerie: Vilar n'en garde aucune, et tout devient plus significatif' (In this plenitude of signification, all the elements of theatricality compete: the play was thought to be written for demonstrations of stage machinery: Vilar gets rid of them, and everything becomes more significant) (I 384). Intelligibility and clarity attain even the stuff of the performers' bodies: Vilar's Don Juan is 'dry' and 'metallic,' Sganarelle moist, all fat and sweat (I 385). Vilar's *Dom Juan* is eventually performed for more than 370,000 spectators, an impressive draw for the austere staging of a classic text. Barthes ends his review by proclaiming the 'popular success' of the production. His choice of qualifier is significant, and suggests that *Dom Juan* not only meets the ideal of an intelligible, semiologically pure and responsible spectacle on the stage, but also draws audiences across the French socio-economic spectrum and brings 'the people' together in a collective appreciation of a worthy text. In short, it meets Barthes's three criteria for a new popular theatre.

A brief report on a visit to Avignon, where Barthes attends a meeting of the Amis du théâtre populaire shortly after he sees *Dom Juan*, reveals the headiness of the moment. As he contemplates the cold and wind-swept courtyard of the papal palace, Barthes imagines its animation during the summer festival: a new theatrical space for a new theatre – and a new public. After a familiar tongue-lashing of bourgeois theatre, he describes Vilar's audiences as a public that transcends the divisions of society that 'bourgeois' theatre continues to enforce: 'un public populaire, vaste, d'origine variée sans doute, mais surtout frais, neuf, où beaucoup découvrent le théâtre, pour la première fois' (a popular public, vast, of varied origin no doubt, but above all fresh, new, where many discover the theatre, for the first time) (I 394). These are not jaded bourgeois spectators dozing off in their seats, but an active public of a new age, 'innocent' and 'fresh,' that 'enters into the dialogue' of the theatrical encounter and actively carves out the meanings from the tabula rasa of the empty space. Barthes all but proclaims the realization of his ideal theatre in Vilar's festival:

> Avignon a été la voie naturelle du Théâtre populaire, parce qu'Avignon est un lieu sans mensonge où tout est remis entre les mains de l'homme. Il n'est que de passer la tête, un jour d'hiver, par la grosse porte de bois qui ferme la cour du festival, pour saisir qu'au théâtre aussi les hommes sont seuls et qu'ils peuvent tout.

> (Avignon has been the natural route of popular theatre, because Avignon
> is a place without lies where everything is put back into the hands of man.
> One need only take a look, on a winter day, through the massive wooden
> gate that closes the festival courtyard, to grasp that in theatre, too, men are
> alone and are capable of anything.) (I 395)

'Man' has been liberated, and the lies of bourgeois theatre laid bare: the
austere courtyard effectively represents a zero degree of both the stage
and the spectator who leaves the burden of class divisions and other
'varied origins' at the door. For a brief moment in early 1954, a new
theatre, adult, semiologically sound, and generously bestowing freedom and responsibility on the spectator, appears to be at hand.

It will not be Jean Vilar, however, who ushers in the new day. No
sooner does Barthes announce the advent of a new popular theatre than
he begins to express disappointment at some of Vilar's production
choices. In a March 1954 review of *Richard II* at the TNP Barthes directs
most of his criticism at the leading actor Gérard Philipe rather than
Vilar's staging, and compares Vilar's own acting favourably to the
'bourgeois' mannerisms of Philipe. However, the article implicates Vilar's
lax stage direction that permits the cinema idol to overact shame-
lessly.[17] In the spring of 1954 Barthes begins to review other theatres
and directors around France that, in his assessment, fare better than
Vilar's most recent efforts.[18] After condemning Philipe's performance
in *Richard II*, Barthes admires a performance of Maria Casarès in a
production of Julien Green's *L'ennemi*. Where Philipe takes recourse to
familiar stereotypes and spoonfeeds the spectacle to a passive audience, Casarès, like the wrestlers and the Greek tragedians, 'inundates
with clarity' the performance for an active, thinking public.[19] Barthes's
praise for Casarès tacitly indicts Philipe and his adoring spectators: 'elle
jette sur la scène un *excès* et une *distance*, qui ne peuvent que lasser les
paresseux et déconcerter les amateurs de salut facile' (she throws onto
the stage an *excess* and a *distance* that can only weary those who are lazy
and disconcert the lovers of easy salvation) (I 412). The lazy spectators
are precisely those to whom Barthes believes Philipe panders, and
though his rendition of King Richard at this point marks an isolated slip
in Vilar's judgment, the TNP no longer represents what Barthes earlier
calls 'l'arche [...] qui tient en soi seule l'avenir du théâtre populaire' (the
ark that holds in itself alone the future of popular theatre) (I 389).
Barthes amplifies his criticism of the TNP in the following month in
another review that sharply reprimands Vilar's choice of Victor Hugo's
Ruy Blas, a play Barthes finds inferior, unworthy of the TNP's public,

and a colossal waste of talent and resources; he will later lodge similar complaints against Vilar's choice of another Hugo drama, *Marie Tudor*, and Claudel's monumental *Soulier de satin*. For Barthes, Both Philipe's cloying charisma in *Richard II* and the melodramatic mediocrity of the repertoire, far from engaging the collective audience in a ritual encounter with a historical moment, betray the defining principles of popular theatre and revert to the weary conventions of bourgeois realism.

The flood of Barthes's admiration for Vilar is therefore already cresting even before he discovers Brecht. The incipient rift with Vilar will widen in the following years, and with hindsight one might wonder if it is inevitable. In his initial enthusiasm Barthes seems wilfully to overlook profound philosophical differences that separate him from Vilar. Vilar's invocations of 'greatness,' of a trans-historical 'man,' of 'truth' in a 'noble' and 'pure' theatre, of the universal appeal of the classics, and his desire to make 'beauty' accessible to the masses who would never otherwise go to the theatre, ring with a patronizing idealism that clashes with Barthes's residual existentialist and Marxist inclinations and his insistence on history, not to mention a nascent interest in signs and structures that will soon displace the individual and free human subject.[20] Moreover, one must wonder how any theatre, Vilar's or anyone else's, could meet Barthes's exigent standards. In *Writing Degree Zero* and *Mythologies*, the unalienated cultural production remains a dream, a utopian vision virtually unachievable in contemporary France, yet Barthes demands nothing less of the stage.[21] He strives towards a goal he already deems impossible in the literary realm, and in his earliest writings on theatre, between the spring of 1953 and the summer of 1954, he appears to be setting himself up for bitter disappointment. Barthes's vast new public, the empowered 'man' of the new era, is already devolving into lazy spectators reluctant to wean themselves from the comfortable and familiar clichés of bourgeois tradition. He appears to believe briefly that he has caught up to the elusive zero degree of theatre when he discovers Vilar and the TNP, only to see it slip away to an ever-receding future. This disappointed hope, increasingly blighted throughout the 1950s, foreshadows Barthes's eventual repudiation of the Théâtre National Populaire and its director, and ultimately his abandonment of French theatre altogether.

Bedazzled by Brecht

If all cultural production, be it literature, theatre, or mass-media artefacts, is as Barthes believes embedded in the material relations of a specific historical moment, it follows that a truly popular theatre would need to come from elsewhere, its productive roots in a society free of the *embourgeoisement* that continues to plague post-war France. When the Berliner Ensemble performs *Mother Courage* in Paris in 1954, Barthes appears to have found such a theatre. Years later he will write that he is 'ébloui' (dazzled) by Brecht's production (II 1181).[22] His initial review in *Théâtre populaire* is no less emphatic: 'Nous avons vu que cette critique profonde édifiait du même coup ce théâtre désaliéné que nous postulions idéalement, et qui s'est trouvé devant nous en un jour dans sa forme adulte et déjà parfaite' ('The performance proved to us that this profound criticism has created that theater without alienation which we had dreamed of and which has been discovered before our eyes, in its adult and already perfected form') (I 1202; *CE* 35–6). Barthes's purpose as a theatre critic abruptly finds sharp focus and new energy. The editorial team of *Théâtre populaire* shares Barthes's enthusiasm and the journal quickly becomes the forum in which Brecht's defenders respond to French critics on the right, who deplore such an overtly political theatre, as well as those on the left who either misunderstand it as a 'great' work of universal appeal or, towing a Zhdanovian line, suspect Brecht of formalism and lament the lack of positive heroes in his plays. Barthes himself writes the editorial for the January/February 1955 issue dedicated to explaining Brecht to a sceptical and misunderstanding French public. His *parti pris* is clear:

> Notre revue s'est trop de fois indignée devant la médiocrité ou la bassesse du théâtre présent, la rareté de ses révoltes et la sclérose de ses techniques, pour qu'elle puisse tarder plus longtemps à interroger un grand dramaturge de notre temps, qui nous propose non seulement une œuvre, mais aussi un système, fort, cohérent, stable, difficile à appliquer peut-être, mais qui possède au moins une vertu indiscutable et salutaire de 'scandale' et d'étonnement.

> (This magazine has too often condemned the mediocrity or the meanness of our theater, the rarity of its rebellions and the sclerosis of its techniques, to postpone a consideration of a great contemporary dramatist who offers not only a body of work but also a strong, coherent, stable system, one difficult to apply perhaps, but which possesses at least an indisputable and salutary virtue of 'scandal' and astonishment.) (I 1203; *CE* 38)

Brecht's arrival in France so impresses Barthes and his co-editors that it precipitates a change in editorial policy: the journal, whose initial mission was to promote popular theatre wherever it might appear and to avoid any appearance of an 'esprit de chapelle,' or clique mentality, becomes a pulpit for disseminating the Brechtian good news with nearly religious fervour.[23]

Barthes wholeheartedly embraces the key tenets of Brecht's dramaturgy. Brecht, like Barthes, does not believe the performer should 'become' the character by creating a realistic interior psychology or emotional state that the spectators recognize and to which they can relate, but should hold up the character's words and actions for the spectators' critical assessment. Brecht's productions do not make the character's actions believable, logical, and familiar to the spectators' sensibilities, as in a realist theatre's bid for verisimilitude, but 'turn the object of which one is to be made aware from something ordinary, familiar, immediately accessible, into something peculiar, striking, unexpected.'[24] By distancing the performer from the characters and revealing to a thinking spectator the social and economic relations that generate the characters' world view and motivate their actions, Brecht's 'epic' theatre furnishes a nearly literal realization of the *larvatus prodeo* figure: the 'finger' of the alienation effects signals the reality that the characters accept as immutable nature, leads the spectators to understand the material conditions that create and perpetuate it, and challenges them to imagine a solution to the contradictions, usually the result of a capitalist society, that plague the characters. This distancing, the *Verfremdung*, serves to reveal the social *gestus* of the represented situation: the relations, to which the characters are often blind, that shape their actions and attitudes towards each other.

Brecht's stage aesthetic and his finely crafted repertoire meet Barthes's first two demands for a new theatre. The third element, the thinking, popular audience that transcends class divisions, is still impossible in contemporary France, but not, Barthes implies, in East Germany.[25] What Barthes might or might not have known about the audiences at Brecht's *Theater am Schiffbauerdamm*, the conditions of his state subsidies, or the general sociological profile of East Germany is unclear. For his purpose as a critic in 1950s France, however, these questions matter little more than the actual sociological constituency of ancient Greek audiences; in Barthes's writing Berlin is another distant, only vaguely invoked home of an ideal theatre, as removed from Paris as his vision of Aeschylus's Athens.

It is perhaps possible to overstate the epiphanic nature of Barthes's first encounter with Brecht's theatre. Barthes's own retrospective comments would make the conversion immediate and complete while his earliest accounts of *Mother Courage*, initially at least, situate Brecht alongside Vilar, Roger Blin, Roger Planchon, and others as part of the same swell of new dramaturgy that counters the dominant 'théâtre de classe' (theater of class) (I 438). There is no doubt, however, that Brecht strikes a far deeper chord than any of his French contemporaries, and in a matter of months eclipses them as the standard against which Barthes thereafter measures all efforts. Barthes's first review of a TNP production following the Berliner Ensemble's visit, a review of Vilar's *Macbeth* in early 1955, is a telling indication of how quickly the discovery of Brecht refigures the parameters of Barthes's criticism. Vilar might succeed in enacting a sort of *Verfremdungseffekt*: 'Vilar *n'est pas* Macbeth. Soit. Mais c'est en fait pour mieux montrer Macbeth [...] éloigné par Vilar, Macbeth *montre* comment il s'est choisi d'être Macbeth' (Vilar *is not* Macbeth. Granted. But this is in fact to *show* Macbeth better [...] distanced by Vilar, Macbeth shows how he chooses to become Macbeth) (I 473); but he ultimately falls short of Barthes's ideal when he fails to reveal the social *gestus*: 'La "conscience" de Vilar n'est certes pas aussi radicale que le "distancement" de Brecht. Vilar ne recrée pas ici le "gestus" social de l'époque' (The 'conscience' of Vilar is certainly not as radical as the 'distancing' of Brecht. Vilar does not recreate here the social *gestus* of the period) (I 473). In the end, Vilar's intelligent nod does not measure up to Brecht's perfected dramaturgy. The Berliner Ensemble's return to Paris with *The Caucasian Chalk Circle* in 1955 only boosts Barthes's admiration and confirms Brecht's ascendency as the model popular theatre he seeks: 'le succès du *Cercle de craie* a été total' (The success of *Chalk Circle* has been complete) (I 516). Barthes's univocal enthusiasm for Brecht does not waver even as his passionate advocacy for a new French theatre begins to falter.

Barthes initially believes that Brecht's revolutionary example will redeem France from the general catastrophe of its theatre by sowing doubt in the minds of spectators conditioned to accept psychological realism and lavish spectacle as the hallmarks of good theatre: 'ces menus doutes seraient le commencement d'un plus vaste mouvement de libération' (these few doubts would be the beginning of a greater movement of liberation) (I 483). It soon becomes clear, however, that Brecht's plays succeed the ancient Greeks as the touchstone against which French productions, mired in the bourgeois and petit-bourgeois sensibilities that dominate late-capitalist France, will inevitably come up deficient. A few productions draw a positive review by displaying a certain Brechtian quality – an amateur production of *Ubu roi* in Annecy, for example[26] – but this qualified endorsement pales when contrasted with Barthes's effusive praise for Brecht's own productions. Many others take a broadside from an impatient Barthes who does not hide his contempt for the mediocrity served up on most French stages.[27] French-language productions of Brecht's own plays betray most starkly the conditions that in Barthes's eyes condemn French theatre ultimately to failure. Roger Planchon, for example, creates a brilliant staging of Brecht's *Fear and Misery of the Third Reich*, but can only do so in a small theatre in Lyon; financial exigencies preclude such a production from reaching a broad audience or from appearing in Paris. Jean-Marie Serreau's 1955 production of *A Man's a Man* does not lack in good will or understanding of Brecht's dramaturgy, and Barthes acknowledges a certain successful alienation of war and its dehumanization that provokes critical thought in the spectator. However, a reprimand for the gratuitous décor and the conventional acting of some members of the troupe mitigates his praise, and he ends his review by rehearsing a now familiar lament: 'nous connaissons les causes du mal, ce statut général de la scène française, qui fait le théâtre tributaire du capital, et place tout l'art dramatique français à la merci de l'Argent' (we know the causes of the problem, the general state of the French stage that makes the theatre dependent on capital, and places all French dramatic art at the mercy of Money) (I 486–7). In a later account of Brecht's 'translation' to the French stage he cites four productions that fall prey to misunderstandings that compromise epic dramaturgy: too much naturalism here, a slouch into the picturesque there, or an excess of sentimentality that counteracts the alienation effects deployed elsewhere. Barthes does not fault the directors of the plays, and even applauds their efforts. The blame lies once again with the institution of theatre in 1950s France, which, as Barthes so often reminds his readers, is a function of a society dominated by a bourgeois class whose tastes inflect even the most avant-garde or purportedly subversive of performances: 'On ne saurait souhaiter une implantation de Brecht en France, sans s'attaquer conjointement à la situation générale du théâtre français' (It would be impossible to wish for an implantation of Brecht in France without conjointly taking on the general situation of French theatre) (I 733–4). Ironically, Brecht's growing acceptance in France only spurs Barthes's exasperation with the contemporary French stage.

Under the Sign of Saussure

Barthes discovers Brecht at a decisive moment when the theoretical and philosophical strands that inform his early writings are beginning to fray and new ones come into play. The year 1955 marks a critical point in Barthes's first 'phase' during which two separate public exchanges compel him to defend, with palpable discomfort, both his Marxist rhetoric and his admiration for Sartre. In a review of Camus's *The Plague*, Barthes roundly criticizes the author for attributing evil to an abstract quasi-divine essence (the plague itself) rather than to human relations – social, political, and economic – against which the protagonists can intervene. In a rebuttal Camus counters that Barthes has missed the point of the book, that it is in fact a meditation on the necessity of human solidarity in a resistant struggle that everyone understands to be the German occupation. He then challenges Barthes to state clearly 'au nom de quelle morale plus complète' (in the name of what more complete morality) he lodges his critique.[28] As one critic puts it, Barthes's 'takes the plunge'[29] when he tersely answers 'au nom du matérialisme historique: j'estime une morale de l'explication plus complète qu'une morale de l'expression' (in the name of historical materialism; I believe a moral of explanation more complete than a moral of expression) (I 479). In the same year Barthes also rallies to the defence of Sartre's highly political and roundly reproved drama *Nekrassov*, a parodic parable of the Kravchenko affair that unsettles the Communist Party in France in the 1950s.[30] By defending Sartre's attempt to deny reports of Stalin's brutality, Barthes again uncharacteristically aligns himself with the very sort of orthodox political position he usually discredits, be it on the right or the left.

These public tiffs, perhaps both skirmishes in the heated exchange between Sartre and Camus begun in 1952, seem to reinforce Barthes's Marxist and Sartrean leanings, but his defensive posture also betrays a growing distance from both figures. In spite of a certain Marxist idea of history that informs his invectives against post-war French society, Marxism is, as Philippe Roger remarks, more of a 'companionship' or an 'accompaniment' to Barthes's writings than an orthodox doctrine or method.[31] The bristling tone of Barthes's response to Camus leaves the impression that he has been forced into a theoretical corner where he is ill at ease, and even while championing a historical materialist critique he carefully inserts some distance between himself and a rigorous 'science' of history: in tacit recognition of the arguably simplistic invocation of Marxism at work in his own criticism of *The Plague*, he seems to doubt that he himself counts among the 'partisans' who meet the exigencies of this approach. In the following months, when another accuser demands to know once and for all if Barthes is Marxist or not, Barthes replies that the inquisitor should read Marx and decide for himself – a decidedly coy response given his own unsure relation to Marx's own writings.[32] Barthes's defence of *Nekrassov* also rings hollow alongside his earlier insistence on the commitment of dramatic and literary form. Despite comparisons of Sartre's wit to that of Beaumarchais, his rebuttals to the play's tepid reviews read more as a *petite mythologie* of theatre criticism in France than a defence of Sartre's dramaturgy, and contain no mention of the responsibility and choice in each aspect of the mise en scène that he admires first in Vilar and then in Brecht. The unstated reason for this notable silence would likely be that, in terms of its form, Sartre's conventional play fails to realize the new dramaturgy Barthes advocates elsewhere.[33]

Years later, Barthes parcels his career into four distinct phases and names the most influential intertexts of each.[34] Sartre and Marx figure alongside Brecht in the schema as the interlocutors of the first phase, which neatly coincides with his tenure as a theatre critic, but they clearly do not enjoy equal favour. From Sartre and Marx Barthes gleans the notions he likes and discards others, thus *Writing Degree Zero* and other early texts can be read as an idiosyncratic digestion of existentialism and historical materialism that harbours misgivings towards both. Such ambivalence is notably absent in his understanding of Brecht, who brings together what Barthes admires in the others: freedom and responsibility on the part of theatre practitioners (echoes of Sartre) and an acute sense of how the material conditions of a historical moment shape the thoughts and actions of his characters (via Marx), all while challenging a thinking public to imagine alternatives to the represented situations. Distinct Sartrean and Marxist overtones resonate in Barthes's praise of Brecht in 1954: '[Brecht] amène le spectateur à une conscience plus grande de l'histoire, sans que cette modification provienne d'une persuasion rhétorique ou d'une intimidation prédicante: le bénéfice vient de l'acte théâtral lui-même' ([Brecht] leads the spectator to a greater consciousness of history, without this modification resulting from rhetorical persuasion or preachy intimidation: the benefit comes from the theatrical act itself) (I 419). A year later Barthes again marries Marxist and Sartrean rhetoric: 'le théâtre de Brecht accomplit une synthèse authentique entre la rigueur du dessin politique [...] et la liberté de la dramaturgie' (Brecht's theatre enacts an authentic synthesis between the rigour of a political design [...] and the freedom of the theatrical act) (I 496). Subsequent reviews further praise Brecht's 'responsibility' in every aspect of a production, including make-up, costumes, and lighting, which leads a knowing spectator to grasp the social *gestus* of the play. Brecht effectively synthesizes Barthes's vision for a popular theatre with what he most admires in his selective and unorthodox distillation of both existentialism and Marxism, without the attendant reservations that as time passes erode his already tenuous subscription to these philosophies.

More than existentialist and Marxist affinities, a third facet of Brecht's theatre justifies the intensity of Barthes's unflinching admiration. Brecht produces not only a theatre of commitment and historical consciousness, but also an exemplary theatre of intelligible signs. In this respect he represents both a culminating figure of Barthes's early years and a forerunner to the next stage in his schema: the semiological phase and the ascendancy of Ferdinand de Saussure, the father of structural linguistics, as a primary theoretical figure. No *coup de foudre* comparable to the discovery of Brecht sparks Barthes's initial appreciation of Saussure, but the Swiss linguist's influence is apparent as early as 1953, when, as noted above, Barthes already views theatre, literature, and popular culture through a distinctly semiological lens.

Barthes articulates his admiration for Brecht's productions in explicitly semiological terms. The well-known essay on 'diseased' theatre costumes, for example, develops the terms of Barthes's earlier appreciation of Vilar's *Prince of Homburg* and concludes with a discussion of a costume's relative 'health':

> D'abord, *le costume doit être un argument* [...] dans toutes les grandes époques de théâtre, le costume a eu une forte valeur sémantique; il ne se donnait pas seulement à voir, il se donnait aussi à lire, communiquait des idées, des connaissances ou des sentiments [...] les théâtres forts, populaires, civiques, ont toujours utilisé un code vestimentaire précis, ils ont largement pratiqué ce que l'on pourrait appeler une politique du signe.

> (First of all, *the costume must be an argument* [...] in all the great periods of theater, costume had a powerful semantic value; it was not there only to be seen, it was also there to be *read*, it communicated ideas, information, or

sentiments [...] powerful, popular, and civic theaters have always utilized a precise vestimentary code; they have broadly practiced what we might call a politics of the sign.) (I 1209; *CE* 46–47)

Barthes cites as his exemplary healthy specimen the deliberately tattered, burned, and worn costumes of Brecht's production of *The Mother*, which receive this favourable prognosis insofar as they undergo semiosis: 'le bon signe doit toujours être le fruit d'un choix ou d'une accentuation; Brecht a donné le détail des opérations nécessaries à la construction du *signe* de l'usure' ('the good sign must always be the fruit of a choice and of an accentuation. Brecht has given all the details of the operations necessary to the construction of the *sign* of wear-and-tear') (I 1210; *CE* 48). The scorched cloth of *The Mother*'s costumes would be little more than meticulously crafted, expensive, but ultimately meaningless rags were they considered outside the systems of signifiers and social relationships established within the production and from which they derive significance. On Brecht's stage, however, they become powerful signs of poverty, much more intelligible and effective than, for example, actual old clothing purchased for the occasion.

The semiological imperative receives programmatic articulation the following year when Barthes outlines the four tasks of the Brechtian critic. The first two tasks resonate with Barthes's Marxist affinities of the early 1950s, and he begins by stating the absolute necessity of Brecht for all contemporary 'revolutionary' theatre:

> Quiconque voudra réfléchir sur le théâtre et sur la revolution, rencontrera fatalement Brecht [...] la connaissance de Brecht, la réflexion sur Brecht, en un mot la critique brechtienne est par définition extensive à la problématique de notre temps.

> (Whoever wishes to ponder theater and the revolution will inevitably encounter Brecht [...] the familiarity with Brecht, thought on Brecht, in a word Brechtian criticism is by definition extensive to the problematic of our time.) (I 1227; *CE* 71)

Barthes first calls for a sociology of theatre audiences, which is still lacking in France, although he notes that the French criticism of Brecht necessarily aligns the critic, right or left, within a certain sector or class of society. The second, 'ideological' task recasts the gesture of demystification and explanation that guides the *Mythologies* in terms of

Brecht's dramaturgy. Another 'moral' task demands an ethic of personal choice and rings with existentialist overtones. Brecht's spectators, like Sartre's heroes, question the apparently 'natural' status quo and are therefore confronted with the difficult question of individual responsibility: how might one act to solve the problems that plague the lives of the characters? To these familiar topoi of the early 1950s, however, Barthes adds a fourth 'semiological' task in distinct and systematic Saussurean terms: dramatic art must signify rather than represent the world; there must be a palpable distance between the signifier and the signified; their relationship furthermore must be at least partially arbitrary, 'faute de quoi on retombe dans un art de l'expression, dans un art de l'illusion essentialiste' ('otherwise we fall back on an art of expression, an art of essentialist illusion') (I 1230; *CE* 75). Despite obvious differences between a materialist grasp of history, Sartre's humanism, and Saussure's synchronic and detached analysis of structure over historical event or autonomous subject, Barthes weaves all three into his appreciation of Brecht.

Barthes's semiologically inflected appropriation of Brecht is arguably no less selective than his earlier borrowings from Sartre and Marx. A critic has remarked that 'if Brecht had not existed, Barthes would surely have had to invent him.'[35] Even without the condition, one could contend that Barthes, ever the theoretical *bricoleur*, did indeed create his own Brecht, selecting the aspects that appealed to him and reworking them into an idiosyncratic notion of 'epic' theatre as an exemplary instance of a committed semiosis.[36] The Saussurean principle that a sign has no value outside the system from which it differentially derives meaning harmonizes with the *gestus* of Brecht's epic theatre, which reveals how the characters' thoughts and actions are shaped by the social, economic, and political relationships in which they are mired. However, a contradiction simmers between a theatre that leads a spectator to participate in history and to form committed responses that will rectify the troubling status quo, and a structural analysis intended primarily to offer an understanding of the system. The political dimension of Brecht's theatre is consequently less enhanced than compromised by the semiological lens through which Barthes's considers it, and in the following years Brecht's masterful deployment of signs overtakes any political objectives as Barthes's primary interest in his dramaturgy. However, for a brief time in 1955 and 1956, a semiologically construed Brechtian theatre serves as the ground on which Barthes continues to juggle the discourses of Marx and Sartre even as the

Saussurean ball comes into play. The four tasks of the Brechtian critic are perhaps less prescriptive, as Barthes intends them, than descriptive of his desire to reconcile the commitment of his earliest 'phase' with an interest in signs and signification that increasingly drives his thought.

Dénouement

The tension between Sartrean/Marxist commitment and an acute sense of the sign, though briefly productive for Barthes, soon resolves in favour of semiological analysis. In 'The Myth Today,' the theoretical treatise that concludes *Mythologies*, Barthes reflects on the limits of his critical stance and recognizes that the project of demythologizing is ultimately negative: he can reveal the political dimension of even the most banal speech, but he cannot do so in the name of any deeper truth. The *larvatus prodeo* figure comes to Barthes via Descartes, but unlike his predecessor he cannot confidently vouch for any truth-wielding *cogito* lurking beneath the mask. The mythologist's speech is merely a displacement: 'sa parole est un méta-langage, elle n'agit rien; tout au plus dévoile-t-elle, et encore, pour qui?' ('His speech is a metalanguage, it "acts" nothing; at the most it unveils – or does it? To whom?') (I 717; *M* 156). The questions betray Barthes's suspicion that the modernized society of post-war France is incapable of producing an unalienated popular culture that encompasses all strata of society, comparable to his ideal Greek spectatorship. Instead, Barthes witnesses the ascendency of the petite-bourgeoisie as the dominant class in an age of mass communication in which any 'truthful' explanation of the material relations of a society, any popular reader/audience to whom this is communicated, and the mythologist himself constitute myths and masks in their own right.

The parameters of Barthes's criticism shift palpably in 1956. In contrast to the earlier exchange with Camus in which Barthes demands in the name of historical materialism a plague be nothing more than a plague, he all but repudiates the revelatory literalness he promoted only two years earlier: 'le vin est objectivement bon, et *en même temps*, la bonté du vin est un mythe: voilà l'aporie. Le mythologue sort de là comme il peut: il s'occupera de la bonté du vin, non du vin lui-même' ('wine is objectively good, and *at the same time*, the goodness of wine is a myth: here is the aporia. The mythologist gets out of this the best he can: he deals with the goodness of wine, not the wine itself') (I 718; *M* 158).

The pure 'literality' of the object no longer concerns Barthes, nor does the notion of a popular culture that represents the zero degree of ideologies of class. Instead of working to strip away the 'masks' that obscure and alienate, the post-*Mythologies* Barthes trains a fascinated critical eye on the same insidious connotations he earlier strives to pare down to nothing, 'second order' meanings that, he concedes, constitute rather than conceal the realities of the world around him. Barthes no longer seeks to replace the ideological 'mask' with any truth, authenticity, or knowing subject underneath, for these are themselves only part of the mask on whose surface meanings and truths migrate and coalesce.

A casualty of the sea change in Barthes's thought is the dream for a viable popular theatre in France. Nineteen fifty-five marks the peak of Barthes's activity as a theatre critic, a year during which he publishes seventeen articles, reviews, and editorials on contemporary French theatre. His interest abruptly ebbs as the number falls to nine in 1956, then only four or five per year, and his final review appears in 1960 followed by near silence on the subject of theatre as performance practice throughout the remainder of his life. These numbers can be explained in part by other preoccupations that compete for his time – in 1956 Barthes accepts a position at the Centre national de la recherche scientifique (CNRS) to engage in a sociological study of fashion. The same year, the Soviet invasion of Hungary and Kruschev's renunciation of Stalinism compel many Marxist and *marxisant* writers to question their convictions. Even earlier, however, the tide of Barthes's criticism is already turning against French theatre. By 1956 the hope and passion of Barthes's earlier writings cedes to a somewhat repetitive explication of Brecht punctuated by fatigued impatience with French theatres.[37] Although Barthes occasionally admires the work of other directors, most notably Planchon, and observes with approval the possible birth of a new theatre in Michel Vinaver's *Aujourd'hui ou les Coréens*, his primary interests already lie elsewhere, and he does not champion the work of these men with the passion that drives his earlier embrace of either Vilar or Brecht.[38]

The fate of the TNP in Barthes's criticism is perhaps the most telling barometer of his disillusionment with French theatre. Reviews in the later 1950s magnify Vilar's shortcomings, and an ever less forgiving Barthes observes how Vilar's critical success compromises his once radical project. Vilar alone represents Barthes's greatest hope for French theatre, and his capitulation to degraded bourgeois norms and the TNP's dependency on bourgeois and state money administer the coup de grâce to an irredeemable French stage:

> Mais si Vilar se met à être complaisant, la partie est perdue: ce n'est plus
> telle ou telle cabale qui le menace, comme aux temps héroïques du TNP,
> c'est toute une France 'irresponsible' qui est prête à lui régler son compte –
> dans la gloire, bien entendu.

> (If Vilar starts becoming complacent, the game is lost: it is not this or that
> cabal that threatens him, as in the heroic past of the TNP, it's a whole
> 'irresponsible' France that is ready to settle his score – in glory of course.)
> (I 740)

In his last review of a Vilar production, Barthes issues a harsh condemnation of the TNP:

> Il y a maintenant un style Vilar, au sens complet du terme: un ensemble de
> normes esthéthiques et idéologiques [...] comme à la Comédie Française,
> où tout comédien venu de l'extérieur est rapidement aplati sous le poids
> des traditions implicites, le TNP semble avoir éliminé toute tension entre
> ses acteurs et son metteur en scène, ses spectacles et son public.

> (There is now a Vilar style, in the full meaning of the term: an ensemble of
> aesthetic and ideological norms [...] as at the Comédie Française, where all
> actors coming from the outside are quickly flattened by the weight of
> implicit traditions, the TNP seems to have eliminated all tension between
> its actors and its director, its spectacles and its public.) (I 777).

Where Barthes earlier remarks bold choices in Vilar's stagings, he sees
mannered, complacent, and aestheticized performances. The spectators
too, once the fresh and innocent 'men' of a new age, draw blame as
irresponsible consumers of ideologically insidious spectacle. The comparison to the Comédie Française, in the 1950s a low blow for *engagé*
theatre if there ever were one, announces Barthes's virtual rejection of
Vilar, the TNP, the dream of a truly 'popular' audience, and finally of
theatre itself as an object of study.

Only Brecht survives the flood of Barthes's discontent, but even he
undergoes an apotheosis, rising out of the hopelessly compromised
world of contemporary French theatre and politics to become a primarily theoretical figure. The semiological gloss of Brecht reaches full
expression in one of Barthes's final considerations of Brechtian dramaturgy, a 1960 preface for *Mother Courage*.[39] Of the four tasks of the
Brechtian critic outlined in 1956, the semiological here clearly eclipses

the others. Barthes cites numerous production choices – costumes, props, gestures – that signify insofar as they are used by the characters in a specific set of social relations; they derive their meaning from the system of both the represented social situation and the stage's economy of signs. The reader, however, is left to wonder exactly what this social situation and these gestic meanings are. The detailed analyses of the semiotics of costumes and acting styles, an early speculation on the semiotics of photography (a topic that will later fascinate Barthes), and a reflection on Brecht's use of significant details far outweigh the cursory concluding comments about what this exemplary staging actually reveals to the spectators, and even there it remains surprisingly abstract: merely that Courage does not see that her commercial activity, which she believes guarantees her autonomy and her family's livelihood, is contingent on the war that destroys her children. Barthes proposes that Courage's daughter, who is mute but sees what her mother cannot, is the true heroine of the play, and a certain vocabulary (her 'ethical act,' her 'free gesture') echoes the Sartrean overtones of his earlier criticism. However, what she does and why, not to mention what this might mean for the spectator – a late-1950s spectator in France at the height of the Algerian conflict, for example – are left unsaid. Questions of who these spectators are, how much they pay for a ticket, where they live, and their social class, former preoccupations of an activist Barthes and crucial for his vision for a popular theatre, are not entertained at all.

The preceding year Barthes writes: 'le sens d'une œuvre n'est pas forcément une leçon' (the meaning of a work is not necessarily a lesson) (I 849); in his later analyses of Brecht the production of meaning all but displaces the meaning itself, a fortiori, any didactic message. This trend culminates in a 1963 interview in which Barthes looks back on his theatre years. His broad, brief, and nearly glib reference to the concerns of Brecht's theatre is in itself telling – 'il prend parti sur la nature, le travail, le racisme, le fascisme, l'histoire, la guerre, l'aliénation' ('it takes sides with regard to nature, labor, racism, fascism, history, war, alienation') (I 1363; *CE* 263) – and is eclipsed by the lengthy and detailed account of theatrical signs that occupies the greater part of the discussion. The interview in question, 'Literature and Signification,' is the final text included in *Critical Essays*, published in 1964, a choice that intentionally or not casts a revisionist gloss over Barthes's theatre criticism and his interest in Brecht. Brecht persists in Barthes's writings as less the founder of a new dramaturgy who engages the problems of modern capitalist society than an exemplary creator and manipulator of signs, a transposition that guarantees his survival in Barthes's structuralist 'phase,' while the dialogues with both Marx and Sartre, from whom any semiological resonance cannot be likewise separated from the considerations of the society in which the 'density of signs' is embedded, precipitously fade into the past.

In 1965 Barthes looks back on his theatre years and their abrupt end with a certain degree of puzzlement:

> J'ai toujours beaucoup aimé le théâtre et pourtant je n'y vais presque plus. C'est là un revirement qui m'intrigue moi-même. Que s'est-il passé? Quand cela s'est-il passé? Est-ce moi qui ai changé? Ou le théâtre? Est-ce que je ne l'aime plus, ou est-ce que je l'aime trop?

> (I have always liked the theatre and yet I hardly go there any more. This is a reversal that intrigues me. What happened? When did it happen? Is it I who changed? Or the theatre? Do I no longer love it, or do I love it too much?) (I 1530)

Though Barthes guesses Brecht's inimitable dramaturgy contributes to his sudden distaste for anything less dazzling, by 1965 even his predilection for Brecht's theatre as performance practice has waned to virtually nothing. Barthes's questions go unanswered, and he does not offer the obvious explanation that between the first theatre review and the last the parameters of his thought, along with that of many other French intellectuals, radically shift from a Marxist-existentialist call for change to a rigorous semiological and structural analysis of the present situation. He leaves this observation to the few commentators who ponder his sudden departure from the theatre, and who do not fail to note the neat coincidence of his tenure as a theatre reviewer with the Marxist/ Sartrean phase of his career. Andy Stafford argues that the tension between a 'Trotskyian cynicism towards popular culture' and a 'typically Communist Party cultural populism' confounds Barthes's impatient call for a viable popular theatre, the very possibility of which he soon begins to question.[40] Stafford concludes that Barthes's exasperation with mass culture, so evident in the *Mythologies*, drives him to quit the popular theatre movement and to undertake the esoteric structuralist enterprise of the early 1960s. Philippe Roger similarly maintains that Barthes champions an idiosyncratic vision of a truly popular theatre that he subsequently deems unattainable.[41] Where Stafford contends that André Malraux's theatre reform of 1959 plays into the hands of bourgeois culture and further alienates Barthes, Roger suggests that through the establishment of theatres and Maisons de la culture throughout France, Malraux, minister of culture under de Gaulle, actually realizes a certain kind of popular theatre, a disturbing success that impels Barthes's silence lest he find himself praising the initiatives of a government he does not support. In both cases, the audience of this new theatre is not the fresh and innocent 'man' Barthes earlier envisions, but an all too familiar bourgeois or petit-bourgeois spectatorship that imbues the purportedly popular national audience with its own ideology and aesthetic sensibilities.

Accounts that chart Barthes's flight into an abstract structuralism, away from a politically conscious theatre rooted in the material conditions of a rapidly changing society, are consistent with Kristen Ross's conclusions in her investigation of post-war French culture, *Fast Cars, Clean Bodies: Decolonization and the Reordering of French Culture*. Ross considers the rise of structuralism as part of a greater ethos of cleansing that inflects images of the new French nation, its culture, and its people in the period of rapid change between 1950 and 1965. Modernization creates a 'national middle class' of mass consumers who supplant the bourgeoisie as the arbiters of culture. The new nation, its institutions, and its cultural artefacts appear to grow out of a levelling of individual distinctions, but Ross is ever mindful of new and as yet less visible lines of exclusion that transect this society. She relates the literal cleansing of the newly available washing machines and bathtubs to the imaginary washing away of the colonial era through decolonization, a gesture that also tidily cleanses the influx of immigrants, many of them workers from former colonies whose labour fuels modernization and ensures the comforts of the new dominant class, from inclusion in the shiny new nation. Ross includes the ascetic ideals that descend from Barthes's zero degree in this cleansing gesture, notably his idealization of Robbe-Grillet's nouveau roman as a 'literal literature,' and she even more pointedly implicates structuralism and semiology: 'Subjectivity, consciousness, and agency – what passed for *l'homme*, in short, under the now obsolete terms of bourgeois humanism – are effaced to the profit of rules, codes, and structures.'[42] This evacuation of the individual political subject occurs at the moment when immigrant populations begin to claim a new subjective identity as inhabitants and even citizens of a rapidly changing France, only to find their struggle less defeated than abstracted from the structuralist vision.

The call for a new national popular theatre begs the same critical pressure Ross brings to novels, film, and advertising, and that Barthes himself applies with a heightened awareness of the colonial dynamic on *steak-frites*, Pierre Poujade, red wine, and other phenomena studied in *Mythologies*. Vilar, for example, arguably 'cleanses' the post-colonial demographics from his ideal audience. Despite the inclusion of translated works by foreign authors in his repertoire, Vilar explicitly addresses 'un public français, indispensable à la naissance de grandes œuvres françaises' (a French public indispensable for the birth of great French works).[43] Envisioning a working public engaged in the most menial chores or hard labour, Vilar invokes a past that is not that of most immigrants from former colonies who often hold such jobs: 'Il s'agit d'apporter à la partie la plus vive de la société contemporaine, aux hommes et aux femmes de la tâche ingrate et du labeur dur, des charmes d'un art dont ils n'auraient jamais dû, depuis le temps des cathédrales et des mystères, être sevrés' (It is a matter of bringing to the most lively part of contemporary society, to the men and women who perform thankless tasks and hard labour, the charms of an art from which, since the time of cathedrals and mystery plays, they never should have been severed).[44] At other times, Vilar adds a racial inflection by tracing the specificity of the national and popular public's lineage to a period before France becomes deeply involved in the colonial experience: 'Nous continuerons donc notre travail, travail pour ce bon public simple et sentimental et raisonnable que l'on appelle, depuis au moins Henri IV, le peuple de France' (And so we will continue our work, work for that simple, sentimental, and reasonable public that has been called, at least since Henri IV, the people of France).[45] In these and other remarks, Vilar fails to consider how the 'national' inflects the 'popular' in an increasingly multi-ethnic country where the effects of the colonial experience and decolonization further baffle the already fraught endeavour of imagining a national popular spectatorship.[46]

Like other proponents of a national popular theatre over the years, Barthes ponders its popular dimension at length and ties its success to a negotiation of class divisions, while the national character of this theatre, in either 1950s France or in his ancient Greek ideal, escapes comparable scrutiny. Does the ancient chorus, the representative of the 'collective' and model for a new French theatre, really speak as the whole of society, or is it also mired in a historical situation, a divided society with a dominant voice that passes as universal and speaks for the nation and the people, namely, that of an enfranchised Greek male spectatorship? In a notorious passage of the *Poetics*, Aristotle excludes women and slaves from the ideal spectator, the 'average man' on whose sensibilities mimesis is contingent, and thereby compromises the universality of the 'human' element in tragedy with an inflection of gender, class, and likely race and ethnicity as well. Barthes's own brand of criticism likewise erects a mythic spectator when the audience he hails as 'national' and 'popular' is, like Aristotle's 'man' of ancient Athens, endowed with ethnic and national specificity, and the all-inclusive levelling of differences that bonds the 'people' of this new society together only emerges after a prior and invisible gesture of exclusion. Years later, well after he has ceased to write on contemporary French theatre, Barthes himself turns a retrospective mythologist's eye on the Greek spectators he and others freely idealized:

> On a fait volontiers du théâtre grec le modèle même du théâtre populaire. Il faut pourtant rappeler que, pour admirable qu'elle ait été, la démocratie athénienne [...] était une démocratie aristocratique: elle laissait à la porte les métèques et les esclaves.

> (One has willingly made Greek theatre the very model of popular theatre. It must be remembered, however, that admirable as it was, Athenian democracy [...] was an aristocratic democracy: it left the foreigners and slaves at the door.) (I 1549)

The innocent spectators Barthes imagines in the Avignon courtyard, washed clean of class divisions and the weight of history to be reborn into a new theatrical age, invite similar interrogation. Barthes offers no further retrospective reconsideration of the ethnic and national constitution of Vilar's spectators, nor of any other theatre audience in his contemporary France. He realizes fully, however, that the ideal audiences and the 'fresh' collectives he briefly envisions in the mid-1950s are anything but innocent. This realization, tinged with a dismayed awareness that he himself might have indulged in myth-mongering in imagining a popular theatre modelled on the ancient Greek ideal, would only hasten his flight from the terms of his early theatre criticism into the 'scientific delirium' of the structuralist abstraction.

'Did I Love It Too Much?'

A narrative of idealistic passion, disappointment, and repudiation therefore emerges as a prevalent explanation for Barthes's abrupt dismissal of the institution of theatre. Exasperated with the theatre he sees around him, weary of the Sisyphian task of advocating an impossible theatre, and armed with a new theoretical discourse, after 1960 a disappointed Barthes abandons this critical project whose origin, methods, and lofty goals are inexorably compromised in the realities of post-war France.

However, when one broadens the enquiry from a narrow focus on Barthes's failed dream for a national popular theatre to a more general consideration of the place theatre and performance occupy in his writings throughout his long career, it is apparent that the account outlined above begs questions that pass unasked, not to mention unanswered. The most evident is why theatre alone among systems of representation is so inextricably linked to Barthes's failure to reconcile his new semiological analyses with a Sartrean Marxism, and why disillusionment with one necessarily entails the rejection of the other. Barthes expresses an impatient dislike of literature on grounds similar to those that kindle his invectives against French theatre, a fact that does not prevent him from investigating literary texts in all phases of his long career. Literature accompanies Barthes throughout his writings, and not only at its most experimental; even the most traditionally canonical of texts draw his attention as rich sites for investigating different modes of *écriture*. Other media that are targets of trenchant critique in *Mythologies*, photography for example, also return as important preoccupations for the later Barthes. Would not the shift from an existentialist/Marxist analysis to a more scientific semiology also open a new critical perspective on theatre as a signifying system? Theatre's 'density of signs' already provided a rich field of enquiry for the theorists of the Prague Linguistic Circle, Barthes's predecessors in the study of signs and signification. Furthermore, while Vilar and others are accused of becoming entrenched in the establishment (Vilar's case will culminate in the protests of the 1968 Avignon festival), new directors and troupes emerge who also grapple, arguably with success, with the same issues of audience, funding, repertoire, and a new stage aesthetic that preoccupy the early Barthes. Many also share a keen sense of the semiotics of performance practice, yet one looks in vain in Barthes's work for comments on the productions of Ariane Mnouchkine, Antoine Vitez, Robert Wilson, Peter Brook, Patrice Chéreau, or others who come into prominence in France in the 1960s and 1970s.

Furthermore, the contention that Barthes abandons theatre after 1960 itself demands revision. If Barthes no longer addresses the institution of theatre in France or specific contemporary productions, 'theatricality' and the 'theatre' re-emerge as privileged terms in his later writings.

Theoretical stagings often serve as the central figures on which his later thought turns: the castrato's stunning performance in *S/Z*, the idealization of Bunraku in *The Empire of Signs*, a curious drag show in *Sade, Fourier, Loyola*, the scene of love in *A Lover's Discourse: Fragments*, to name only a few instances. A figurative and textual theatre flourishes; it is only a literal theatre and specific moments of live performance practice in his contemporary France that disappear in his later work.

The resurgence of a theoretical or textual theatre, neatly extracted from live performance, raises further questions when the body, *le corps*, also emerges as a key theoretical trope in Barthes's later 'phases.' Why, when Barthes examines the body's inflection in literary texts, painting, photography, music, and other media, does he deploy the word 'theatre' either as an epithet for stereotyped and arrogant political language, or in a more general sense, as so many contemporary critics do, as a metaphor that denies performance any specificity, or even a place at all, in the theatricality he invokes? Why must the body, *le corps*, his 'mot-mana' and privileged figure, be mediated by language and technology or else remain abstract, and only on the rarest occasions be the living and present body of performance practice?

Finally, one cannot ignore the significance of a studied silence in Barthes's writing. Far from a mark of irrelevance or dismissal, a refusal to shed knowing light on certain topics is a tactical gesture in Barthes's oeuvre. From the zero degree through the figure of the photographic image's *punctum* in his last published book, the carving out of an elusive, ephemeral space for the unsayable informs Barthes's idiosyncratic position as a writer who resists the uncritical repetition of stereotyped discourses, even when these are discourses of liberation and even if this means favouring a watchful silence in the place of more active intervention. Writing, the body, sexuality, subjectivity, pleasure and *jouissance*, music, love, photography and other key Barthesian topoi find their ideal manifestation not as what can be captured in language, but as fascinating, troubling remainders that fissure the purportedly smooth surfaces of meaning and carve out blind fields in the overbearing discourses of truth that blithely and arrogantly circulate around him. If silence is a lack, it is also refuge from the nauseating babble of received knowledge, and in this apparent gap churn the most cherished, intriguing, and contested critical figures of Barthes's writings.

Do I no longer love it, or do I love it too much? Clearly, a disappointed Barthes sours on the institution of theatre in France, and ultimately relinquishes his vision for a national popular theatre. However, the place of a certain theatricality, the body, and the tropes of the unsayable in Barthes's later work bid us refrain from answering his question too quickly, and to wonder if some part of live performance so enthrals him, touches him so deeply, unsettles his thought so completely that he can not – or will not – subject it to the knowing theoretical scrutiny he brings to other media. *Does he love it too much?* Entertaining seriously this question opens a new perspective not only on Barthes's theatre criticism, but on the entire oeuvre of the man who, before he ever publishes a word, as a young student feels a powerful and anxious fascination with the possible failure of words, meaning, and subjectivity, as he peers from behind his mask in the courtyard of the Sorbonne.[47] These sentiments mark the beginning of a long, rich, and often conflicted reflection on live performance that is illuminating, though often frustrating as well, for if performance acts as a useful interpretive lens through which we might consider Barthes's work, it is often a transparent one, discernible only through subtle refractions and uncharted blind spots. Those who seek a coherent and detailed program that practitioners of theorists of performance might follow will still be disappointed, as ultimately Barthes himself is. Whether a young man playing Darius, a theatre critic in the 1950s, or the aging critic looking back on this scene, Barthes continues to find live performance practice an ambivalent trap, a stage on which his political and linguistic subject is never able to shake off the compromising mask. He bestows on it nothing more than some early articles and a later spangling of oblique figures – and nothing less than a loving regime of silence.

2 Performance and Its Double: The 'Live' and the Structuralist Abstraction

Roland Barthes and his fellow post-war critics inherit a rich legacy from the preceding generation of theorists of theatre and performance. There is of course Brecht, who articulates the principles of his epic theatre, the alienation effect, and the 'gestic' potential of the theatrical apparatus in the 'Short Organum for the Theater' and other treatises of the 1930s and 1940s. Barthes's public and forceful advocacy of Brecht is widely recognized as the most noteworthy thrust of his writings on theatre. However, an exclusive focus on Barthes's embrace of Brecht risks eclipsing his encounter with the thought of other theorists. Although he rarely invokes them by name, the terms of two influential accounts of performance practice, Antonin Artaud's 'theatre of cruelty' and the work of the Prague School linguists in the field of theatre semiotics, also resonate through Barthes's theatre criticism in the 1950s.

The common ground shared by Artaud's celebration of raw presence and a semiotic reading of the stage is not immediately apparent, and it further evinces Barthes's willingness to weave diverse and even contradictory theoretical strands into the fabric of his writing. Artaud is best known for envisioning theatre as the brute experience of life itself, not its double, its representation, or its simulacrum. He calls for the liberation of the theatrical apparatus – body, voice, space, movement, music – from the straitjacket of a conventional theatre grounded in logic, language, and rational psychology. A 'theatre of cruelty' effectively divests both performer and spectator of rational thought and other psychological trappings in favour of a more immediate and unsettling life underneath: a corporeal presence liberated from the 'disorders of consciousness' that troubled Kleist, although where Kleist admires the grace of innocent youth, Artaud most often envisions a nightmarish unleashing of basic and universal human instincts and drives.[1]

Accounts of twentieth-century theatre often situate Artaud in opposition to Brecht, but in terms of the performer's presence a more stark contrast can be found in the work of the linguists and theorists of the Prague Linguistic Circle, also called the Prague School. From 1926 until the Communists seize power in Czechoslovakia in 1948, this group of international scholars produces pioneering work in the study of language and literature as systems of signification and are notably innovative in their transposition of semiotic and linguistic theory to non-verbal forms of signification, including theatre. Jiří Veltruský succinctly puts forth the fundamental principle of *semiosis* that governs much of their thought: although less arbitrary than the phonemes and graphemes of written and spoken language, 'all that is on the stage is a sign.'[2] The simplicity of this principle belies the Prague Schoolers' subtle sensitivity to theatre's idiosyncracies as a system of representation and the difficult duality of the material object and its semiotic properties. Petr Bogatyrev cites the example of a diamond to illustrate the complexity of semiosis in theatre. A diamond is already a sign, for it is not only the thing itself (a glittering stone) but also signifies wealth or elegance. On the stage, the 'reality' of the diamond matters little; indeed, in most cases one would presume a stone to be fake. Already both reality and sign, on the stage it becomes both a sign and the *sign of a sign*, and even if the diamond is genuine the semiotic properties effectively displace the reality of the 'thing itself,' to which the spectator might be entirely indifferent.[3] The performer, too, is ostensibly bound by the same principle. Jindřich Honzl writes: 'The fundamental nature of an actor does not consist in the fact that he is a person speaking and moving about the stage but that he *represents someone, that he signifies a role in the play.*'[4] Honzl discounts the difference between the live performing body and its inanimate replica: 'hence it does not matter whether he is a human being; an actor could be a piece of wood as well.'[5] Veltruský similarly concludes that in certain cases 'it follows that people in these roles can be replaced by lifeless dummies.'[6] Semiosis erodes the distinction between the live and the inanimate, between a living body and its simulacrum.

Artaud and the Prague Schoolers strive simultaneously towards the two poles – unmediated corporeality or the inanimate simulacrum, a purification of presence or its elimination, an inimitable 'here and now' or an iterable signifier – between which, at least for Kleist, the human experience unfolds. Unlike Kleist, they posit ideal theatres that accommodate rather than displace the live performing body in their ideal, be it innocent immediacy or inanimate perfection. However, neither Artaud nor the Prague School theorists escape the anxieties of the 'live.' In both cases the question of the performer's presence prompts theoretical gestures that blur the distinction between their otherwise starkly opposed positions and betray the resistance of the live performing body to their theoretical ideals.

Artaud articulates in detail the power of the body's living presence and reserves it a place of honour in his theatre, but he also envisions an ideal theatre secured through, or that at the least provides for, the abstraction of the live performing body itself. In *The Theatre and Its Double* Artaud proposes shadow puppets, masks, and giant marionettes as powerful staging strategies for a theatre of cruelty, and invests these inanimate objects with the same immediacy and powerful presence as the live performing body: 'the sudden appearance of a fabricated Being, made of wood and cloth, entirely invented, corresponding to nothing, yet disquieting by nature, capable of reintroducing on the stage a little breath of that great metaphysical fear which is at the root of all ancient theatre.'[7] The monstrous puppet appears to strip away logic, reason, and the coherent cogito as well as a live performer can, and arguably evacuates an interior, rational subject more definitively than a live body that risks, à la Kleist, serving as the fetish for a rational consciousness. The repeated calls for the body's dismemberment (in *Spurt of Blood*, for example) or its replacement with an inanimate simulacrum in no way constitute a disavowal or even a suspicion of the performer's body, which remains the privileged figure of Artaud's vision, but they nonetheless challenge the necessity of a live performer for a 'cruel' performance.

Inversely, the Prague School linguists, despite observations to the contrary, at times concede that the live performing body is a singularly problematic sign. The apparently exhaustive semiosis of the stage notwithstanding, the Prague Schoolers, as Michael Quinn observes, recognize in the body 'unique patterns of coherence that are different from those exhibited by larger theatrical structures.'[8] Veltruský revises his earlier contention that the body's apparent presence can be reduced to a 'zero degree' (his term) and maintains that, like other material objects on the stage, 'the stage figure created by a live actor oscillates between being a sign, that is, a reality standing for a reality and reality in its own right.'[9] Bogatyrev goes further by recognizing the performer's body as a uniquely rich component of theatre, at once part of a sign system and, by virtue of its 'liveness,' a more real phenomenon and an exception to the rule of semiosis: 'The only live subject in the theatre is the actor [...]

we see in him not only a system of signs but also a living person.'[10] One might anticipate that the semiotic complexity of live performer would guarantee it a central place in subsequent enquiries as a singularly rich site for further study, but this is not the case; Bogatyrev concludes this discussion of the compromised corporeal sign with yet another invocation of the inanimate puppet's semiotic purity.[11] Veltruský and Bogatyrev concede and even admire the body's exceptional status, but this recognition remains within a parenthesis outside of which they carry on their analyses as if the body were little different from any other sign.

A replica or an exaggerated representation of the body realizes Artaud's immediate presence, while the body resists semiosis through a measure of 'liveness' that sentences it to a marginal place in the Prague Schoolers' discussions. The live performer is disclaimed, granted an exemption, and in certain passages displaced from both a 'cruel' performance and the semiotic stage. Despite obvious differences, the question of 'liveness' blurs the otherwise stark opposition between these conceptions of theatre, and raises the question of whether their ideal theatres are best expressed through the abstraction of the live performing body itself.

Barthes is an heir of both Artaud and the Prague School linguists. Although there is no evidence Barthes explores the full reach of Prague School criticism, he admires and often cites the work of one member of the group, Roman Jakobson, and invokes other figures who engage this body of theory: Louis Hjelmslev and Viggo Brøndal, among others. The principle of semiosis guides his analysis of the stage, and the bodies that populate it, as he moves towards a more rigorous semiology throughout the 1950s. More surprising perhaps, especially for those who closely identify Barthes's theatre criticism with his admiration for Brecht, is the intermittent but distinct Artaudian strain that runs through his early writings. On rare occasions Barthes invokes Artaud by name, usually only in a list of writers who envision the outer limits of language (Lautréamont and Mallarmé often fill out the roster). Nonetheless, a body's inarticulate 'being there' haunts Barthes's writings in the 1950s, emerging through a vocabulary of fascination and anxiety more evocative of Artaud than of Brecht. The performing body's elusive presence, fleeting and exempt from meaning, makes only rare appearances but its significance is far-reaching. Not only does it offer a counterpoint to the intelligible body-as-sign Barthes more frequently proposes, but it also represents an early articulation of the figure of *le corps*, the open, generative, neutral figure exempt from meaning around which so much of his later thought turns.

Artaud and the Prague School semioticians bequeath Barthes an unsettled theoretical terrain on which the live performing body holds an exceptionally dynamic place even as provisions are made, at least parenthetically, for its evacuation from consideration. The ambivalence of this legacy threatens to compromise Barthes's own competing theoretical ideals: the pure 'zero degree' and 'literality' on one hand, and on the other a semiological analysis that tolerates poorly any unresolved tension between the body-as-sign and its live or present double. The conundrum of the live performing body's 'presence' haunts Barthes, not only in his theatre reviews but throughout his early writings: in his euphoric moments, his discontents, and finally the abrupt and enigmatic end of his theatre criticism and the striking failure of his subsequent structuralist phase to accommodate live performance practice in its ambitious project.

The Theft of the Body

Competing accounts of the body's role in representation unsettle Barthes's terms from his first published writings. In the opening pages of *Writing Degree Zero* Barthes draws a propaedeutic distinction between language, style, and writing (*écriture*). Language constitutes the field in which the author writes, a 'reflex response,' a determined limit a single author is free neither to set nor to choose. Style likewise offers no choice to a writer, but differs from language in that the writer's individual experience determines it rather than an externally imposed and shared cultural situation. It is a 'personal and secret mythology,' a 'form without destination,' the 'closeted memory' that demands no responsibility on the part of the writing subject. Language and style are both givens, fixed systems, horizons within which a writer must navigate. Powerless to change these two invariables, only in writing can the author as conscious subject find a narrow freedom to make ethical choices and committed gestures. In the greater part of *Writing Degree Zero* Barthes sets language and style aside to address the possibilities and pitfalls of *écriture*.

The brief remarks on style nonetheless sketch a startling portrait of the body's role in both the generation and the reception of the literary text. Style fascinates Barthes for reasons other than the measured arguments that characterize his discussion of *écriture*. It springs from the 'hidden, secret flesh' of the writer's body and forms a second axis of possibilities 'whose frame of reference is biological, not historical.' The contact of this 'deep' and 'dense' corporeality with language provokes a 'transmutation': 'une metamorphose aveugle et obstinée, partie d'un infra-langage qui s'élabore à la limite de la chair et du monde' ('a metamorphosis starting from a sub-language where flesh and reality come together') (I 146; *WDZ* 11). With further vocabulary worthy of an alchemist, Barthes continues:

> Aussi le style est-il toujours un secret; mais le versant silencieux de sa référence ne tient pas à la nature mobile et sans cesse sursitaire du langage; son secret est un souvenir enfermé dans le corps de l'écrivain [...] ce qui se tient droit et profound sous le style [...] ce sont les fragments d'une réalité absolument étranger au langage. Le miracle de cette transmutation fait du style une sorte d'opération supra-littéraire, qui emporte l'homme au seuil de la puissance et de la magie [...] C'est l'Autorité du style, c'est-à-dire le lien absolument libre du langage et de son double de chair, qui impose l'écrivain comme une Fraîcheur au-dessus de l'Histoire.

> (Style is always a secret; but the occult aspect of its implications does not arise from the mobile and ever-provisional nature of language; its secret is recollection locked within the body of the writer [...] what stands firmly and deeply beneath style [...] are fragments of a reality entirely alien to language. The miracle of this transmutation makes style a kind of supra-literary operation which carries man to the threshold of power and magic [...]. It is the Authority of style, that is, the entirely free relationship between language and its fleshly double, which places the writer above History as the freshness of Innocence.) (I 146; *WDZ* 12–13)

Those familiar with Barthes's later work might be surprised to find in *Writing Degree Zero* a corporeal figure that would seem more at home in *The Pleasure of the Text, Roland Barthes by Roland Barthes,* or 'The Grain of the Voice' and other later essays. The body of style anticipates the blissful post-structuralist dissemination of the subject of his later career, where *le corps* emerges as the figure of exemption from meaning, a gap in which desire, secret or otherwise, circulates under the 'masks' of meaning, of self, and of ideology.

Barthes's brief, undeveloped thoughts on style jar with the greater argument of *Writing Degree Zero*. Rhapsodic enthusiasm over mystical excesses to the social, to history, and to language clashes with the Marxist and existentialist urgency that drives the theorization of *écriture.* Style is a sensuous underside to the mask of writing, a 'fleshly double' beyond ideology, not an authorial self but a living, fragmented, desiring body somehow manifest in the literary text and complicit in its production. Style also precedes and exceeds the gesture of writing as commitment in the given historical moment. The opening pages of *Writing Degree Zero* house a profound ambivalence between the call for the writer's responsibility in an alienated historical moment and fascination with a quality of writing situated outside history, where the author withdraws from society to inhabit 'un nouveau monde adamique où le langage ne serait plus aliéné' ('some new Adamic world where language would no longer be alienated') (I 186; *WDZ* 88). The Edenic utopia of literature only puts into relief its present predicament. The problematics of modern form condemns the writer to look, in Barthes's comparison, as Moses upon the promised land he will never enter. Even texts that approach the ideal zero degree, Camus's *The Outsider*, for example, still wear the mask of literature and remain the emblem of a specific historical moment, namely, the ongoing societal reconfiguration of post-war France. Style remains elusive: 'il est la "chose" de l'écrivain, sa splendeur et sa prison' ('the writer's "thing," his glory and his prison') (I 146; *WDZ* 11). With his lingering search for freedom and ethical choice, after a brief moment of breathless fascination Barthes evades the prison-house of style, however glorious, to explore the possibilities and pitfalls of *écriture,* the writer's sole possibility for commitment.

Barthes limits his comments on the body in *Writing Degree Zero* to the discussion of an abstract notion of literature. When he examines representations of photographed, filmed, or live performing bodies, the distinction between a historically situated body-as-*écriture* and a corporeally manifest *style* meets resistance. In Barthes's primary preoccupations of the mid-1950s, the *Mythologies* and his theatre criticism, the body- as-*écriture* uneasily cohabitates and competes with its elusive double of 'decorative flesh' – literal flesh in the case of performance. A gesture of historical or ideological significance produces the figurative 'mask' of the body-as-writing while a 'magic' and 'secret' body haunts intelligibility from beyond the threshold of meaning.

The numerous bodies that populate *Mythologies* attest to the overwhelming prevalence of the intelligible corporeality and to Barthes's desire to establish the performing body as a mode of *écriture.* 'Professional' wrestling, for example, endows its bodies with 'absolute clarity,' and the wrestlers' intelligible bodies tidily exhaust any 'parasitic' remainder that eludes signification; no secret flesh lurks under these masks. In a similar vein, 'une intention de totale extériorité' (an intention of complete exteriority) characterizes the stylized signs of femininity inscribed by the Folies-Bergère showgirls (I 198). In the unclothed human body Barthes sees neither nature nor truth but a system at work: the dancers' bodies circulate freely as both signs in a system of gendered codes and as commodities in an economy of exchange (the seats at the Folies-Bergère are expensive and the spectators demand a product in return for their money). The showgirls thereby achieve the evacuation of presence that Kleist deems impossible for a live dancer or performer. Barthes writes: 'J'ai dissipé le mystère le plus tenace de l'existence, celui du corps d'autrui [...] ce visage humain qui d'habitude *n'est jamais qu'un présent*, voici qu'il m'est enfin manifesté comme un produit' (I have cleared up the most tenacious mystery of existence, that of the other's body [...] this face which normally *is nothing more than present*, is here at last manifested to me as a product) (I 199, emphasis added). Many other mythologies feature a semiotically pure corporeality unencumbered by presence or secret remainders. The men of ancient Rome portrayed in Hollywood films are riddled with internal conflict. How does the spectator know this? Not by apprehending the characters' interior psychology or deep corporeality, but by viewing a simple exterior sign: the beads of sweat on their foreheads. L'Abbé Pierre's face seems to exude a goodness that wells from within, testifying even to the manifestation of a divine presence on earth in this tireless crusader against homelessness; Barthes, however, sees an insidious montage of signs borrowed from a cultural code of saintliness. The myth 'Striptease' perhaps best illustrates the exhaustive semiosis of the body. As the stripper progressively peels off her clothes the conventions of the dance and the signs of eroticism reclothe her body under a code of nudity so opaque that it effectively cloaks any more 'natural' state of nakedness or brute reality under its intelligible surface. Barthes derides the tendency of the petit-bourgeois public to lend depth to these ideologically moulded masks, hence his evident delight in the wrestlers and to a lesser extent the showgirls who, unlike those who would obscure the body's mythic charge, unabashedly parade their status as signs.

Even in the world of myth, however, a 'fleshly double' shadows Barthes's intelligible bodies, interrupting the self-conscious saturation in signification with a euphoric ascesis of meaning. Like 'The World of Wrestling' and 'Folies-Bergère,' the lengthy *petite mythologie* 'Visages et figures' also dates from 1953, but appears only in truncated form as 'L'acteur d'Harcourt' in the 1957 anthology.[12] In the longer original, a typology of cinema idols frames the short passage that constitutes the revised essay on studio portraits of stage actors. Barthes outlines the beginnings of a sociology of physiognomy, a study of the 'authoritarian typology' of faces that the cinema industry, by virtue of its ubiquity, imposes on the public of 1950s France. The preponderance of Gérard Philipe and Daniel Gélin lookalikes on the street attests to a morphology of the human face that is not biological but sociological. Philipe and his youthful contemporaries are not treated as individuals nor even as living bodies, but as a 'look' circulating in the semiotic economy of a historical moment. Barthes appreciates the Philipe type because its youth and its intellectual quality suggest a becoming, an open text, part of a dialectical historical movement towards a new future in post-war France (more echoes of Marx and Sartre) rather than the immobility evident in older film stars, contemptuously dubbed 'de beaux insectes peints et vides' (beautiful, painted, and vacuous insects) (I 232).

Some exceptional faces, however, are so singularly ethereal that they resist typification and cannot circulate as infinitely repeatable signs. Rudolph Valentino and Greta Garbo both possess a beauty Barthes qualifies as a mysterious and 'divine' apparition that leaves the awe-struck viewer mute with fascination. Garbo and Valentino transcend history and language; they simply 'are,' preserved forever in their immobile perfection by either death or retreat from the public eye, cleansed of the clutter of meaning that defines the more contemporary star. Barthes opposes the impenetrable and inaccessible Valentino, 'condamné à sa trajectoire de pur spectacle' (condemned to his trajectory of pure spectacle), to Philipe's historicized sociability (I 230). The awe of Garbo's singular face similarly puts into relief the 'complexité infinie de functions morphologiques' ('infinite complexity of morphological functions') that constitute Audrey Hepburn's much more earthly and analysable charm (I 605; M 57). The inarticulate divine faces are not hollow shells or masks that circulate in an economy of signification, nor are they ideal essences that shed their materiality; in Barthes's eyes they testify to an inert density denuded of the patina of meaning 'où la chair développe des sentiments mystiques de perdition' ('where the flesh gives rise to mystical feelings of perdition') (I 604; M 57). The star's secret flesh is not of this world, not bound by the system of social relations, but rather 'l'essence de sa personne corporelle, descendue d'un ciel où les choses sont formées et finies dans la plus grande clarté' ('the essence of her corporeal person, descended from a heaven where all things are formed and perfected in the clearest light') (I 605; *M* 57). Even for Hollywood divinity this is an untenable state, and Garbo betrays a 'rapport volontaire et donc humain' ('voluntary and therefore human relation') when her arched eyebrows too deliberately match the curvature of her nostrils, a tinge of morphological readability that defaces the magical essence with a touch of the changeable, reproducible, and no longer inimitable mask (I 605; *M* 57). This slight degradation marks the beginning of the transition between the divine 'âge valentinien' and the era when the cinema begins to make its stars readable as humans, as women or men, as sociological selves. The decadence of the star image culminates in the 1950s tabloid magazine, where awe cedes to intelligibility, essence to history, and mystery to a myth begging demystification. Even at their most divine, Barthes therefore does not extract these faces from history – only in the early golden age of silent cinema was such deification possible – but neither does he treat them as the insidious masks of myth. The faces of Valentino and Garbo are more magical than mythic, more a mute void of meaning than a socially embedded *écriture*, more likely to inspire inarticulate pleasure and fascination than a rational appreciation of intelligible, readable signs.

Valentino and Garbo might exude divine splendour, but as strictly photographic or filmed images their faces, while inimitable, are also infinitely repeatable and circulate widely in movies and photographs. One continues to see them long after their bodies have withdrawn: they are not *live*. In the closing passage of 'Visage et figures,' the inarticulate face finds a second manifestation in a living and present body different from both the mythic masks of Romans in the cinema, L'Abbé Pierre, et al., and the cinema deities frozen in their silent perfection. While riding a commuter train Barthes notices a shabbily dressed woman reading a movie magazine, and the juxtaposition of her tired and affectless face with the countenances of the degraded 1950s stars on the page draws a poignant observation:

> La caméra, détournée de son olympe et fixée une fois sur ce visage terrestre, n'y aurait saisi aucun pathétique de la fatigue et de la pauvreté. Le réalisme est bien sot de nous montrer des visages-en-train-de-souffrir. La vérité était au-delà de l'expression, elle était sous la peau, dans la densité même de ce visage fatigué à vie, amené par la longue sédimentation des peines, à l'état d'une substance têtue, inaltérable, sinon par la mort. Nul effet d'apitoiement ne sortait de cette figure trop humain, mais

il suffisait de la confronter avec son double de luxe pour comprendre qu'on a volé à l'homme jusqu'à son propre visage.

(The movie camera, turned from its Olympus and fixed for once on this earthly face, would not have captured any pathos of fatigue or poverty. Realism is indeed foolish to show us faces-in-suffering. The truth was beyond expression, under the skin, in the very density of this world-weary face, led by a long sedimentation of difficulties to the state of a stubborn substance, inalterable except in death. No pity-inspiring affect issued from this all-too-human face, but it sufficed to contrast it with its luxurious double to understand that man has been robbed even of his own face.) (I 232)

This woman's face, impenetrable as Garbo's, likewise does not figure in the stock of sociological masks that Barthes catalogues elsewhere. No system, no code, no classifiable morphology lends it meaning; she is not exhibiting the appropriate 'mask' even of her supposed poverty or years of hard work. Instead Barthes finds a density, a stubborn substance that is beyond expression, beyond signification, that has nothing to say. The mythic body of the insectoid 1950s French movie actors is all surface, pure mask, but here we have depth, a body stripped of its intelligible sociological double, the inaccessible lived (and living) experience of an individual's body, of the 'thing itself': body degree zero. The woman's face differs from Valentino's and Garbo's in that, though also inarticulate flesh, it has no preservation in photography or film. It cannot be repeated, frozen, viewed, and reviewed; it has no token of value that circulates in an economy of signs, nor any mark to immortalize its inimitable, unsayable presence. This corporeal excess to intelligibility is, however, neither a divine apparition nor any magical miracle situated on the threshold of power and magic; Barthes views her expressionless face as a gap, as alienation, as absence, loss, and theft.

'Visages et figures' vividly illustrates the methodological dilemma that plagues the mythologies that follow: if the ideological masks that pass as nature constitute rather than obscure the 'realities' of the modern world, the possibility of rescuing anything underneath – a greater truth, a less alienated world – is precluded. Barthes recognizes the paradox of the mythologist's task: 'il risque sans cesse de faire s'évanouir le réel qu'il pretend protéger' ('he constantly runs the risk of causing the reality which he purports to protect to disappear') (I 718; M 158). As a mythologist, Barthes therefore has no words to express the truth about the woman's situation. He is consequently complicit in the very 'theft' he decries when in the greater part of the *Mythologies* he, too, unloads the 'thing itself' and trains his attentions on the tidily semiotized bodies of the wrestlers, strippers, and mythic faces such as those in the pages of her magazine. Barthes recognizes the sacrifice inherent in this gesture:

> il n'y a qu'un choix possible, et ce choix ne peut porter que sur deux méthodes également excessives: ou bien poser un réel entièrement perméable à l'histoire, et idéologiser; ou bien, à l'inverse, poser un réel *finalement* impénétrable, irréductible, et, dans ce cas, poétiser.

> (there is as yet only one possible choice, and this choice can bear only on two equally extreme methods: either to posit a reality which is entirely permeable to history, and ideologize; or, conversely, to posit a reality which is *ultimately* impenetrable, irreducible, and in this case, poetize.) (I 719; *M* 158)

As Barthes sets style aside to explore writing, he chooses the historical, ideological, and mythic mask at the expense of its living, poetic, inarticulate double.

A longing for the utopian zero degree of corporeality nonetheless leads Barthes occasionally to 'poetize.' The star portraits represent Barthes's earliest reflections on photography, a medium that will fascinate him as the threshold between the analogue imprint of the real and a coded system of representation. Photography has its own codes and rhetoric, but for Barthes it also bears the trace of something more, both euphoric and mournful, that he later will name a 'message without a code,' 'an "obtuse" meaning,' or a *punctum*.[13] The photographs of the vanished Valentino and reclusive Garbo are tinged with a melancholy quality, and the feelings of loss and wonder they inspire already suggest the inexpressable attraction of certain photographs and the irreducible body that they preserve. In the case of the stars, the fascination nonetheless remains historical and cultural, and Barthes shares it with society as a whole. More 'poetic' is the woman on the train, whose impassive face exceeds the sign system and moves Barthes deeply not despite but through his inability to assign it a social and historical value.

Even in his *petites mythologies* Barthes leaves open a narrow gap for a desiring subject to navigate, and the body, most poignantly a live and present body, is the site of this 'poetic' gesture. The figure of *le corps* he will develop in his later writings, far more 'poetic' than ideological, finds early expression in the first phase of his career. The body is the privileged site of the inexpressible, and the 'fleshly double' of style becomes a more literal 'absolute state of the flesh,' irreducible, dense, and in the case of the woman on the train inexorably *present*, for there is no iterable sign to mark its absence.

Troubling and Trivial Bodies

The spectre of the intelligible body's inarticulate double assiduously haunts Barthes's first published writings on theatre. 'Powers of Ancient Tragedy,' as noted in the previous chapter, is for the greater part a manifesto for a theatre of exterior, readable, and responsible signs that lead the spectator to a deeper understanding of the world both on stage and off. Barthes reconfigures Aristotle's catharsis in semiotic terms as a purification of autonomous individuality from the stage, leaving only a readable historical situation (a 'jubilation of intelligence') that enmeshes both spectator and performer even unto the most personal depths of their bodies. However, in the midst of this celebration of meaning, in which Barthes goes so far as to catalogue the 'fundamental modes' of the human body (discontent, surprise, etc.), the poetic body makes a surprising apparition that defeats corporeal intelligiblity:

> Mais si l'on prend la tragédie grecque dans sa pureté originelle, les larmes collectives du peuple ne sont rien de moins que sa plus haute culture, son pouvoir d'assumer dans l'abîme de son propre corps, les déchirements de l'idée ou de l'histoire.

> (But if Greek tragedy is taken in its original purity, the collective tears of the people are nothing less than their highest culture, their power to assume in the depths of their own body the rending of the idea or of history.) (PTA 217)

The nature of tragedy's *déchirements* is not immediately clear. If they implicate even the deepest interiority of both mind and flesh in a historical moment or signifying system to reveal 'une saisie immédiate des rapports, et non des choses, qui est la définition même de la culture' (a grasping of relations, and not things, which is the definition of culture itself) (I 217), tragedy would effectively cleanse the performance – and the performer – of inexplicable remainders, of any 'presence' sheltered from history and ideology in some inner precinct of being. However, the *déchirements* also suggest something that tears through the meanings of culture and its system of relations in the alienated historical moment. As Barthes continues, he appears to invoke a performance cleansed of history, not implicated in it, and a performer whose 'fresh' body lives and breathes in the here and now of the *present*:

> Il n'est pas indifférent, il est même essentiel que le spectateur soit cet homme de peau, dont la sensibilité, plus organique que cérébrale, accueille à chaque moment du drame, le mystère et l'intérrogation diffuse qui naissent du vent et des étoiles [...] La puissance du plein air tient à sa fragilité: le spectacle n'y est plus une habitude ou une essence, il est vulnérable comme un corps qui vit *hic et nunc*, irremplaçable et pourtant mortel à la minute. D'où son pouvoir de déchirement, mais aussi sa vertu de fraîcheur, qui purifie les planches de leur poussière, l'acteur de son métier, les vêtements de leur artifice, et fait de tout cela le faisceau hasardeux d'une beauté qu'on croit ne jamais plus revoir ainsi ordonnée.

> (It is not indifferent, it is even essential that the spectator be this man of skin, whose sensitivity, more organic than cerebral, at each moment of the drama welcomes the diffuse mystery and interrogation that are born of the wind and stars [...] The power of the open air demands fragility: there the spectacle is no longer habit or essence, it is vulnerable as a body that lives *hic et nunc*, irreplaceable and still mortal at any time. Hence its rending power, but also its virtue of freshness, that purifies the boards of their dust, the actor of his profession, the clothes of their artifice, and makes all of this the hazardous bundle of a beauty that one can believe never to see arranged in such a manner again.) (PTA 217–18)

The Artaudian resonance is unmistakable: the living body purifies the stage, cleansing not only the 'parasitic remainders' that muddy intelligibility, but also the rational and intelligible themselves. The *hic et nunc* of performance penetrates the spectator's body much like the visceral hunger Artaud proposes as a metaphor for spectatorship, and the immediacy of the performance rips through the masks of meaning to reveal a 'fresh' and organic presence underneath.

The intelligible body's rending double makes another appearance in Barthes's 1954 preface to an edition of Baudelaire's theatre. Barthes begins with a definition of theatricality that could have been culled

from the Prague School studies: 'une épaisseur de signes et de sensations [...] qui submerge le texte sous la plénitude de son langage extérieur'
('a density of signs and sensations [...] that submerges the text beneath
the profusion of its external language') (I 1195; *CE* 26). In Barthes's
assessment, Baudelaire's failed theatre projects lack a sufficient sense of
this theatricality, with one notable exception: 'ce qui appartient chez lui
à une théâtralité authentique, c'est le sentiment, le tourment même,
pourrait-on dire, de la *corporéité troublante* de l'acteur' ('his authentic
theatre is the sentiment, indeed one might say the torment, of the
actor's *disturbing corporeality*') (I 1195; *CE* 27, emphasis added). Barthes
initially defines this corporeality as consummate artificiality: Baudelaire
calls for a girl to play the son of Don Juan, for example, and for
attractive women to populate the stage as his many servants. These
cross-dressed, soft-porn production choices recall the showgirls and
strippers of *Mythologies*, and through obvious artifice enact a sort of
Brechtian distantiation that undermines any alibi of realism or historical accuracy.[14] However, alongside the alienating artifice of the spectacle, the 'vénusté' of these bodies is also a phenomenon in itself: 'le
corps de l'acteur est artificiel [...] mais non factice, et rejoint par là ce
léger dépassement, de saveur exquise, essentielle, par lequel Baudelaire
a défini le pouvoir des paradis artificiels' ('the actor's body is artificial
[...] but not factitious, and thereby a part of that delicate transcendence,
of an exquisite, essential savor, by which Baudelaire has defined the
power of the artificial paradise') (I 1196; *CE* 27). A delectable corporeality exceeds the mask of semiosis, if only delicately, and an explicitly live
performing body far more evocative of Artaud's alchemical theatre and
of the style in *Writing Degree Zero* once more interrupts Barthes's ode to
intelligibility:

> On peut deviner par là que Baudelaire avait le sens aigu de la théâtralité la
> plus secrète et aussi la plus troublante, celle qui met l'acteur au centre du
> prodige théâtral et constitue le théâtre comme le lieu d'une ultra-incarna-
> tion, où le corps est double, à la fois *corps vivant* venu d'une nature triviale,
> et corps emphatique, solonnel, glacé par sa fonction d'objet artificiel.

> (This suggests that Baudelaire had an acute sense of the most secret and
> also the most disturbing theatricality, the kind which puts the actor at the
> center of the theatrical prodigy and constitutes theatre as the site of an
> ultraincarnation, in which the body is double, at once a *living body* deriv-
> ing from a trivial nature, and an emphatic, formal body, frozen by its
> function as an artificial object.) (I 1196; *CE* 27–8, emphasis added)

The apparition of the performing body's secret double sows neither contradiction nor unease in Barthes's arguments. The body-as-sign and its disturbing excess work in concert to purge the stage of the false natures of bourgeois consciousness enshrined in realist theatre: one in a gesture of alienation that implicates all naturalness in an unmistakable artificiality, and the other through the palpable *liveness* of a performer that exceeds the artifice as a trace of the 'thing itself' and lends the performance a powerful and exquisite savour.

Barthes therefore follows both of Kleist's opposing ideals when he imagines two ideal performing bodies: one as pure signification, an inanimate mask, or a depthless body-as-sign that would satisfy the Prague School linguists' principle of *semiosis*, and the other a troubling evacuation of social meaning and rational intelligibility characteristic of Artaud's visceral here-and-now. For Kleist, it is between the ideals of pre-conscious innocence and inanimate grace that the drama of human imperfection unfolds. Barthes similarly decries a self-present consciousness that claims autonomy from historical and signifying systems, and that both muddies the clarity of the corporeal sign and adulterates the fresh and inarticulate purity of the stubborn substance lurking underneath.

Barthes's two ideal corporealities, one completely exhausted in semiosis and the other stripped bare in a radical zero-degree ascesis, find uneven advocacy in his early work. *Writing Degree Zero* already confines 'style' to little more than a lyrical aside, and in *Mythologies* Barthes casts his lot with the intelligible. Though stunning apparitions of a troubling, tormenting, poetic, and fresh performing body haunt his early theatre criticism, Barthes relegates his transport over the body's secret double to a parenthesis. The two ideals nonetheless coexist peacefully in Barthes's earliest criticism, at least briefly, before the growing interest in signs and signification diminishes his tolerance for an inarticulate corporeal *saveur*, on stage or off.

An Unhealthy Sign

As Barthes enters the 'scientific delirium' of his structuralist phase in the mid-1950s, the imperatives of a more rigorous semiological analysis accommodate poorly any deep and secret corporeality in performance. Barthes's enthusiastic espousal of Brecht, conjugated with a Saussure-inspired semiology, predictably lowers his threshold of tolerance for the occult and 'magical' excesses of the 'absolute state of the flesh,' situated outside of history as the 'freshness of innocence.' The early texts in which Barthes rhapsodizes over the body's poetic double appear before his incendiary experience as a spectator of *Mother Courage* in 1954. Thereafter, the lingering intrusion of an inarticulate corporeality generates more worry than fascination when it competes with an intelligible body-as-sign for Barthes's favour.

In 'Diseases of the Costume,' published in 1955, Brecht and Saussure loom large as Barthes proposes gestic properties as the touchstone of a production's semiological 'health.' He charges the costume, like all aspects of a production, with a basic function:

> Le costume n'est rien de plus que le second terme d'un rapport qui doit à tout instant joindre le sens de l'œuvre à son extériorité. Donc, tout ce qui, dans le costume, brouille la clarté de ce rapport, contredit, obscurcit, ou falisifie le *gestus* social du spectacle, est mauvais.

> (The costume is nothing more than the second term in a relation which must constantly link the work's meaning to its 'exteriority.' Hence everything in the costume that blurs the clarity of this relation, that contradicts, obscures, or falsifies the social *gestus* of the spectacle, is bad.) (I 1205; *CE* 42)

Barthes deplores costumes that impress an audience through aesthetic appeal and historical accuracy, parasitic alibis that do not contribute directly to the argument of the play. A costume is 'healthy' when it is a readable sign, a clear and meaningful decision on the part of designers, directors, and performers. Barthes echoes the Prague School theorists by first noting the duality of the object on stage (both material object and sign) before insisting on its semiotic qualities, which all but eclipse the trace of the 'object itself.' The semiological imperative is clear: 'La cellule intellective, ou cognitive du costume de théâtre, son élément de base, c'est le *signe*' ('The intellectual or cognitive cell of the costume, its basic element, is the *sign*') (I 1209; *CE* 46).

When the performer's body comes into question, however, the 'thing itself' tenaciously persists. The Prague Schoolers prevaricate on semiotic properties of the performer's body, and for Barthes, too, the prognosis of the body's semiological health is less favourable than that of the costume. As noted in the previous chapter, his earlier review of *Le Prince d'Hombourg*, in many ways a forerunner of 'Diseases of the Costume,' ends with a vindication of the 'admirable exteriority of situations, objects, and bodies' that situates the performer's corporeality as one more layer in theatre's density of signs. The later essay, however, does not so freely extend its diagnostic tool to the human body on stage, and in the midst of this discussion of healthy, readable signs, the tormenting corporeality of the 'mystic' body makes an unexpected intrusion: 'Autre fonction positive du vêtement: *il doit être une humanité*, il doit privilégier la stature humaine de l'acteur, rendre sa corporéité sensible, nette, et si possible déchirante' ('Another positive function of the costume: it must create a humanity, it must favor the actor's human stature, must make his bodily nature perceptible, distinct and if possible affecting') (I 1210; *CE* 48–9). The recurring terms *sensible* and *déchirant* (both inadequately conveyed in the translation) are noteworthy and, again more evocative of Artaud than Brecht, suggest a body that tears through the surface of 'healthy' intelligible signifiers. No less surprising is the invocation of a nature and an inherent human quality that distinguish the body and conscript other apparently subordinate elements of theatre (set, costume) to its service: 'le théâtre exige ouvertement de ses acteurs une certaine exemplarité corporelle; quelque morale qu'on lui prête, le théâtre est en un sens *une fête du corps humain* et il faut que le costume et le fond respectent ce corps, en exprimant toute la qualité humaine' ('theater demands of its actors a certain corporeal exemplarity; whatever ethic we attribute to it, the theater is in a sense *a celebration of the human body*, and costume and background must respect this body by expressing its entire human quality') (I 1210–11; *CE* 49, emphasis added). Barthes does not define any further this 'corporeal exemplarity' beyond a surprising appeal to a vague humanism. Is he, like Kleist, staking out a site for the 'human' between the sign and its zero degree, between the consummate readability of the wrestlers (suggested in the qualifier *nette*) and the mute density of the woman's face on the train (*sensible* and *déchirante*)? In any case, it is doubtful that the 'humanity' would indicate the conscious subjective agent whose hands were already tied in *Writing Degree Zero* and whom Barthes generally views more with suspicion than mute fascination.

In 'The Diseases of Costume' Barthes's Artaudian inclination to celebrate the 'rending' phenomenon of the performing body collides with both a Brechtian worry over parasitic values that muddy the gestic clarity of a healthy performance, and his semiologist's suspicion of an aberrant corporeality that fails to conform to the model of the healthy and functional sign. Barthes also charges the ideal costume with another important function. When the healthy costume respects the troubling corporeality of theatre, it does not merely reveal a body's human nature but actively shapes the performer into a sign, sculpting the body, carving out its silhouette for the spectator, becoming 'parfaitement consubstanielle à sa chair' ('perfectly consubstantial with its flesh') (I 1210; *CE* 48). This transformation is particularly important for the performer's face: 'Le costume doit savoir *absorber* le visage, on doit sentir qu'invisible mais nécessaire, un même épithélium historique les couvre tous deux' ('The costume must be able to *absorb* the face; we must feel that a single historical epithelium, invisible but necessary, covers them both') (I 1211; *CE* 49). While purportedly respecting the body's exceptional nature, Barthes's healthy costume exercises the opposite function, less revealing the singularity of the performing body than mitigating it, enclosing it, even obscuring it altogether under its sheath as a mask does a face. The costume guarantees the body's semiosis by effectively abating its unique and 'miraculous' properties, reconciling it with the systems of language and history Barthes brings together in his conjugation of Brecht and Saussure. Barthes effectively prescribes a remedy to the corporeal sign, which, thus pathologized, less inspires mute admiration than demands the concerned vigilance of designers and directors. The body might still be cause for celebration, but by Barthes's diagnostic standards it is also an ailing sign in need of care. The task of a good costume is to nurse the body back to semiotic health.

Clothing interests Barthes from his earliest writings, and soon after he writes 'The Diseases of Costume' he wins an appointment as a researcher in sociology at the Centre national de la recherche scientifique (CNRS) to study fashion. From its start a more rigorous semiology shapes this project, which will culminate in his most methodical structuralist work, *The Fashion System* (1967). Barthes's first article on the vestimentary code, 'Histoire et sociologie du vêtement,' appears in the journal *Annales* in 1957.[15] Barthes evokes Saussure by name and profusely deploys a vocabulary borrowed from linguistics – 'signifiers,' 'signifieds,' 'index,' 'structures' – that signals a departure from earlier criticism in which he does not embrace the terms of linguistics and structural analysis so systematically. A comparison of 'Histoire et sociologie du vêtement' with 'The Diseases of Costume' reveals a telling restriction of purview. Where the discussion of costumes in the first article becomes mired in the question of the performer's body, the more structuralist Barthes is solely interested in the mutations of costume within an impersonal system, and any idiosyncratic deviations draw his interest only as permutations of a greater structure. Barthes studies clothing as it appears in drawings, documents, painting, photographs, or most often in the abstract, and an impersonal taxonomy of generic categories and populations replaces any individual body actually wearing the clothes. In the earlier 'Diseases of Costume,' Barthes proposes a course of treatment for the unhealthy sign of the performing body, but in the later article he no longer needs to charge the clothes with the task of serving the body's 'humanity' for the simple reason that the body is absent, and he proceeds untroubled by the 'tormenting' excesses of its presence. Purging the body underneath the clothing permits a more precise semiological study. The robust semiotic health of the garment system in these later writings owes less to any cure for the illness of 'liveness' than to the neat elimination of the offending element, namely, the live human body itself, from consideration.

The volume of Barthes's theatre criticism begins to fall sharply at the same moment he turns his critical attention to fashion. The demands of his new research position and his scholarly ambitions (*The Fashion System* was intended to be a doctoral thesis) might explain this shift in interests, but his structural analyses also clearly benefit from the live performing body's eviction from his purview. The replacement of the body with a hollow shell of clothing and of the individual with an abstract system betrays a preference for a 'healthy' structural simulacrum of the body immune to the maladies endemic in the 'tormenting' *hic et nunc* of the body's presence. If theatre is a celebration of a 'fresh' and 'troubling' body, as Barthes undertakes more rigorously semiological studies he chooses more and more to stay home from the festivities.

On the rare occasions when Barthes continues to consider a specifically live performance, inarticulate presence is not so easily defeated and a 'poetic' body stubbornly continues to shadow its intelligible double. In one of his last and longest articles on Brecht's theatre, a 1960 preface for an edition of *Mother Courage*, Barthes offers his final and most impassioned articulation of the double performing body.[16] After praising once again the intelligible artificiality of the costumes that is Brecht's hallmark, Barthes issues a surprising disclaimer:

> Mais peut-être faut-il aller plus loin: derrière ce sens il y a encore un chiffre. Bien plus que dans les matières dégradées [du costume] [...] ce chiffre peut se découvrir dans quelques substances fraîches, fragiles [...] dans le col entrouvert d'une chemise, la peau d'un visage, un pied nu, le geste enfantin d'une main, une casaque trop courte ou à moitié attachée. Ce chiffre, qui est le vrai chiffre brechtien, c'est la vulnérabilité du corps

humain. Et comme cette vulnérabilité, Brecht ne la dit jamais mais en confie l'évidence au spectacle, et comme précisément la tendresse corporelle de l'homme est le chiffre au-delà duquel il n'y a plus rien à déchiffrer, le sens le plus offert devient le sens le plus caché: l'homme est aimable.

(But perhaps it is necessary to go further: behind this meaning there is still a cipher. Even more than in the range of materials in the costumes [...] this cipher can be discovered in some fresh, fragile substances [...] in the half-open collar of a shirt, the skin of a face, a bare foot, the childlike gesture of a hand, a topcoat that is too short or only half-buttoned. This cipher, which is the true Brechtian cipher, is the vulnerability of the human body. And like this vulnerability, Brecht never says it aloud but confides its evidence to the spectacle, and just as man's corporeal tenderness is the cipher beyond which there is nothing more to decipher, the most clearly offered meaning is the most hidden: man is lovable.) (I 893–4)

Barthes concedes a body that somehow exceeds the costume and the rest of theatre's 'density of signs'; the gap in clothing is no longer foreclosed with a nudity that is just another sign, as with the strippers and showgirls, but is left open, exempt from meaning. The gaping clothing both conceals and reveals a body that represents the failure of signification, only here it is not pathologized, nor is the costume charged with enclosing it. The lyrical foray into abstract language and ideas – 'tenderness,' 'lovable,' the 'beyond' – contrasts sharply with the drier scientific discourse of his sociological studies of clothing, further suggesting a filiation from his theatre criticism to the bodies that populate his later works. If Barthes no longer situates this vulnerable body absolutely outside of history it nonetheless lingers at the threshold of intelligibility, on the brink of the unthinkable and fascinating *au-delà*, the 'beyond.'

More remarkably, instead of worrying over this excess Barthes marvels at it as the horizon of semiosis and the raison d'être of theatre itself. His vocabulary again takes a rhapsodic turn, and the usage of the distinctly Artaudian term 'cipher' (*chiffre*) to describe the performing body of Brecht's theatre is particularly striking. His vision of an ideal theatre is, in effect, where Brecht and Artaud meet, where history, ideology, and writing reach their utopian outer limit beyond which there is nothing more to alienate, nothing more to say, where one can only affirm: the zero degree of performance, a body not of writing but of 'style.'[17] The *Mother Courage* preface is the last article Barthes writes about a specific theatre production in contemporary France. He thereby closes his career as a theatre critic by indulging in a final celebration of the performing body's attributes – its 'human' quality, the presence and depth of the flesh, the resistance to meaning, the excess to the signifier – that the rigorous structuralist analyses to follow will not allow.

The Flesh Made Word

The structuralist tide sweeps over the French intellectual world in the early 1960s. Riding its crest, Barthes joins Claude Lévi-Strauss, Jacques Lacan, Michel Foucault, Louis Althusser, and others in an often contentious displacement of the rational human subject from its privileged place as the centre of knowledge. These men rose to the status of academic superstars by levelling, in a loose (though not always harmonious) alliance of mutual influences, an ambitious assault on the foundational discourses of traditional disciplines. They uproot philosophy by splitting the subject and dissolving it into impersonal language and codes, rebuke traditional historiography by mapping a series of synchronic systems and successive epistemes whose rifts defy causal logic, and evacuate the empirical and perceived realities of positivistic enquiries that characterize the 'human sciences' and literary studies, with no exemption for conventional Marxist enquiries.[18]

In the 1963 essay 'The Structuralist Activity,' Barthes hails the 'structural man' of a new age whose defining task is to pull apart the world, sort out the pieces, divine their function in the system that organizes them, understand the rules of this system, and finally recompose the world as a 'deeper' structure, the intelligible simulacrum of surface reality. Structural signification is not defined as inherent quality, content, or a secure and stable signified, but as a function. The world is a system of relations, and the individual a variable in the algorithm, separated, analysed, and reinstated as a figure divested of inherent meaning, though ready to be assigned any number of meanings. Barthes christens this new species *Homo significans* (I 1332; *CE* 218), not 'man' as autonomous subject moving through an unfolding sequence of historical events but as a map of virtual subjectivities in a synchronic system of possibilities. Where in *Writing Degree Zero* the literary work testifies to capitalism in crisis and to the writing subject's limited range of responses, the 'structural man' sees writing as a field of signification to be tilled by critics and readers who unearth a 'deeper' structure of pure relations: commitment cedes to permutation, the historical moment to a deeper synchronic system.

In the early 1960s, for Barthes as for other 'structural men' (whether they identified themselves as such or not), the world is primarily one of language. Linguistics, until the 1960s a marginal field of study in the French universities, quickly finds itself at the forefront of a new mode of thought: linguists Saussure, Hjelmslev, and Jakobson are frequently invoked, Lacan's unconscious is structured like a language, Lévi-Strauss examines the mythic narratives of 'primitive' cultures, and Foucault analyses discursive formations.[19] Barthes's semiology also grants primacy to the word. In *Elements of Semiology* he explicitly overturns Saussure's contention that linguistics is a branch of semiology and makes semiology a category of linguistics instead. Barthes devalues non-verbal forms of signification as the impoverished subordinates of language, and through his reversal of Saussure's declaration imagines an ambitious synthesis of the new structuralist activities under the linguistic banner: 'By this inversion we may expect to bring to light the unity of the research at present being done in anthropology, sociology, psycho-analysis and stylistics round the concept of signification' (*ESm* 11).[20] A few years later Barthes reiterates his suspicion that non-linguistic codes are a 'utopia,' and that language penetrates all objects of 'real culture' through and through.[21] Given this orientation towards language, *Elements of Semiology* could more aptly be titled *Problems of Semiology*, for when the discussion turns to non-linguistic forms of signification it generally raises more questions than it answers.

The live performing body and the 'secret' of its presence find no place under the new reign of language, systems, and codes over Barthes's thought. Nothing could be more inimical to the reconstituted structural simulacrum of lived reality than the inarticulate and irreplaceable flesh of the double body, the body of style that has no signifier other than its own presence. Years later, Barthes reconciles a body exempt from meaning with the terms of a structural analysis by naming it his *mana*, the word structural anthropologists use for a force that freely flows through the structures that shape a society, but that has no form itself. In the early 1960s, however, he makes no such concessions to the body's 'miraculous' double; instead the inarticulate 'density,' 'freshness,' and impenetrable 'poetry' that attend the bodies of his early phase abruptly and unceremoniously vanish. There is no gesture of reconciliation, nor even of repudiation, only the fact that *homo significans* has no substance, no body worthy of celebration, neither a phenomenological reality of a singular lived experience that would serve as the index of an individual subject nor a 'secret' flesh beyond history; 'man' becomes a contentless function in the reconstituted code, a variable in the structural simulacrum of the world.[22]

The eradication of the 'poetic' body entails an evacuation of its primary precinct, the theatre. When Barthes is asked about his tenure as a theatre critic in the 1963 interview 'Literature and Signification,' he initially reconciles theatre with semiology when he again remarks theatre's 'density of signs,' calling it a 'cybernetic machine' that emits a range of contrapuntal messages. Theatre's richness offers the semiologist a desirable field of study: 'on peut même dire que le théâtre constitue un objet sémiologique privilégié puisque son système est apparemment original (polyphonique) par rapport à celui de la langue (qui est linéaire)' ('one can even say that the theater constitutes a privileged semiological object since its system is apparently original [polyphonic] in relation to that of language [which is linear]') (I 1363; *CE* 262). Barthes again hails Brecht's theatre as an exemplary theatre of signifiers, not of signifieds, that does not communicate a message but leads the spectator to realize that the world, like the stage, is an object to be deciphered. In short, the ideal theatre transforms the active, decoding spectator into 'structural man' who grasps the deeper system under the lived experience of the characters. The question of the troubling 'double body' also appears definitively resolved by a semiotic study: 'ce que nous appelons le *naturel* d'un acteur ou la *vérité* d'un jeu n'est qu'un langage parmi d'autres' ('What we call the *naturalness* of an actor or the *truth* of a performance is merely one language among others') (I 1363; *CE* 263). Theatre, even a theatre of performing bodies, would therefore seem entirely capable of thriving under a structural analysis.

Barthes's optimistic vision of an ideal performance, however, obscures the fact that he has already abdicated his role as a theatre critic. Despite the range of enticing attributes that would draw a semiologist's critical eye, Barthes notes theatre's apparently privileged status as a marginal curiosity that only draws commentary in response to the interviewer's question before he drops the matter to move on to more pressing preoccupations of the moment. Theatre's polyphony might distinguish it from language, but in 'Literature and Signification' this concession is only a passing nod, into which one might read a certain regret, towards a field of study Barthes has already ceased to pursue. In the rest of the interview, as in his other writings of the early 1960s, he sets his critical sights nearly exclusively on the written word. It is just two years later that he wonders 'did I love [theatre] too much, or not enough?'[23] Was the disappointment too great, or did interest merely wane? Theatre might have enjoyed privilege as a 'density of signs,' but for Barthes as for other structuralists the study of language inspires his most sophisticated and precise semiological analyses.

Theatre continues to draw Barthes's interest only as a linguistic phenomenon. *On Racine,* Barthes's study of the seventeenth-century playwright, also appears in 1963, and it sparks a heated controversy that brings widespread attention to the challenge that structuralism, in literature and other domains, mounts against the traditional and entrenched humanist establishment of the Sorbonne. A heated public exchange with Raymond Picard, a Racine scholar of the 'old school' biographical criticism that dominated French literary criticism since the nineteenth century, propels Barthes to international intellectual stardom as the champion of structuralism in a latter-day quarrel of the ancients and the moderns. The battle, however, is fought on the turf of the written word, with little consideration of the incarnation of Racine's texts in a moment of live performance practice.

In *On Racine* Barthes studies theatre as pure language, cleansed of the clutter of any 'density' that would adulterate the spoken or, more often, the written word. The Racinian conception of space justifies this approach. The religiously respected unity of place makes the stage an intermediary zone between the sacred chamber, where the absent father or God silently lurks, and the exterior, where any event or dramatic action takes place. Unlike Shakespeare, who did not spare the audience even the grisliest of deeds, in this eternal antechamber all one can do is speak, and in Barthes's study the Racinian characters shed their physicality, their material substance, to become purely linguistic figures that emerge from the text alone. Bérénice is charming not because of the actions or appearance of any body on stage but solely because another character says so in the text: 'Bérénice a de belles mains; le concept débarasse en quelque sorte de la chose' ('Bérénice has beautiful hands, the concept somehow gets rid of the thing') (I 997; *OR* 12). The statement encounters no interference from a performing body whose attributes might or might not justify its claim, for the 'thing itself' has been purged from consideration. Barthes aptly deploys a vocabulary of cleansing to describe the linguistic filter of Racinian convention, *bienséance,* that screens out the adulterating incursions of bodies, actions, and extra-linguistic realities:

> on dit que c'est par bienséance; mais ce que la bienséance écarte dans la mort charnelle, c'est un élément étranger à la tragédie, une 'impureté', l'épaisseur d'une réalité scandaleuse puisqu'elle ne relève plus de l'ordre du langage, qui est le seul ordre tragique.

(this is reputedly for reasons of propriety, but what propriety rejects in carnal death is an element alien to tragedy, an 'impurity,' the density of a reality scandalous because it no longer proceeds from the order of language, which is the only tragic order.) (I 993; *OR* 5)

The intermediary characters who recount events that occur outside the walls of the antechamber spare the hero contact with reality by 'distilling' the action down to a pure cause: 'Car face à cet ordre du seul langage qu'est la tragédie, l'acte est l'impureté même' ('Confronting this exclusive order of language which is tragedy, action is impurity itself') (I 994; *OR* 7). Although Barthes attributes this purification to the spatial configuration of Racine's own dramaturgy, by choosing to focus exclusively on language, by removing Racine from the moment of performance, and by making his characters pure language indifferent to the specific performing bodies that populate the stage in practice, he, too, plays the role of the intermediary who screens out any residual 'thing itself' and cleanses the object of his study of any corporeal excess to tragedy and language, or more precisely to tragedy *as* language.

The gesture that unloads the performing body clears the way for a tidy structural analysis. *On Racine* reveals the system that governs time, space, and action in Racine's plays, making them each homologous manifestations of a shared network of relationships despite the variety of characters, situations, and locales. Barthes distils the Racinian conflict down to a system even more stark than Vladimir Propp's permutations of the Russian fairy tale or the structuralist *modèle actantiel*: 'A a tout pouvoir sur B. A aime B, qui ne l'aime pas' ('A has complete power over B. A loves B, who does not love A') (I 1005; *OR* 24). The meanings assigned to A and B, be they male or female, Greek or Hebrew, sexually frustrated queen (Phèdre) or murderous son (Néron), matter little; it is the place in the system, 'A' or 'B,' that determines the deeper, functional signification of the character. Even the sexes become an abstract structure into which the characters, regardless of their own particular biology, find their place: Agrippine and Athalie are 'viriloid' in the system, Taxile and Hippolyte 'feminoid.' Gender, race and ethnicity, nationality, age, even beauty are mere variables in a greater equation that is the world inhabited by the disembodied *homo racinianus*: 'il s'agit au fond de masques, de figures qui reçoivent leurs différences, non de leur état civil, mais de leur place dans la configuration générale qui les tient enfermés' ('we are dealing, essentially, with masks, with figures that differ from each other not according to their public status but according to their place in the general configuration that keeps them confined') (I 995; *OR* 9). A sub-species of *homo significans, homo racinianus* is not an individual but a figure, a function, a hollow mask.

By reducing the characters to variables in an algorithm, Barthes divests them not only of a 'civil status' but cleanses Racinian dramaturgy of a body and of its 'poetry' as well. They are substitutable figures in a pattern, ciphers in an equation, who derive meaning solely from their place at any given moment in the system of relationships that constitutes the Racinian world. As purely linguistic phenomena they are indifferent to the specific historical moment of performance practice and shielded from any static resulting from their 'incarnation' by a performing body, be it in the seventeenth century or the twentieth. 'Racinian man' is a lifeless simulacrum, as inanimate as Kleist's puppet, and Barthes similarly dismisses both a body and a conscious subject – or, again, the living body as the index of a conscious subject – from his account. Racine's theatre, Barthes's pure tragedy, is no longer live.

In contrast, within the diegesis of the Racinian world the body continues to act as a figure of disruption and maintains its fascinating, troubling appeal. The inhabitants of this cloistered universe experience the presence of the loved one's body or the sight of the adored face as a profoundly disturbing experience, an affect that resembles closely – remarkably – Barthes's earlier reactions to 'magical' and 'tormenting' bodies on stage. In words that match nearly verbatim his own ambivalent remarks on theatre, Barthes observes that when faced with the body of the other the Racinian character can only say *'je vous aime trop'* ('I love you too much') or *'je ne vous aime pas assez'* ('I don't love you enough') (I 1000; *OR* 16). For the Racinian hero, as for the structural analyst, the evacuation of the 'lovable' body, not its presence, brings happy resolution to this impasse:

l'Éros racinien ne met les corps en présence que pour les défaire. La vue du corps adverse trouble le langage et le dérègle [...] Le héros racinien ne parvient jamais à une conduite *juste* en face du corps d'autrui: la fréquentation réelle est toujours un échec [...] Le corps adverse est bonheur seulement lorsqu'il est image.

(the Racinian Eros brings bodies into confrontation only to destroy them. The sight of the adverse body disorders language, troubles it [...] The Racinian hero never achieves *adequate* behavior towards the adverse body: real frequentation is always a failure [...] The adverse body confers happiness only when it is an image.) (I 1001; *OR* 17)

In *On Racine*, however, only the characters are troubled by the body's presence. Barthes, the scientific 'structuralist man,' encounters not the face of a disturbing corporeality but merely variables derived from words on a page, and looks with cool analytical detachment on this world of language with none of the mute wonder he experienced as a spectator during his theatre years. *On Racine* effectively displaces Barthes's own experience as a spectator and permits him to consider the stage through the lens of a written language that filters out any of the impurities, dangers, torments, or semiological infirmities of the live and present body.

The sole discussion of performance practice in *On Racine* lies sequestered in the brief second section of the book, 'Dire Racine' (Racine Spoken), and here Barthes's studied silence on the performing body becomes deafening. This short essay reads as a brief mythology of Racinian acting and reprises many of the themes that dominate Barthes's theatre criticism. Jean Vilar's 1958 production of *Phèdre* at the TNP draws a trenchant commentary. The apparent lack of any coherent mise en scène permits designers and performers to indulge in the myth of Racine, most notably in the actors' conflicted effort to infuse the stylized alexandrines with expression and psychology while also preserving their musicality. Barthes imagines an ideal alexandrine, 'un *être-là* pur et simple de la parole' ('a pure and simple *dasein* of speech') (I 1083; *OR* 147), unadulterated by the psychological motivation that the performers strive to invest in it. Barthes again deploys a vocabulary of purification throughout the essay: 'ascesis' is the cure for Racine's theatre, which must be 'swept clean' of its mythic trappings; the ideal alexandrine 'exhausts the actor' entirely, leaving no mystic remainders, no mythic alibis, nothing but the 'pure' word in its wake. The ideal interpretation of Racine's text is a language of prescribed sound and rhythm unadulterated by individual inflection, alibis of naturalness, psychological realism, and, a fortiori, any secret, tormenting corporeality that exceeds language itself. Acting has become solely a question of speaking, theatre a matter of language, and the performer a voice as static and impersonal as the text's transcription into the phonetic alphabet (no 'grain of the voice' here).

If the disembodied theatre of *On Racine* marks the most egregious abstraction of the live performing body from an ideal theatre of language, a crowning example of the flesh made word occurs in the lengthy and painstakingly methodical structuralist analysis of *The Fashion System*, the culmination of Barthes's decade-long study of clothing. Barthes establishes the rhetoric and syntax of fashion not by studying the clothing itself, nor even fashion photographs, but by examining instead the written text of the photographs' captions and the accompanying magazine articles. In the brief mention of the body in this work, he amplifies his earlier remarks on the costume that echo his assessment of the Folies-Bergère showgirls and strippers of the *Mythologies*: the body interests him only when it enters the language of fashion ('small, fine traits are in style this year') or when the clothes, or more accurately the description of the clothing, shape the body into a complex of clearly intelligible signs. The body enters his analysis not as an excess, certainly not as the 'humanity' that the costume serves, but as a variable, a signifier that is a function of the clothing system itself: the bare arm between the shoulder and the glove is part of the whole look. Where on the stage he saw vulnerability and freshness in the half-open collars and gaping garments, here the glimpse of the body, conveyed though language, becomes just another figure in the equation. In a 1967 interview Barthes justifies his exclusive focus on language through a familiar rhetoric of purification: '[les descriptions] sont de l'ordre de l'intelligible pur, et par là même hétérogènes à toute imagerie, qui ne peut que les encombrer, les altérer' ([the descriptions] are on the order of pure intelligibility, and thereby different from all imagery, which can only burden or alter them) (II 455). Indifferent to the messy non-linguistic encumbrances of photography, not to mention of any live body wearing the clothing, and apparently lacking interest in their adulterating potential, Barthes neatly cleanses such troubling excesses from consideration in favour of a pure study of the 'literature' of fashion journalism. The body has become just another sign among others, and even then one worthy of little more than passing mention.

Human Sacrifice

The year 1966 sees the publication of *Criticism and Truth*, Barthes's answer to the attack on *On Racine*, as well as Lacan's *Ecrits*, Greimas's *Structural Semantics*, Foucault's *The Order of Things*, Pierre Macherey's Althusser-inspired *For a Theory of Literary Production*, and the eighth issue of the journal *Communications*, which assumes the stature of a structuralist manifesto. The fervour of this moment marks the zenith of structuralism as an intellectual force, what François Dosse dubs its *Annum Mirabile*.[24] However, structuralism's triumph comes at a price not everyone in the 1960s is willing to pay. Though it is unfashionable at the time of structuralism's greatest vogue, some critics, and not only reactionary denizens of the Sorbonne, voice their reticence over structural analysis's radical evacuation of both the individual human subject and of a dialectical conception of history. In the field of anthropology, Africanists, for example, note the indifference of Lévi-Strauss's neat and purportedly universal systems that underlie human culture, based mostly on isolated American peoples, to the less stable after-effects of colonialism in the newly independent African nations.[25] The structuralist seeks first and foremost to explain the world, not to change it, and the synchronic study of cultural systems that evacuates both human agency and the particular conditions of an individual's struggle seems inadequate to account for the radical, even revolutionary changes of this dynamic period. The rise of a faceless *homo significans* in Barthes's writing is not exempt from this critique. As noted in the previous chapter, Kristen Ross specifically cites this abstract figure as the emblem of a technocratic post-human world cleansed of the contradictions of the historical moment of decolonization, and she reproves semiology and structuralism as an intellectual retreat from new struggles emerging in 1950s France: 'Precisely at the moment that colonized peoples demand and appropriate to themselves the status of men [...] French intellectuals announce the "death of man."'[26]

For Barthes, the structuralist abstraction impels an evacuation of the theatre, or, to be precise, of live performance practice. Clearly, he has ample reason to reject the contemporary French stage as a compromised bourgeois institution, but the 'secret' and 'miraculous' qualities he attributes to the body in his early criticism offer a second compelling motive for his sudden silence on a mode of representation on which he earlier pinned his highest hopes. Barthes loses faith in the dream of a less alienated society whose emblem is precisely this elusive body: the Adamic zero degree manifest in the writer's style, the 'fresh' and 'innocent' spectators of a new age, and the tender and lovable bodies of live performance that linger in the margins of his theatre criticism as figures of fascination. In their place Barthes offers the written word, a dematerialized sign, and a disembodied voice that yield more easily to the critical activities of structural man. The gesture that banishes the chronically 'ill' performing body also secures the conditions that guarantee the health of his systematic analyses in *On Racine*, *The Fashion System*, and other writings of the 1960s.

It seems fitting that the dismissal of liveness culminates in a death. Barthes opens 'The Death of the Author' by once again eliminating a body: 'l'écriture est destruction de toute voix, de toute origine. L'écriture, c'est ce neutre, ce composite, cet oblique où fuit notre sujet, le noir-et-blanc où vient se perdre toute identité, à commencer par celle-là même du corps qui écrit' ('Writing is the destruction of every voice, of every origin. Writing is that neuter, that composite, that obliquity into which our subject flees, the black-and-white where all identity is lost, starting with the very identity of the body that writes') (II 491; *RL* 49). Barthes's evacuation of the body from the gesture of writing seems explicit, yet even these lines carve out a space for an open term that resists the investment of meaning. Is it the body itself that is being purged, or is it only its assigned 'identity' that is lost, leaving behind a body presumably purified of this imaginary construct? The essay that follows, however, leaves little doubt that the *scripteur*, the figure of a subject that appears in writing, has no life, and no body, outside of the gesture of writing itself. In a reversal that echoes Kleist's contention that the live body is the copy of the puppet, Barthes writes:

> Le scripteur n'a plus en lui les passions, humeurs, sentiments, impressions, mais cet immense dictionnaire où il puise une écriture qui ne peut connaître aucun arrêt: la vie ne fait jamais qu'imiter le livre, et ce livre lui-même n'est qu'un tissu de signes, imitation perdue, infiniment reculée.

> (The *scriptor* no longer contains passions, moods, sentiments, impressions, but that immense dictionary from which he draws a writing which will be incessant: life merely imitates the book, and the book itself is but a tissue of signs, endless imitation, infinitely postponed.) (II 494; *BL* 53)

Writing is a horizontal plane across which meanings move; there is no depth, no *déchirement* through which anything underneath becomes palpable: 'l'espace de l'écriture est à parcourir, il n'est pas à percer' ('the space of writing is to be traversed, not pierced') (II 494; *BL* 54). Barthes theorizes writing as a surface that no point (later theorized as the *punctum*) might pierce, a mask with no face underneath, deprived of a body and the 'secret' of style: signs without life.

With hindsight, we know the exigencies of Barthes's structuralist delirium enforce the abstraction of the body only to prepare the terrain for another corporeality to emerge. The death of the author might free the text from the spectre of an individual, a writing subject, and an intention that structuralism cannot tolerate, but it also destabilizes the system with the concomitant birth of the reader announced in the essay's closing passages. In Barthes's writing, this new 'phase' is heralded by, among other things, the lifting of the injunction against the inarticulate body that exists beyond language and returns with force in his writing in the 1970s. Theatre too will return as a privileged figure, though only rarely as a moment of performance practice; Barthes's rejection of the hopelessly compromised institution of contemporary French theatre proves to be definitive.

Barthes's structuralist abstraction does not resolve the worries of presence; on the contrary, his silence on live performance is a telling symptom of presence anxiety. The contours of the blind field to which Barthes relegates the 'poetic' body and the theatre it inhabits become discernible as he gingerly treads around the very questions he raises only a few years earlier as a spectator enrapt with the 'tender' and 'lovable' performing body. Paradoxically, Barthes's silence, both a prison and a sanctuary, shelters live performance from the 'structuralist activity' of his scientific bid; the 'pure' analysis of *The Fashion System*, had Barthes brought it to descriptions of the body instead of clothing, would doubtless have stripped the body of any 'poetry' it managed to retain, not to mention its power to challenge the system that demands the exhaustive parsing of all potential meaning. The live and present performing body lies beyond the reach of the discourse of structuralism and its totalizing claims. *Did I love theatre too much or not enough?* The resurgence of a troubling, excessive corporeality in the following post-structuralist years might lead one to answer with the axiomatic title of the article Barthes left unfinished at the time of his death: *One always fails to speak of what one loves.*

3 Staging Theory: Theatricality and the Displacement of Desire

Theatre occupies a paradoxical place in the body of theory known as French post-structuralism: it seems to be everywhere and almost nowhere. On one hand, theatricality provides a versatile figure for articulating philosophical, psychoanalytical, and historical conceptions of subject, truth, and language. As Timothy Murray remarks in the introduction to *Mimesis, Masochism, and Mime: The Politics of Theatricality in Contemporary French Thought*, a collection of essays by Jacques Derrida, Michel Foucault, Luce Irigaray, Gilles Deleuze, Julia Kristeva, and others in the post-stucturalist pantheon who deploy prolific theatrical imagery to illustrate their thought, 'theatricality is what performs and lays bare the mediating procedures of reflexivity that give rise to thought, text, and image while proving false the utopian postwar notion of the unprejudiced.'[1] However, the proliferation of theatricality as a fruitful figure does not similarly entail the restitution of a literal theatre as a similarly privileged site of enquiry. While some (Hélène Cixous, Josette Féral, Louis Althusser) address theatre specifically, in many of these discussions live performance practice as a distinct mode of representation finds a much narrower niche and often escapes consideration altogether. The evacuation of the live performing body from figurative theatricalities takes various forms: it is displaced by the voice in some cases, while in others it is absorbed into parity with non-live media such as cinema; most often a literary, metaphorical, or purely conceptual 'staging' precludes specific consideration of performance's liveness and a performer's presence.

The advent of post-structuralist thought ushers in a remarkably prolific moment in Barthes's career. *S/Z*, *Empire of Signs*, and *Sade, Fourier, Loyola* appear in rapid succession between 1970 and 1971, along with a number of important essays on music, photography, and other visual arts. For many readers this is the most familiar face of Barthes, yet these years arguably represent less the zenith of any single phase than a moment of intense and rapid transition. *S/Z*, *Empire of Signs*, and *Sade, Fourier, Loyola* all maintain palpable ties to the structural analyses of the preceding years and contain only early articulations of the eroticized textuality that will reach full flower in 1973 with *The Pleasure of the Text*. Perhaps *Sade, Fourier, Loyola* illustrates this straddling most starkly: by the time Barthes finishes the study of the three writers he feels compelled to append a second, fragmented, and much more 'textual' Sade section in which he responds to the earlier essay that opens the book.

Theatre, or at least a certain theatricality, returns after years of inattention to reclaim prominence in Barthes's writing at this critical juncture in his career. Theatrical metaphors again proliferate, and stunning performances illustrate the new parameters of Barthes's thought as he exits the structuralist 'delirium' to embark on the adventure of the text. The performing body also returns, and Barthes's theoretical stagings often feature a provocative corporeality. A castrato, Bunraku puppetry, a Kabuki actor, and a surprising drag performance inspire euphoric transport in a reader-cum-spectator identified to some degree as Barthes himself.

Changing vocabularies chart the migration of diverse discourses through Barthes's work as new terms and figures appear, often borrowed from his interlocutors of the moment, while older ones fade and fall into disuse or are redefined to suit a new theoretical climate. Theatre's resurgence marks only one of the many swerves, departures, and returns that defy a linear mapping of Barthes's career. The particularly pronounced reversals of fortune of writing (*écriture*), for example, also measure the rise and ebb of Barthes's structuralist zeal. Among the many casualties the structuralist tide leaves in its wake – history, the subject, philosophy, 'man,' literature, and of course theatre – writing, as defined in *Writing Degree Zero*, also finds itself stranded in the early 1960s. *Ecriture* demands responsible choices of a knowing (if not free) subject at a specific historical juncture; in short, writing requires a writer. The death of the author, which occurs in fact in Barthes's work several years before he rings its knell in 1968, effectively divests *l'écriture* of its currency as a critical term in favour of the impersonal systems, languages, and codes of signification purified of an individual agent and less sensitive to the specific moment of writing's production or consumption.

Barthes does not forsake writing for long. A fresh theoretical investment soon restores the term to buzzword status when it finds a champion in Jacques Derrida, who makes *écriture* the prime term of the
deconstruction of Western metaphysics. *Speech and Phenomenon, Writing
and Difference*, and *On Grammatology* appear in rapid succession in 1967,
and together launch a formidable assault on the self-present thinking
subject of Western thought. Derrida targets the cogito, meaning, and
truth, of which the spoken word is the emblem, to reveal the inevitable
point where their apologists – Plato, Rousseau, and Husserl, to name
only a few – betray the subject's authoritative presence and mastery
over meaning as always a repetition, as already an iteration of something else, as *writing*. Both meaning and the subject are spirited (*soufflé*)
to an elsewhere, deferred to an inexorably absent truth or pure state of
being. Difference becomes the order of the day, or, as Derrida writes,
différance, neatly encapsulating in this neologism both deferral and
difference, alternate meanings that always bear the trace of the excluded inflection of the term.

Writing redefined offers a welcome way out of an approach to literary texts whose drive to gather apparently diverse entities under a
shared deeper structure proves somewhat sterile. As early as 1967
Barthes opposes an *écriture* of distinctly Derridean resonance to the
scientific language of structuralism:

> Le structuralisme ne sera jamais qu'une 'science' de plus (il en naît quel-
> ques-unes par siècle, dont certaines passagères), s'il ne parvient à placer
> au centre de son enterprise la subversion même du langage scientifique,
> c'est-à-dire, en un mot, à 's'écrire' [...] seule l'écriture a chance de lever la
> mauvaise foi qui s'attache à tout langage qui s'ignore.

> (Structuralism will never be more than just another 'science' [a few are
> born every century, some fleeting], if it does not succeed in placing the
> subversion of scientific language itself at the centre of its project, that is to
> say, in a word, to 'write' itself [...] only writing has the opportunity to
> remove the bad faith attached to any language that ignores its own work-
> ings.) (II 431–2)

A few years later he writes: 'Derrida a été de ceux qui m'ont aidé à
comprendre quel était l'enjeu (philosophique, idéologique) de mon
propre travail: il a déséquilibré la structure, il a ouvert le signe' (Derrida
was among those who helped me to understand the stakes [philosophi-

cal, ideological] of my own work: he unhinged the structure, he opened the sign) (II 1417).

Difference, deferral, absence, and dissemination would not appear to favour the return of theatre, nor of the 'poetic' and 'secret' bodies of Artaudian resonance that linger in the margins of Barthes's early writings. Derrida directly addresses the question of presence in performance and dedicates two essays in *Writing and Difference* to a deconstructive reading of *The Theater and Its Double*. Artaud envisions a theatre that does not pay tribute to an absent author or a master text, but manifests a living existence in the here and now that claims precedence over the derivative, compromised, impure gesture of repetition inherent in language, even in the phenomenological subject's rational 'presence of mind';[2] Derrida joins Artaud in discrediting this self-present voice. However, in the assault on Western theatre, and more generally on Western thought, Artaud posits a life before writing, before a rational subject and speech, a purer state of being of which language is the 'double' and that therefore, for Derrida, ultimately 'fulfills the most profound and permanent ambition of Western metaphysics.'[3] Derrida homes in on the passages where Artaud himself betrays his brute, primitive, archetypal theatre as the 'image of something subtler than Creation itself,' and the purported theatre of the here and now as always already a repetition of an absent and irrecuperable origin.[4] For Derrida, Artaud's raw scream lays no less specious a claim to metaphysical self-presence, to *being*, than the phenomenological voice and its bid for primacy over the long-discredited writing. Despite Artaud's claims, a cruel theatre manifests the 'gratuitous and baseless necessity' of representation and can guarantee no presence, live, corporeal, or otherwise, exempt from language or lurking behind the sign.[5]

Barthes hails Derrida's reading of Artaud as a watershed: 'Ses interventions littéraires (sur Artaud, sur Mallarmé, sur Bataille) ont été décisives, je veux dire par là: irréversibles' (His literary interventions (on Artaud, on Mallarmé, on Bataille) have been decisive, by that I mean: irreversible) (II 1417). However, as Lawrence Schehr notes, if Barthes's work echoes Derridean notions it also resonates with competing strains of those who would revise or contest the terms of deconstruction.[6] A rival impulse betrays the influence of the other interlocutors Barthes lists alongside Derrida at this point in his career: Jacques Lacan, Phillipe Sollers, and perhaps with the most marked enthusiasm his former student Julia Kristeva. Where Derrida indicts the psychoanalyst as a suspect purveyor of truth and maintains representation's 'baseless necessity,' Kristeva, with a heavy psychoanalytic inflection, posits a body of generative drives that precedes language and the imaginary unity of the writing subject: 'pre-verbal gesturality,' a realm of production and process ('le sujet en procès') also invoked in the 'geno-text,' *signifiance*, the *chora*, and the 'semiotic.' Kristeva offers a competing reading of Artaud, locating in his texts an 'investment without delay and without *différance* in an asymbolic biological and social matter which is nevertheless already organized.'[7] Her deliberate disavowal of the Derridean term draws attention to the dissonance between their thoughts on representation: Kristeva identifies an originating corporeal impulse that precedes the symbolic function where Derrida sees only 'gratuitous and baseless necessity,' and imagines an unfathomable bodily impulse where deconstruction only allows for a 'fold.'

Poetry and other written texts generally dominate Kristeva's discussion, but in passing she identifies performance – dance, theatre, and gestural painting – as the privileged site where 'the text has no other justification than to give rise to this music of pulsions.'[8] Kristeva suggests that a revolutionary theatre can manifest a generative creative impulse whose absence and deferral Derrida deems inexorable, and her reading of Artaud would seem to accommodate better the return of the 'magical,' 'tender,' and 'lovable' bodies that inflect Barthes's theorization of the zero degree and sow contradiction in his early theatre criticism. It remains questionable, however, whether Kristeva's vision for theatre offers a model for a new performance practice, or if the envisioned theatre's revolutionary breach in the symbolic can withstand the closure of representation.[9] In a gesture that resonates with Kleistian worries, Kristeva displaces theatre into the figurative realm as a trope for literary and textual representation more generally, effectively evacuating the specificity of live performance practice per se from her theoretical ideal. The experimental texts that 'stage' a palpable semiotic drive, for example, efface the distinction between cinema and theatre – 'the old cinema/theater distinction disappears' – and announce the future 'elimination' of theatre altogether.[10] 'Modern theater does not take (a) place,' proclaims the title of a short article in which even Artaud comes to represent a 'theater/cinema' of cruelty that holds the problematics of presence at an arm's length, and *à la limite* provides for its elimination from Kristeva's consideration of theatre altogether.

In his theoretical flitting of the early 1970s Barthes alights on the critical terms of both Derrida and Kristeva, on both the inexorable 'always already' and the euphoric dream of its fissure.[11] *The Theater and Its Double* is once more a tacit intertext of Barthes's writing, and theatre returns as the arena of the contested Artaudian legacy. As in his earlier criticism, Barthes again observes both theatre and its double, both the inexorable 'masks' of meaning and a hint of what lurks beneath, both the imposition of representation's code and the fleeting reminder of the underside that threatens to undo it. However, the re-emergent theatre little resembles the compromised French stage Barthes decries in the 1950s, no more than *le texte* duplicates the terms of *l'écriture* articulated in *Writing Degree Zero*. Both theatre and the written text return differently, into the parameters and preoccupations of a new theoretical moment announced by, among other figures, the appearance of a desiring reader who makes choices, accepts or rejects the 'masks' of convention, and actively participates in the weaving and unravelling of the meaning that flows through the text.

There are a mask and a desire that Barthes is loath to signal, even to discredit them. As the consummate reader, Barthes himself, more than he previously recognized as a mythologist or structural analyst, finds his own subjectivity, his own body, and his own individual desires implicated in his writing. However, while he openly assumes his class identity as bourgeois and his social status as an intellectual and freely interrogates the contradictions they bring to his writing, Barthes situates his sexuality in a blind field where the desires and pleasures of his own body remain nameless. Before the posthumous publication of *Incidents* demands recognition of homosexuality as both a biographical fact and an important figure in Barthes's writings, his critics, too, despite the hints and oblique references that begin to appear in his work in the early 1970s, respect his injunction of silence. These passages have now drawn considerable attention, but the implications of Barthes's discretion remain contested.

A number of critics take Barthes to task and seek to excavate or amplify his nearly invisible and elusive homosexuality. D.A. Miller stages his own 'homosexual encounter' with Barthes's texts, and from his own very 'out' position proposes to 'to develop Barthes's gay muscle.'[12] Some refuse even this degree of complicity. Ross Chambers, for example, pointedly indicts Barthes's willful 'forgetting' of both sexuality and the conditions (post-colonialism, class privilege) that shape it.[13] However, if Barthes's careful dance on the closet's threshold threatens to compromise the utopian terms of a 'zero degree' of sexuality, others wonder if Barthes's studied and not entirely complete refusal to assume this identity in his writing is also a gesture of resistance, a tactical ploy that shelters sexuality from the code, from the stultified stereotype of myth, and from the closure of representation that suffocates pleasure. Murray Pratt attempts to rescue Barthes's autobiographical texts from more pessimistic readings by signalling their potential to 'contest dominant homophobic ideologies of production and individual identity.'[14] Pierre Saint-Amand defends Barthes's 'voluptuous suspension' against those who would have him erect a stronger, less ludic identity.[15] In her deconstruction of D.A. Miller's own gay voice in *Bringing Out Roland Barthes*, Barbara Johnson writes: 'What if sexuality were not a type of identity but a type of loss of identity? [...] The civil status conferred by identity – each must go to his native land and enroll himself – is precisely what Barthes is arguing *against*. But when writing makes you *not* know yourself, he implies, something sexy is happening.'[16] While the muted gay voice represents for some the inexorable demand that Barthes claim an identity (or that an identity claim him), Johnson reminds us that Barthes situates pleasure in the failure of any system that would pigeonhole his sexuality and his subject according to an oppressive classificatory regime. The conflicting perspectives on Barthes's homosexuality therefore take the shape of a familiar Barthesian trope: an ideal term exempt from meaning, but that in any given situation inexorably risks the imposition of a meaning, potentially as brutal as it is provisional.

The coincidence of theatre's return, the birth of the reader, and the implication of Barthes's own desires and pleasures in the theorization of the text stake out an unsettled theoretical terrain in his writings of the early 1970s. Barthes's interlocutors evacuate presence from the theatres that serve as figures for textuality and ultimately strip live performance of its specificity among systems of representation. Barthes also envisions ideal theatres and bodies secured through the abstraction of a suspect corporeality, at times his own. However, in Barthes's case the displacement fails, anxiously and repeatedly, and the persistent return of a 'lovable' performing body and its hold on the spectator's desire mires his theoretical flitting in the thorny conundrum of 'presence' further embarrassed with an unavowed sexuality. The relegation of homosexuality and live performance to a blind field of unspoken pleasures and worries leaves its imprint on Barthes's critical terms, and invites an interrogation of the conditions that enable and police both the prodigal return of theatre and the birth of the desiring reader/spectator at this remarkably prolific point in his career.

A Writerly Theatre

S/Z opens with a resounding repudiation of structuralism's totalizing imperative:

> On dit qu'à force d'ascèse certains bouddhistes parviennent à voir tout un paysage dans une fève [...] tâche épuisante (*'Science avec patience, le supplice est sûr'*) et finalement indésirable, car le texte y perd sa différence.

> (There are said to be certain Buddhists whose ascetic practices enable them to see a whole landscape in a bean [...] a task as exhausting [ninety-nine percent perspiration, as the saying goes] as it is ultimately undesirable, for the text thereby loses its difference.) (II 557; *S/Z* 3)

Difference, Barthes's notes, springs not from authorial genius or originality, nor from the unique nature of a given work, but from the movement of plural discourses through the provisional playground of the literary text. In opposition to the Buddhist's lone bean – dry and demanding: adjectives that could easily qualify the 'high structuralist' *Elements of Semiology* and *The Fashion System* – Barthes proposes a galaxy of signifiers to be traversed and connected in an infinite number of ways. Writing is the productive practice of weaving and unravelling the multiple strands of signifiers that form the fabric of the *text*. A 'writerly' text is therefore open to 'le jeu infini du monde' (the infinite play of the world), in which the process of structuration and the production of meaning take priority over any single definitive structure or produced meaning (II 558; *S/Z* 5). Readers who ascertain this process can therefore participate in the gesture of meaning's production and effectively become writers in their own right. The 'readerly' text, on the contrary, is a product whose meaning is frozen, packaged, and consumed according to the rules of ideology, truth-wielding criticism, narrative convention, and common sense.

Certain texts of the literary avant-garde shatter narrative, logic, and character into a stream of words so opaque they compel the reader to acknowledge the plurality and provisionality of any possible reading. Mallarmé, Lautréamont, and Artaud, frequent icons of *Tel Quel* criticism, blaze this trail, and contemporary writers including *Tel Quel* editor Philippe Sollers produce writing that resembles words strewn across the white field of the page.[17] For his study, however, Barthes chooses a story by the highly readable Balzac, the same author whose realist prose he historicizes out of his purview in *Writing Degree Zero*. *Sarrasine*, a novella little known previously, offers a wealth of literary conventions for Barthes's incisive critique along with a touch of the writable, a 'parsimonious plural' that permits an early articulation of the pleasures of the text.

The method in *S/Z* is deceptively simple. Barthes identifies the five codes that constitute the plurality of Balzac's story, and then shatters the novella into units of reading (*léxies*) to map the codes as they overlap and thread together to weave the fabric of a tightly woven text. Throughout he intersperses critical commentary to explicate the terms and conditions of this 'slow-motion' reading of classic realist prose. Four of the codes occupy familiar topoi in Barthes's thought. The *proairetic* code aligns the sequence of actions within the story, and the *hermeneutic* code poses enigmas and defers their resolution, stringing the reader along and preserving the necessity and logic of the storytelling itself; these are the codes of linear narrative. The appendix of *S/Z* contains a schema of proairetisms, the desiccated skeleton of Balzac's rich text whose austerity and in this case expendability illustrate all that is lost in the sole armature of the readerly. The *semic* code accounts for connotation, the second order of meaning that covers the apparently inconsequential detail or action with the 'gold dust' of signification that, when it returns insistently, as it inevitably does in the economy of a 'classic' text, slowly coalesces to form a meaning: the compendium of details in the opening sequence, for example, adequately signifies the wealth of the Lanty family before either character or narrator broaches the subject directly.[18] The *referential* code draws on science, common sense, and references to general cultural knowledge to support Balzac's narrative. This is the most ideological of codes and in many cases reeks of the *doxa*, the 'natural' assumptions of truth and received ideas so trenchantly discredited in *Mythologies*. The interplay of these four codes echoes the project outlined earlier in the 1966 'Introduction to the Structural Analysis of Narratives,' and alone does not mark a radical break with Barthes's earlier criticism other than by permitting him to listen to all four at once instead of directing his attention to one at a time.

It is the remaining *symbolic* code that heralds the text and leads Barthes's thought out of the closed systems of his structuralist phase.[19] The narrative maintains suspense and preserves its secrets until the end of the novella – What is the narrator's story, which he hopes to exchange for sex? Who are the old man at the party and the beautiful youth in the painting? Where do the Lanty family and their immeasurable wealth come from? The answer to these questions is an impossible neutral term: a castrato, a former opera star of legendary talent and beauty whose symbolic lack annihilates the barriers that guarantee meaning and anchor truth, be it of the sexes, the represented body, or the Parisian economy. *Sarrasine* is not just one realist story among many, a mere literary *fait divers* regarding the curious legacy of a castrato that happens to have the right measure of the writerly. The novella's symbolic register (castration) and the enigmatic figure on which its narrative structure turns and falters (a castrato) provide a parable for the breakdown of the 'vast symbolic structure' and 'immense province' of symbolic relations – the very systems structuralism sought to divine – that drive the production of meaning and, as they fail, threaten its collapse. The oppositions that establish meaning begin to ease, wreaking havoc on literature's representative function:

> il n'est plus possible de *représenter*, de donner aux choses des *représentants*, individués, séparés, distribués: *Sarrasine* représente le trouble même de la representation, la circulation déréglée (pandémique) des signes, des sexes, des fortunes.

> (it is no longer possible to *represent*, to make things *representative*, individuated, separate, assigned; *Sarrasine* represents the very confusion of representation, the unbridled [pandemic] circulation of signs, of sexes, of fortunes.) (II 700; *SZ* 216)

The contagion also touches the reader who, no longer the passive observer of the novella's plural voices, becomes a participant implicated in the forging and undoing of signification itself: the reader/writer barrier also dissolves, leaving the active navigator of the text to appreciate the play and return of meanings with no beginning and no end. Barthes's symbolic code is not just another thread in the smooth weave of a tidy realist text (text, he reminds us, shares an etymology with textile); it is the loose strand that, if tugged, risks bringing apart the apparently seamless whole. The symbolic breakdown leaves no clear terms to order, no stable system to divine: the structure is undone.

After the bodiless abstractions of the 1960s, corporeality stages a stunning comeback in *S/Z* as the site of symbolic excess and of the 'parsimonious plural' where Balzac's readerliness falters to reveal the instability and play of an otherwise tame textuality. The emblematic figure of symbolic disruption is the castrato's body itself. Throughout the novella this body is repeatedly remade, painted, sculpted, and narrated as both male and female: first on stage as woman, recreated by the sculptor as a nude ideal of feminine beauty, then re-executed in a marble copy that serves as the model for a painting of Adonis, which in turn Girodet is alleged to have copied for his androgynous though clearly male *Endymion* that today hangs in the Louvre. Within the story itself the castrato appears as the opera diva La Zambinella, a frightened girl, a Neapolitan *ragazzo*, and a grotesque centenarian. The castrato's body provides the perfect metaphor for the writerly text. Voyeurs, listeners, artists, authors, narrators, spectators, and readers perpetually create this body anew, according to their own desires, but there is no stable truth about the castrato's gender, no language, no painting, no sculpture in which to express it definitively. In Barthes's reading the castrato's body is a realm of possibilities, of the production of meaning and gender, of meaning *as* gender, but any given reading or meaning produced is always provisional and fails to secure its truth. The figure of the castrato is not sterile, indeed it is very productive. It nonetheless fails to be reproductive, literally, of course, but also as the figure of the elusive 'third term' that upsets the male/female binary, a neutral figure of excess (composite of both genders) and lack (the figure of neither gender), both the answer to all the enigmas and a void that betrays the factitiousness of any truth. The castrato is 'la tâche aveugle et mobile de ce système' ('the blind and mobile flaw in the system'), the joker in the deck that must be assigned a meaning but that for gender categories, as for the species, cannot guarantee the future as an iteration of the terms of the present (II 579; *SZ* 36).

If the castrato's body is the figure of the writerly text in this parable of textuality, the sculptor Sarrasine is the emblematic reader caught haplessly in the tradition of literary reception already decried in *Writing Degree Zero*. In the Sarrasinean artist one might see the truth-seeking reader/critic of 'old' criticism (the spectre of Raymond Picard, perhaps), who strives to look behind or through the fictive world of Balzac's texts to establish its origin in a biographical or historical referent. Sarrasine believes in the transparent intelligibility and readability of the world, as much as the petit-bourgeois readers and spectators of the *Mythologies*, and maintains faith in a stable truth behind the signs that constitute his reality. Neither the Roman world nor the system of reference, however, is what it seems. The French sculptor, like the traditional reader of Balzac's text, is the consumer of the readerly who has wandered into an at least partially writerly world where he unknowingly becomes an active accomplice in generating its meanings. When he is convinced he has found the ideal woman of his dreams in La Zambinella, and recreates her as a sculpture, a nude of ideal feminine beauty, he fails to understand until it is too late that he himself has shaped this body according to already coded desires. He ultimately dies for his obstinate subscription to readerly aesthetics that demand any gaps in the knowable and the sayable be filled with a plausible truth, even if only a hallucinated one. The sculptor is the unwitting victim of representation's 'baseless necessity,' and his misreading is therefore as inevitable as it is disastrous: 'l'esthétique sarrasinienne de la statue est tragique' ('the Sarrasinean aesthetic of the statue is tragic') (II 695; *SZ* 208). Hence the sculptor's panic and the general catastrophe when the truth, or rather the impossibility thereof, is revealed: it is nothing less than his world, whose meanings he experiences as nature itself, collapsing before his horrified eyes.

There is one place, however, where instead of recoiling at the symbolic horror of castration even the stubborn sculptor wallows blissfully in the annihilation of meaning, of language, and of his own imaginary self. Sarrasine strays into a theatre. Already before the curtain rises, the music steals the sculptor's speech and provokes a violent physiological transformation. The triumphant entrance of the prima donna further intensifies the pleasure of the sculptor, who swoons in ecstasy, emitting involuntary cries of pleasure as he appreciates the perfection of each part of the diva's body. He believes he has discovered ideal feminine beauty, but the enumerated parts do not add up neatly to a recognizable whole. In Balzac's text the sculptor's own thoughts recognize a bodily supplement: 'this was more than a woman; this was a masterpiece!'[20] Barthes reads the recourse to the masterpiece as a ploy, a smokescreen 'jamming' of the code of reference that betrays the failure of metalanguage: the 'masterpiece' stopgap both hides and draws attention to the something more – or less – that distinguishes the castrato from a woman. The sculptor does not derive pleasure from a familiar knowledge of science, culture, or masterpieces that have come before. On the contrary, in the theatre knowledge, language, and the sculptor's rational subject spectacularly fail him as he experiences, in Balzac's description, 'rapture,' 'delirium,' 'madness,' 'frenzy,' 'intoxication,' 'convulsions,' the collapse of 'fame, knowledge, future, existence, laurels,' and finally a pleasure so intense that it obliges him to leave the theatre and return to a familiar readability where he can recompose both himself and the meanings that anchor his understanding of the world.[21] He will feel similar emotions again in his blind rage at the end of the story when he can no longer uphold the fiction of the castrato's ideal femininity. The difference is that in the theatre he experiences the upheaval not as horror at the pandemic of annihilated sexuality and signification, but as pleasure of the highest order. It is the one place, the one time, the sculptor *gets it off*, not, as he later believes, because he has found the ideal woman enshrined in the Code (he will later execute the 'masterpiece' of sculpture, frozen, hollow, and sterile), but because he experiences something more, both excess and lack, the breach in meaning, the dissolution of the paradigm, the collapse of the Code, the interstice of *signifiance*, and the pleasure of the text.

Barthes's commentary on the castrato's performance reopens the theatre whose doors the structuralist 'delirium' keeps tightly closed. The devastating performance in the Roman opera house bears a resemblance to the Artaudian ideal that will again surprise those who align Barthes more closely with Brecht: the body is (figuratively) dismembered, rationality fails, and limits are abolished. Psychology, language, narrative, and character are dismissed, and ecstatic sound assails the senses and penetrates the spectator viscerally. Moreover, this stunning performance owes its power to a specifically theatrical setting. Only after leaving the theatre does repetition close the gap; only then does Sarrasine revert to his readerly ways and attempt to represent his ideal woman in an inanimate statue, to set his pleasure in stone. He returns to the theatre nightly to experience the annihilating pleasure, though after the first night even this is tempered: he has already begun to rewrite the castrato as the woman of his dreams, believing he is truthfully depicting her sex. When he finally sees La Zambinella off stage in the guise of a woman, her body, though still remarkable, is 'wrapped in the modesty of a young girl' and her glorious voice becomes the banal speech of an uneducated and shallow person.[22] Thoughts of marriage and future domesticity replace Sarrasine's unbridled ecstasy. La Zambinella removed from the stage conforms to an exigent and crushingly banal code of what a woman and a wife should be: beyond the theatre's walls the closure of representation enforces repetition, however baseless.

The Sarrasinean parable illustrates the necessity of representation as much as its failure. One might call this double movement the Orpheus syndrome, after the mythological figure Barthes so often invokes: to lay eyes on utopia is to destroy it. The zero degree lurks over a forever receding horizon. The many readings/rewritings of the castrato indicate that although this body serves as Barthes's emblem of the 'neuter/

neutral' exempt from the imposition of gendered meaning, it represents as much what cannot be thought or written as what the reader *must* rewrite. The castrato reveals the failure of the epistemological and linguistic claim to knowledge, meaning, and truth, even as it demands to be assigned a place in these same systems. Utopia and tragedy again circulate as conjoined terms in Barthes's writings.

The castrato's performance nevertheless keeps *Sarrasine* from being an entirely cautionary tale. There is a moment of happy textuality, of pleasure in the loss of identity and the failure of the intelligible, that briefly eludes the closure of representation. The Roman opera is more than a Derridean fold; it opens a space, a privileged sanctuary where even Sarrasine, the most obstinate zealot of the readable, can hear the 'music of pulsions' and delight in the process instead of the product, the performance instead of the performed, a signifier liberated from a signified, and *signifiance* unhinged from meaning. Balzac's Rome therefore might be added to the list of Barthesian utopias, although with the pleasures confined to a single theatre it remains as parsimoniously utopian as the realist prose of *Sarrasine* itself.[23]

Unsung Pleasures

The castrato might incite symbolic mayhem in the circulation of meaning in the literary text, but there are no more castrati, and Barthes does not suggest that a similarly annihilating and pleasurable performance is possible in his contemporary France, or for that matter in eighteenth-century Italy. *S/Z* does not herald Barthes's own return to the theatre as a spectator and critic. However, the erotically devastating performance at the heart of Balzac's novella demands scrutiny in light of the anxiety and contradictions that historically attend Barthes's assessment of performing bodies. The once-abandoned performance serves as the privileged figure of textuality, but something has been evacuated from the hopelessly 'ill' theatre to guarantee the symbolic neutrality of the castrato's performance. The walls of the textual theatre enclose a utopian space, but what do they keep out?

It is illuminating to consider Barthes's remarks on the singing voice's relation to the body that produces it. The castrato's voice plays an instrumental role in inciting the sculptor's pleasure: 'this voice attacked his soul so vividly that several times he gave vent to involuntary cries torn from him by convulsive feelings of pleasure.'[24] Barthes seizes on Balzac's choice of the term 'lubricated' – 'the young sculptor's senses were, so to speak, lubricated'[25] – to describe the voice's ability to draw together the fragmented parts of the castrato's body, and the text of which it is the emblem, under a guise of seamlessness that would restitute an imaginary unity to both, uniting 'dans une même plénitude le sens et le sexe' ('in the one plenitude both meaning and sex') (II 628; *SZ* 110). He therefore appears to join Derrida in his suspicion of the voice, *la voix*, the term of alleged plenitude and presence opposed to the absence and deferral of *écriture*. However, La Zambinella's is a voice unlike any other. The voice annihilates the dramatic signified of the performing body and undoes the binary gender paradigm that the visual element reinforces: 'La voix est diffusion, insinuation, elle passe par toute l'étendue du corps, la peau; étant passage, abolition des limites, des classes, des noms' ('the voice is a diffusion, an insinuation, it passes over the entire surface of the body, the skin; and being a passage, an abolition of limitations, classes, names') (II 628; *SZ* 110). The 'internal recitation' of the phenomenological subject falters, replaced by a vocal gesture that empties any meaning ascribed to the body (performer) or voiced language (performed song) into a connecting interstice: the breach of the *phrased*, a term Barthes calls 'preciously ambiguous' because it refers both to music and to language, opened between language and the body's breath. The voice's lubricating 'plenitude of pleasure' *liquidates* the epistemological body of truth, and melts the paradigmatic slash of difference ('/') that anchors meaning and guarantees the stability of a *somebody*, be it the performer or the watching, desiring spectator. The body does not produce the voice; it is the vocal performance that briefly opens a gap in the chain of imagined, narrated, sculpted, and painted copies that assert the body's truth.

As Barthes observes, Sarrasine is effectively in love with a voice, not a body. The castrato's aria finds an ancestor in the pure diction Barthes favours in *On Racine*, cleansed of expressive static through the displacement of the performing body itself. The voice is the index of nobody, of *no body*, 'la trace pleine, liée, du manque' ('the complete, connected evidence of a deficiency') (II 628; *SZ* 110). It is significant, though Barthes does not note it, that the voice of the castrato has no gender markings in the theatre episode, and that Balzac gives no information regarding either the libretto or the character for the vocal performance other than the fact that La Zambinella is dressed as a woman. There is no aural diegesis in Balzac's account of the opera, no diegesis mentioned at all other than the exterior trappings of femininity the sculptor accepts as truth. The voice effectively evacuates the body a readerly spectator would invest with meaning.

A body persists nonetheless, and even the stunning symbolic breakdown of the castrato's aria cannot entirely displace it. Barthes betrays the purity and primacy of the subjectless, liquid voice when he writes that 'un délire follement érotique se reverse sur ce corps' ('a wildly erotic frenzy is returned to that body') (II 628; *SZ* 109), thereby invoking a corporeality *before* the vocal gesture that invests it with lubrifying, erotic qualities in the first place: a body, if not somebody, is already there, as stubborn as the substance 'unalterable except in death,' as Barthes noted in 1953 while spying on the anonymous woman in the commuter train.[26] The voice, in Balzac's words 'supple as thread shaped by the slightest breath of air,' conserves this faint trace of a *souffle*, the living, breathing, *animate* body that produces it.[27] Two years later Barthes will more fully theorize the 'grain' of the voice, a palpable trace of the body that piques the listener's desire: 'quelque chose est là, manifeste et têtu (on n'entend que *ça*), qui est au-delà (ou en deça) du sens des paroles [...] quelque chose qui est directement le corps du chantre' ('something is there, manifest and stubborn (one hears only *that*), beyond (or before) the meaning of the words [...] something which is directly the cantor's body') (II 1437; *IMT* 181). In this later essay, and in following years, Barthes will recognize his desire as a reader for such 'direct' traces of the body, but in *S/Z* he is less sanguine in his assessment of these excesses. The castrato's voice is marked with a remainder, with a body, whose claim on the reader's, listener's, or spectator's desire remains the suspect motor of the readerly and drives the sculptor's frenzied and doomed attempts to capture La Zambinella's form. For Barthes, Sarrasine's effort does not represent a 'loving' expenditure but failure: 'Ce mouvement [...] conduit à un échec – à l'Echec – dont *Sarrasine* est en quelque sorte l'emblème' ('This impulse [...] leads to a failure – to Failure – of which *Sarrasine* is in a way the emblem') (II 637; *SZ* 122).

The performing body and its persistent presence occupy a paradoxical place in Barthes's reading of *Sarrasine*. On one hand, the body adulterates the ideal purity of the voice and must be eliminated to secure a pure gesture of production. On the other, the excessive body appears necessary to rescue the text from inert sterility. In Barthes's parable of textuality, it is not the ideal vocal gesture but the persistent body's demand to be rewritten according to the spectator's desire that unleashes a never-ending chain of provisional copies and drives literary and artistic production.

The necessary failure of the post-structuralist ideal and the demand the text places on the reader's or spectator's desire invite an interrogation of Barthes's own abstruse position as a reader of Balzac's text and the castrato that is its emblem. Barthes asserts that *Sarrasine* does not enact but rather represents symbolic mayhem, yet he also recounts in meticulous and methodical detail the moments where the text itself slips on a 'reversible' plural (however parsimonious), where meanings flicker and fade, and where the anchors that guarantee symbolic stability slide underneath even Balzac's readerly prose. As a reader of *S/Z*, Barthes himself takes a seat alongside Sarrasine in the theatre of representation to participate in the spectacle of meaning's production: 'je nomme, je dénomme, je renomme: ainsi passe le texte: c'est une nomination en devenir' ('I name, I un-name, I rename: so the text passes: it is a nomination in the course of becoming') (II 562; *SZ* 11). The 'I' reading the text must generate its own chain of provisional meanings and names, none of which is definitive, each ultimately relinquished in a forgetting: 'une valeur affirmative, une façon d'affirmer l'irresponsabilité du texte, le pluralisme des systèmes [...] c'est précisément parce que j'oublie que je lis' ('an affirmative value, a way of asserting the irresponsibility of the text, the pluralism of systems [...] it is precisely because I forget that I read') (II 562; *SZ* 11).

Who is the 'I' that reads *Sarrasine* so carefully in *S/Z*, and what are the forgotten names, the waste product of the writerly, that Barthes so casually discards? The textual desires that motivate the project of *S/Z* and inflect its critical voice are dismissed as inconsequential. Unlike the sculptor and his unseemly public display, the calm, collected commentary of *S/Z* never openly 'loses it' and again echoes the impersonal voice of *On Racine*: both coolly recount from a critical distance the workings of a text and the emotional turmoil caused by the presence of a desired body. Chaste, dispassionate, and with lingering scientific detachment, the critical voice of *S/Z* most often speaks with an editorial 'we' – appropriate, perhaps, when one considers that this essay is the fruit of the collective effort of a seminar – and explicitly discredits the 'I' who reads and rereads the text as a pronoun of imaginary plenitude to be analysed and interrogated. In the most extensive passage on the reader's voice, Barthes carefully moves the 'I' (the *'moi'*) whose voice narrates the reading of *S/Z* into quotes to suggest that it, too, is a character of sorts generated by the text (II 261–2; *S/Z* 10–11). Only once does Barthes relinquish the impersonality of the critical voice to identify it as his own, and his first-person commentary is confined (in the original French) to a parenthesis:

Quant au texte qui a été choisi (pour quelles raisons? Je sais seulement que je désirais depuis assez longtemps faire l'analyse d'un court récit dans son entier et que mon attention fut attirée sur la nouvelle de Balzac par une étude de Jean Reboul; l'auteur disait tenir son propre choix d'une citation de Georges Bataille, ainsi je me trouvais pris dans ce *report*, dont j'allais, par le texte lui-même, entrevoir toute l'étendue), ce texte est *Sarrasine*, de Balzac.

(The text I have chosen [Why? All I know is that for some time I have wanted to make a complete analysis of a short text and that the Balzac story was brought to my attention by an article by Jean Reboul, who in turn is supposed to have been inspired by Georges Bataille's reference; and thus I was caught up in this 'series' whose scope I was to discover by means of the text itself] is Balzac's *Sarrasine*.) (II 565; *SZ* 16)

Why indeed? The question goes unanswered. Barthes's own desire as a reader of *Sarrasine* is the forgotten term of S/Z, his own rewriting of the text its untold tale.

Commenting on Barthes's discreet neutrality in articulating the writerly ideal, Ross Chambers cautions that 'a story that goes untold can't for that matter be regarded as inoperative: rather, it becomes significant by virtue of having been omitted, and as an object of forgetting.'[28] Chambers is one of many critics who challenge the exemption Barthes claims for himself from the realm of politics, of desire, and of both the pleasures and pains that attend the inexorable 'tragedy' of representation. The castrato's status as *neutre* in particular draws the scrutiny of those who for whom gender urgently matters. When Barthes abstains from ascribing value to the 'joker' in the textual deck others often fill the gap in meaning for him. They do so, however, at their own risk.

Two recent and opposing readings of the castrato's voice reveal the gamble of assigning value to Barthes's unspoken terms. Musicologist Joke Dame decries Barthes's refusal to recognize La Zambinella's masculinity, most apparent in the 'penetrating' phallic voice that brings the sculptor to orgasm, and considers Barthes's insistence on the neutrality of the castrato an obfuscation of homoeroticism in the sculptor's desire for the castrato as a male singer: for Dame, the voice is distinctly masculine and betrays the homosexual desire that a discreet Barthes tidily keeps in the closet.[29] In *The Acoustic Mirror: The Female Voice in Psychoanalysis and Cinema*, Kaja Silverman similarly reads the ideal *neutre* as a false and even disingenuous fantasy, a suspect evacuation of gender difference and an abdication of concomitant political and ethical responsibilities: 'no discourse of the body can foreclose for very long upon sexual difference.'[30] Other feminist readings of Barthes lodge a similar critique.[31] However, unlike Dame and most others who fill in Barthes's blank to reveal an unspoken homosexuality, Silverman identifies the castrato's singing voice as neither the liquidation of the gender paradigm nor a muted masculinity insidiously passing as neutral, but as the figure of a *female* voice that emerges in the wake of the male author's divestiture: 'The castration which Zambinella undergoes not only 'unmans' him, making it impossible for him to speak any longer from a masculine position, but it produces a *female* singing voice [...] The Barthesian fantasy would thus seem to turn not only upon the death of the paternal author, but upon the production of a female authorial voice as well.'[32] Silverman joins Dame in calling Barthes's poker-faced bluff. Both denounce his refusal to forge his own link in the chain of copies as a disingenuous retreat to a utopia of subjectivity and representation that Barthes himself so often deems unattainable, or at least unsustainable. However, the contradictory gender values assigned to Barthes's wild card would also confirm the provisional nature of any definitive reading of this body and justify Barthes's suspicion of the identity politics that demand such truths. Like the painters, sculptors, writers, and readers before them, the critics' acoustic hallucinations of the castrato's gender are only two more links in the ever-growing chain of provisional copies whose truthfulness cannot be guaranteed.

Dame, Silverman, and others who would pin down Barthes's elusive terms stake out what musicologist Carolyn Abbate, in her study of the operatic singing voice's resistance to semiotic and linguistic analysis, names a 'utopian position of interpretive certainty.'[33] Barthes, however, situates himself in a no less utopian position sheltered from the body's inexorable demand to be read and rewritten. The neutral voice – both the castrato's and Barthes's own as the virtuoso reader/commentator of *S/Z* – bears the trace of a body that demands reconciliation with the Code, with the 'name,' and impels the 'outing' of spectators and readers, Barthes and his critics included, as subjects endowed with individual desires. Abbate continues, with terms that capture the ambivalence of the castrato's song for both Barthes and his commentators, '[music] is the beast in the closet; seemingly without any discursive sense, it cries out the problems inherent in critical reading and in interpretation as unfaithful translation. For interpreting music involves a terrible and unsafe leap between object and exegesis, from sound that seems to signify nothing (and is nonetheless splendid) to words that claim discursive sense but are, by comparison, modest and often unlovely. What is lost in the jump is what we all fear: what must remain unsaid.'[34] The leap is terrible, yet, Barthes tells us, jump we must. He does not take the plunge himself in *S/Z*, and the price of this discretion is nothing less than the body, *his* body, and its own specific desires. However, Barthes's efforts to keep his feared beast in the closet and his failure entirely to mute its cry betray his symbolic weightlessness as a reader. When in the same year (1970) Barthes opens this closet door a crack and allows a faint strain of 'splendid sound' to resonate through the account of his travels through Japan, *Empire of Signs*, the anxieties of the body's presence both secure and threaten his utopian pleasures. In Japan Barthes himself again takes a seat in a literal theatre, but far from inducing the ecstatic *jouissance* of the Roman opera the performing body's inescapable claim on the reader/spectator's desire leads to an unequivocal condemnation of Western performance practice as an irredeemably compromised mode of representation.

Chaste Utopia

In the opening passages of *Empire of Signs* Barthes again invokes a text that breaches stable meanings to open a space for the circulation of desire:

> Cette situation est celle-là même où s'opère un certain ébranlement de la personne, un renversement des anciennes lectures, une secousse de sens, déchiré, exténué jusqu'à son vide insubstituable, sans que l'objet cesse jamais d'être signifiant, désirable.

> (This situation is the very one in which a certain disturbance of the person occurs, a subversion of earlier readings, a shock of meaning lacerated, extenuated to the point of its irreplaceable void, without the object's ever ceasing to be significant, desirable.) (II 748; *EpS* 4)

This same passage would aptly characterize Sarrasine's experience in the theatre, faced with the symbolic lack of the castrato's body, or of the reader negotiating the writerly text. Here, however, Barthes expands the interstice confined to the Roman theatre in *Sarrasine* to the vast scale of an entire country, Japan, and the person who tumbles into the fissure of the symbolic is neither a fictive character nor an impersonal critical voice but identified as Barthes himself.

Japan, or rather the semiological neverland Barthes names Japan, offers the antidote to the infirmities of the hopelessly myth-ridden society dissected in *Mythologies*. The food, wrestlers, literature, games, and popular culture of 1950s France find their healthy counterparts in the 'empire of signs.' In the act of giving a gift, eating a meal, demonstrating in the streets or merely saying hello, Barthes revels in the gestures of production – of food, of play, of meaning – that do not insidiously congeal into a suspect product. By the time one has opened an elaborately wrapped gift, offered with great ceremony, the trinket inside is an irrelevant afterthought: the gestures of giving and receiving all but eclipse the gift itself. Food, too, assembled and often cooked while one eats it, does not culminate in a 'dish,' but instead the meal's fabrication and consumption coincide; the end of the meal marks the end of its preparation. The pleasure of the signifier likewise supplants the desire for a signified or a referent, and the generative gesture that would in the West produce something – a gift, a meal, a meaning – in Barthes's Japan eliminates it.

Writing also finds a utopian form in Barthes's Japan. Haiku poetry represents an ideal *écriture* that exhausts meaning in the gesture of its production. The vast number of the short poems proliferates into infinity, each one revealing 'une répétition sans origine, un événement sans cause, une mémoire sans personne, une parole sans amarres' ('a repetition without origin, an event without cause, a memory without person, a language without moorings') (II 801; *EpS* 79). The incidents invoked in haiku – seeing rain on a mountain, hearing a distant bell, discovering a flower at one's feet – are infinitely repeatable and unremarkable, referential trinkets with little inherent value, yet the poems are always different, always unique events in themselves. Barthes professes at last to have found weightless writing liberated from the tragic situation of Western literature that demands even the most pure 'white writing' produce a second-order meaning for the critic-as-sleuth to uncover. Haiku stages the utopian failure of writing as the representation of anything other than what it is, and also of anyone behind it, be it god-like author or the self-present subject whose voice Derrida discredits: 'une suspension panique du langage, le blanc qui efface en nous le règne des Codes, la cassure de cette récitation intérieure qui constitue notre personne' ('a panic suspension of language, the blank which erases in us the reign of the Codes, the breach of that internal recitation which constitutes our person') (II 798; *EpS* 75).

Haiku's deferral of meaning more generally characterizes the immense text of Japan. Barthes witnesses innumerable haiku-like gestures, or 'incidents,' in the streets of Tokyo: a man playing Pachinko, a café client drinking a soda. These incidents inspire a new poetics of writing liberated from character, plot, allegory, or reference to anything beyond its own signifiers. The producers of these gestures, along with their bodies, are again exhausted in the gesture itself. The innumerable acts that constitute the great spectacle of Japan depend not on a hysterical 'théâtralité' with its factitious etiologies of interior psychology and motivation, but rather on a productive gesture that does not express anything, an *écriture* 'qui n'exprime pas, mais simplement fait exister' ('that does not express but simply *causes to exist*') (II 802; *EpS* 80). In haiku or on the street, the incident renders interpretation, criticism, and metalanguage useless, for there is no depth, no hermeneutics, nothing to say about it other than to affirm simply that it is, *as such.*

The exemption from meaning Barthes locates in Japan typifies the impulse towards the neutral that drives his thought since *Writing Degree Zero.* However, Barthes's utopias are inexorably girded by a tragic reverse side, and failure is inscribed in the very terms of their articulation. This double movement is again the Orpheus syndrome: to lay eyes on utopia is to destroy it; to attain the desired neutrality is to invest it once more with meaning, if only as a sign of neutrality. As Barthes so pointedly demonstrates in *S/Z*, Balzac's novella reveals as much the tragic compulsion to impose meaning of the most conventional sort as the failure of these meanings, even when the 'text' is the impossible term of the castrato's body itself. The similarities between the enrapt spectator in Balzac's Roman theatre and Barthes as a Western tourist raise the question of whether his Japan also tragically fails as a utopian space, and whether the voice of the phenomenological subject travelling through the empire of signs, which like Sarrasine's appears to falter in a panic suspension of meaning, continues to intone the inexorable continuo of an 'internal recitation' even if it speaks so softly only a trained ear can hear.

At approximately the same time he is idealizing haiku in *Empire of Signs*, Barthes is also composing haiku-like fragments of his own: the short textual snapshots in prose of his travels through Morocco published posthumously in *Incidents*. These textual fragments resemble the 'novelistic' everyday incidents Barthes observes in Japan with one notable difference: they often testify to an overt and at times graphic homosexuality entirely uncharacteristic of the writings he chooses to publish during his lifetime. Throughout, a post-colonial situation mediates the adventures of the unnamed and (comparably) wealthy European observer with Moroccan men, many of them clearly very poor and often only boys. The exploitative nature of the observer's success as a sex tourist, secured with European privilege and wealth, burdens the purportedly weightless textual incidents with the baggage of history and raises troubling questions Barthes neglects to entertain. The narrator is himself a blind field in these texts, an unobserved observer who witnesses and records the incidents with the psychological detachment characteristic of attempts at 'write writing,' but this narrative position is neither a neutral term, nor a zero degree, nor what Barthes calls in another text from this period, again referring to haiku, '[une] sort de balafre dont est rayé le sens (l'envie du sens) [...] une dépense sans échange' ('a sort of gash rased of meaning [of desire for meaning] [...] an expenditure with no exchange') (II 880; *IMT* 62).[35] A voice whispers into the breach, quietly incanting 'that internal recitation which constitutes our person' and endowing the haiku-like signifiers with the weight of a signified: an unavowed, and for some critics unflattering, confluence of Westernness and homosexuality in the enunciator of these texts, who is marked as Barthes himself.[36]

The gay inflection can also faintly be heard in *Empire of Signs*. The recent quarrying of homosexuality in Barthes's work has unearthed a wealth of material, including telling instances in his encounter with Japan where an unnamed desire discreetly determines his trajectory through the empire of signs. In the passage entitled 'Center-City, Empty Center,' Barthes describes how the forbidden compound of the imperial palace opens a void in the centre of Tokyo where the Westerner would expect to find the pithy kernel of a city's meaning; the 'essence' of Tokyo is not anchored in a central nucleus, but diffused through a vast network of unhinged detours and returns, not unlike the text's multiple threads, which the readers/tourists navigate according to their own desire. But this is not just any desire leading down any random street. As D.A. Miller notes with surprise, the scrawled schematic street directions reproduced in *Empire of Signs* provide detailed maps of a well-known gay area of the Shinjuku quarter.[37] Diana Knight observes, with a certain judgmental distaste, that Barthes's handwritten 'phrasebook,' photo-reproduced in the book, consists almost entirely of pick-up lines, a 'parodic *Gay Guide to Tokyo*, whereby he himself is ironically inscribed in the text as a sexual tourist of the worst sort.'[38] The exemption of meaning, 'the breach of that internal recitation which constitutes our person' Barthes so admires in Japan, appears to harbour a secret of its own.

Empire of Signs contains Barthes's first substantive account of performance practice since he abandoned his theatre criticism nearly ten years earlier and, significantly, the last in any detail he will write before his death ten years later. Three chapters on Japanese Bunraku theatre occupy the centre of *Empire of Signs*. The intertext of *S/Z* bids Barthes's reader pay heed: were it to inspire anything resembling the experience of Sarrasine at the opera, the Japanese theatre would open a utopian space in a utopian land, an ideal situation of *écriture* raised to the second power, a *sanctum sanctorum* of blissful, eroticized textuality.

Barthes's method as a critical spectator in Japan appears to follow the method of textual analysis deployed in *S/Z*. Barthes identifies the plural gestures, or *écritures*, into which Bunraku separates performance: readers and musicians on a dais to the side of the stage produce the dramatic vocal gestures, punctuated with percussive music; manipulators of the puppet visibly execute the gesture of the performance's production; and finally there is the the puppet/character itself. Like the loose weave of the writerly text, Bunraku is another lacework of multiple strands:

> Comme dans le texte moderne, le tressage des codes, des références, des constats détachés, des gestes anthologiques, multiplie la ligne écrite, non par la vertu de quelque appel métaphysique, mais par le jeu d'une combinatoire qui s'ouvre dans l'espace entier du théâtre.

> (As in the modern text, the interweaving of codes, references, discreet assertions, anthological gestures multiplies the written line, not by virtue of some metaphysical appeal, but by the interaction of a *combinatoire* which opens out into the entire space of the theater.) (II 786; *EpS* 55)

As in Balzac's opera scene, there is no diegesis in Barthes's account of the performance. The spectacle of production, combination, and interweaving, perhaps a function of Barthes's happy ignorance of the declaimed Japanese language and hence of the narrative as it unfolds, exhausts meaning in the gesture that produces it. Like Balzac's text, the appeal of Bunraku for Barthes, if not for the Japanese spectators, lies not in character, narrative, or theatrical illusion, but in the spectacle of their fabrication.[39]

Barthes's enthusiasm for Bunraku rekindles the arguments of his 1950s theatre criticism, and he again invokes Brecht as a 'healthy' alternative to the myth-mired theatre of France. The Bunraku puppet establishes a distance between the performer as demonstrator and the character being demonstrated even more radically than Brecht's Chinese actor. The gestures are literally divided among bodies and puppets, while the additional distancing of a third gesture, the displacement of speech to the sidelines, further discredits any alibi of the 'natural.' Moreover, Brecht was ever mindful that the gesture of production comes from somewhere, a point of view, and also has material consequences and social objectives: the *gestus* is not a weightless, neutral gesture that exists simply 'as such.' The early Barthes gradually relegates the political dimension of Brecht's dramaturgy to a parenthesis, but his idealization of Bunraku altogether evacuates the historical contradictions, moral questions, and ethical considerations that the spectator carries away to ponder after having seen a Brechtian production: 'ce qui est soigneusement, précieusement donné à lire, c'est qu'il n'y a rien à lire [...] Avec le *Bunraku*, les sources du théâtre sont exposées dans leur vide' ('what is carefully, preciously given to be read is that there is nothing there to read [...] with *Bunraku*, the sources of theater are exposed in their emptiness') (II 790; *EpS* 62).

If there were any doubt the live performing body profoundly unsettles Barthes's thought on theatre, his remarks on Bunraku confirm the depth of his unease. In *Empire of Signs* the performing body's 'liveness' serves as the grounds for a scathing indictment of Western theatre practice. In the West, the live performer's body unites the three gestures Bunraku so elegantly disperses: '[le corps] emprunte à la physiologie l'alibi d'une unité organique, celle de la "vie"' ('[the body] borrows from physiology the alibi of organic unity, that of "life"') (II 788; *EpS* 58). As in *S/Z*, Barthes again deploys the term 'lubrified' to characterize a live performer, only here it loses the delectable ambiguity that induces wild and ecstatic frenzy. Instead, the live body of Western theatre is chronically readerly, the 'single tissue' that congeals the plural strands into meanings and identities of imaginary seamless plentitude. In the West even the marionette is slave to the alibi of life:

'caricature de la «vie», [la marionette] en affirme par là meme les limites *morales* et prétend confiner la beauté, la vérité, l'émotion dans le corps de l'acteur, qui, cependant, fait de ce corps un mensonge. Le *Bunraku*, lui, ne signe pas l'acteur, il nous en débarasse.

(caricature of 'life,' [the marionette] thereby affirms life's *moral* limits and claims to confine beauty, truth, emotion within the living body of the actor, who, however, makes this body a lie. *Bunraku*, however, does not sign the actor, it gets rid of him for us.) (II 788; *EpS* 58)

Barthes wields the term *animate* as an epithet, both in its etymological meaning of 'breathing' or 'alive' and as a suggestion of subjective interiority (endowed with a soul), to deplore Western performance practice, while Bunraku wins ethusiastic approval by exploding the animate/inanimate opposition: '[Bunraku] refuse l'antimonie de *l'animé/l'inanimé* et congédie le concept qui se cache derrière toute *animation* de la matière, et qui est tout simplement "l'âme"' ([Bunraku] rejects the antinomy of *animate/inanimate* and dismisses the concept which is hidden behind all animation of matter and which is, quite simply, "the soul"') (II 789; *EpS* 60). For Barthes, Bunraku's productive possibilities neatly relieve the corporeal signifier of the 'disorders of consciousness' that troubled Kleist, while the performing body of Western theatre, by virtue of its 'liveness,' makes an insidious appeal to the imaginary stability of meaning, selves, and truths that exist outside of and before the performance itself. No disclaimer exempts even Brecht's knowing demonstrator/actor/agent from Barthes's blanket dismissal of Western theatre practice.

Only in Japan, *là-bas*, can even a live performance realize a pure gesture of writing. When Barthes takes the place of Sarrasine as a spectator of live performance during his travels in Japan he does not assume a similar role in the tragedy of representation. Echoing Brecht's appreciation of Chinese acting techniques, Barthes praises the crossdressed Kabuki actor who signifies 'woman' without attempting to imitate her. Unlike the Western drag performer, the actor's face becomes writing: 'le visage théâtral n'est pas peint (fardé), il est écrit [...] mais un pur significant dont le *dessous* (la vérité) n'est ni clandestin (jalousement masqué) ni subrepticement signé [...] simplement *absenté*' ('The theatrical face is not painted [made up], it is written [...] but a pure signifier whose *underneath* [the truth] is neither clandestine [jealously masked] nor surreptitiously signed [...] simply *absented*') (II 807; *EpS* 88–9). Barthes does not, however, thrill in this 'absence' as an interstice of desire, nor does he experience the orgasmic panic of *S/Z*'s symbolic catastrophe. Opposite a photo of the actor playing a feminine role, Barthes shows an image of the same man, dignified and unmasked, flanked by portraits of his two sons. The photograph does not reveal any deeper truth for Barthes; the actor is wearing just one mask among others: the family father, *le père de famille*.[40] Like the castrato, the kabuki actor's body can be rewritten as male or female, but between the distinguished actor and the signified woman Barthes situates no impossible body, no neutral third term, no wild card that opens an inarticulate breach in the symbolic and lays claim to his desire. Unlike the 'blind flaw' of the castrato, the Kabuki character and the photograph of the actor, side by side, exhaust the body in the signs of femininity and paternity and leave no remainder 'après la vérité de laquelle on court éperdument' ('whose truth we madly pursue') (II 809; *EpS* 91). Though live, Kabuki purifies the body of any excessive third term that interpellates the spectator as a subject, whose demand to be rewritten reveals the nature of the spectator's desire, and that, as it slips, madly unleashes semiotic panic and pleasure. Displaced by the puppet, emptied by the Kabuki actor's make-up and costume, exhausted in the gesture of producing a meaning, the vacated bodies of Japanese theatre effectively relieve the spectator Barthes of the necessity and responsibility of being somebody, *some body*.

Barthes's desiring body stubbornly persists nonetheless, and even in the utopia of pure signifiers an excessive corporeality demands reckoning. As in the Morocco of *Incidents*, Barthes's privilege as a Westerner and subtle traces of his homosexuality betray the weightlessness of the bodies of Japan, and of his own body in Japan. A discussion of physiognomy and an accompanying pair of photographs echo the juxtaposed images of the Kabuki performer in and out of costume: a 'westernized' Japanese actor's studio photo alongside Barthes's own 'Nipponized' image in a Japanese newspaper together denaturalize the facial signifier and illustrate its hollowness and arbitrary nature. Barthes intimates that racial attributes, like those of gender in Kabuki theatre, similarly detach from a natural body and float freely as signifiers from face to face: 'Qu'est-ce que donc que notre visage, sinon une *citation*?' ('What is our face, if not a "citation"?') (II 808; *EpS* 90). He neglects, however, to observe that the cited meanings do not migrate with equal ease. As D.A. Miller remarks, Barthes overlooks the obvious dissymmetry between blepharoplasty, a surgical procedure used to westernize the Asian eyelids, and the mere retouching of a photograph.[41] How many Western actors, one might wonder, undergo surgery to look Asian? As in *Incidents*, an unavowed Western privilege loads the purportedly weightless corporeal signifiers of *Empire of Signs* with the burden of a signified. A dissymmetry also thwarts the free migration of gender identity between the Kabuki character and the dignified performer. Though Barthes dismisses any 'true' body under these masks of identity, in Kabuki tradition it is the female body specifically that is evacuated; the performing body behind the mask of either gender is always already marked as male. It is therefore not exemption from the gendered that so appeals to Barthes in the Kabuki actor, for an inflection of maleness already ascribes, faintly, a signified to the performing body he finds so appealing.

The discussion of Kabuki is brief, and Barthes reserves his more effusive enthusiasm for the inanimate Bunraku puppet stripped of any elusive excess that might betray the nature of his unspoken pleasures. Barthes's ideal performance is purchased with the live performing body's abstraction and the consequent immobilization of his desire. The tempered, almost parenthetical suggestion that the Bunraku puppet is in its own way 'lovable' and produces a certain 'exaltation' falls markedly short of the rhapsodic descriptions of the 'trouble' and 'torment' he experiences as a spectator in the 1950s, not to mention the delirious seizures of Balzac's sculptor. Where Western theatre exhibits living, breathing performers that raise Barthes's guard, where the Roman opera offers an impossible body-as-excess that sends the spectator swooning, Bunraku produces nobody, no body, only a puppet, a mere piece of wood analogous to the trinket in the elaborately wrapped gift, inconsequential in itself. No remainder under the corporeal signifier, no index of a 'blind and mobile flaw in the system' invests Bunraku's productive *combinatoire* with 'wildly erotic frenzy' or anything approaching jouissance that might awaken Barthes's desire.

Between Balzac's Rome and Barthes's Tokyo the place of theatre has been reversed: it is not as a spectator in a theatre but as a tourist exploring the decentred city that Barthes finds a performance that lays claim to his desire. In everyday Japan, 'le corps existe, se déploie, agit, se donne, sans hystérie, sans narcissisme, mais selon un pur projet érotique – quoique subtilement discret' ('the body exists, acts, shows itself, gives itself, without hysteria, without narcissism, but according to a pure – though subtly discontinuous – erotic project') (II 753; *EpS* 10). On the streets of Tokyo, navigated according to his unstated desires, Barthes relishes a living, productive body that promises to fulfil an 'erotic project' as the wooden puppet never could. As a man gesticulates, scrawls maps, and writes proper names in a struggle to arrange a rendez-vous (a date?), Barthes savours the labouring body, and seems entirely indifferent to the prospect of a future appointment he may or may not keep. The making of the date, rather than the date itself, appears the sole source of Barthes's pleasure in his interlocutor's body: 'C'est tout le corps de l'autre qui a été connu, goûté, reçu, et qui a déployé (sans fin véritable) son propre récit, son propre texte' ('it is the other's entire body which has been known, savored, received, and which has displayed [to no real purpose] its own narrative, its own text') (II 753; *EpS* 10). The authorial voice of *Empire of Signs* does not indicate whatever comes of this incidental street scene, and disregards the rendez-vous itself as little more than an irrelevant pretext of the performance that is the exclusive cause of his pleasures. However much the veiled references to homosexuality, like the faint coating of connotative 'gold dust,' might suggest that a 'real purpose' of the rendez-vous indeed exists, by dismissing anything or anybody that exceeds the gesture as inconsequential Barthes diverts the reader's knowing eyes from any 'hysteria' of his own. He is unwilling to reveal the nature of the demand the body places on his desire, and discourages the extrapolation of any further meaning or other purpose. Even when he is engaged in an apparent act of cruising, the pleasures Barthes discloses remain surprisingly chaste.

Barthes's encounter with the Japanese language as a bodily act of performance and production, rather than a produced meaning, exemplifies the cool moderation of pleasure that more broadly characterizes his Japanese idyll:

> la langue inconnue, dont je saisis pourtant la respiration, l'aération emotive, en un mot la pure signifiance, forme autour de moi, au fur et à mésure que je me déplace, un léger vertige, m'entraîne dans son vide artificiel, qui ne s'accomplit que pour moi: je vis dans l'interstice, débarassé de tout sens plein.

> (The unknown language, of which I nonetheless grasp the respiration, the emotive aeration, in a word the pure significance, forms around me, as I move, a faint vertigo, sweeping me into its artificial emptiness, which is consummated only for me: I live in the interstice, delivered from any fulfilled meaning.) (II 750–3; *EpS* 9).

'Faint vertigo' falls far short of the panic breakdown of the Roman opera; indeed, the bliss and terror of the Sarrasinean tragedy are precisely what Barthes purges from the theatres of *Empire of Signs* when he idealizes a gesture of meaning's production that exhausts the performing body, leaving nothing 'madly' to pursue or to which 'wildly erotic frenzy' might return. From Balzac's Rome to Barthes's Japan the spectator's vertiginous spiral into convulsive orgasm has been reduced to a middle-aged tourist's dizzy spell. On the streets or in the theatre, Barthes's empire of signs is a frigidly elegant place disturbed by only a shiver of something more volatile.

The Touch of Hysteria

Kleist's dancer would have admired both the castrato's song and Bunraku; the former purifies the live body of adulterating subjectivity, while the latter replaces the performer with the unencumbered grace of an inanimate puppet. He would no doubt have been less keen on the excessive corporeality that betrays the theoretical purity of these performances: the silent body, and Barthes's unspoken desire for it, which leave an imprint on the discourse of his post-structuralist phase. One might wonder why the discreet Barthes, subtly but persistently, allows this body and hints of his specific desire to adulterate the ideal stagings of his thought. Could a wisp of meaning or a bit of 'hysteria' be complicit in the pleasures of the text?

In the preface to *Sade, Fourier, Loyola*, published one year after *S/Z* and *Empire of Signs*, Barthes again invokes an ideal theatricality cleansed of the infirmities of live performance practice. The three writers impress Barthes not because of their respective philosophies or didactic designs for living, but as founders of new languages, or *logothetes*. The libertine, the utopian, and the visionary all engage in the structuralist activities of dissection and articulation (*découpage* and *agencement*): they isolate their language to purify it of outside 'noise,' exhaustively identify and catalogue the terms of this secluded space, and then order this world according to an economy of ecstasy, jubilation, or ascetic indifference that leaves no gap, no breach, and no supplement. Even the excesses of Sadien pleasure are a term, 'excess,' that is part of the economy of pleasure.

To schematize the terms and conditions of these closed worlds would be a dry and joyless affair, however, were it not for the operation of 'theatricalization' (*théâtraliser*). Barthes's delight in the three writers lies not in what they express, which he glibly brushes aside, but in their engagement in a productive mise en scène of language: 'Sade n'est plus un érotique, Fourier n'est plus un utopiste, et Loyola n'est plus un saint: en chacun d'eux il ne reste plus qu'un scénographe' ('Sade is no longer an erotic, Fourier no longer a utopian, Loyola no longer a saint: all that is left in each of them is a scenographer') (II 1043; *SFL* 6). The theatrical metaphor captures the distinction between the logothete and the (late) author, between the text produced for an active reader/writer and the passively consumed 'readerly' work. It is the ordering and undoing of the carefully catalogued elements and situations, not any given combination, that allows the reader to partake in the pleasures of the writer: 'savourer avec Loyola la volupté d'organiser une retraite, d'en napper le temps intérieur, d'en distribuer les moments du langage' ('savoring with Loyola the sensual pleasure of organizing a retreat, of covering our interior time with it, of distributing in it moments of language') (II 1044; *SFL* 8). Barthes approaches these texts not as pornography, a social/political treatise, or a spiritual exercise, but as the productive 'theatre' of language, whose pleasures lie in the arrangement of the conditions of their respective retreats (the 'systematics') rather than in following them as a rigid rule (the 'system').

The delectable textual mise en scène offers no vision for a new theatre practice. On the contrary, in an interview given the year after *Sade, Fourier, Loyola* appears in print Barthes explicitly distinguishes between the 'combinatoires mobiles' (mobile combinatives) of the logothetes' figurative theatricality and the 'hysteria' of Western performance practice (II 1485; *GV* 167). Barthes deplores in particular the current popularity of the happening; nothing could be farther from the savoury scenography of signification than a happening's claim to liberate the individual (spectator or performer) from any such structuring gesture. Barthes again indicts the live performer specifically as the stumbling block of Western theatre that must, to achieve his ideal theatricality, defer to the ascendancy of the scenographer: 'Cela consisterait à donner un primat à celui qui met en scène par rapport à celui qui joue. Notre théâtre est un théâtre d'acteur, par tradition' ('It would consist of giving primacy to the director instead of the actor. Our theater is traditionally a theater of actors') (II 1485; *GV* 167). As in *Empire of Signs*, Barthes's again distances the actor, along with the compromised performing body, its attendant anxieties, and its hysterical pathology, from his ideal theatrical figure.

Barthes is not the first to propose hysteria as the diagnosis of theatre's illnesses. The modern history of hysteria is closely tied to performance (e.g., Charcot at the Salpêtrière), and nowhere, perhaps, do hysteria and theatre collude more clearly than in fin-de-siècle realism and its enduring legacy. In *Unmaking Mimesis* Elin Diamond traces the confluence of realism and hysteria to Ibsen's plays. In addition to the symptomatic hysteria of the characters in *Hedda Gabler* and *A Doll's House* she cites Freud's interest in *Rosmersholm* as a parable of spectatorship: 'The analyst's magisterial role in translating the hysteric's signs is transferred to the audience. The spectator takes on the role of seeker/knower, is assured of completing the narrative, of discovering the secret, of judging the truth.'[42] Barthes views this secret etiology as a fiction, an insidious side effect of realist acting and more broadly of all live theatrical performance that is no more true than any of the copies of the castrato's body that proliferate in a never-ending chain in *S/Z*. In an idiosyncratic usage that drifts away from psychoanalytical orthodoxy, 'hysteria' becomes Barthes's epithet for militant or combative expression that asserts a claim to truth and enforces closure on the play of signification.[43] In *Empire of Signs* Barthes levels the charge of hysteria specifically against the Western performer whose living body is the symptom of a factitious self, truth, or signified. Succinctly summarizing the paradox of theatre in his writings, Barthes writes that in Bunraku, 'ce qui est expulsé de la scène, c'est l'hystérie, c'est-à dire le théâtre lui-même' ('what is expelled from the stage is "hysteria," i.e., theater itself') (II 790; *EpS* 62). Ideal *theatricality* demands the elimination of hysterical *theatre*, of hysteria *as* theatre. Barthes does not reserve his distaste for dramatic theatrical productions; public displays, demonstrations, activism, happenings, or performed 'scenes' of any sort draw the scornful epithets of 'hysterical' and 'theatre.'

When the body returns alongside an ideal theatricality as the site of writerly pleasures in *Sade, Fourier, Loyola*, Barthes carefully displaces it, too, from the hysteria of live performance practice. Barthes announces the 'amicable return of the author' as a scattering of 'charms' across the surface of the text. These delectable moments, akin to the 'horizon' of style outlined in *Writing Degree Zero*, represent dispersed fragments and inflections, 'glimmers' and flashes of the body that produces the text. Much as he defines the logothete's theatricality against live theatre practice itself, Barthes again demands the evacuation of any literal or living body from its charmed corporeal figure. Barthes goes to telling lengths to establish the figurative nature of this productive body, which can only resurge in the wake of the author's death, and though it touches the reader, it is a site 'en quoi néanmoins nous lisons la mort plus sûrement que dans l'épopée d'un destin' ('in which we nevertheless read death more certainly than in the epic of a fate') (II 1044; *SFL* 9). The animate/inanimate opposition remains critical, and lest a reader overlook this distinction Barthes employs rich funereal imagery to make his point:

> Car s'il faut que par une dialectique retorse il y ait dans le Texte, destructeur de tout sujet, un sujet à aimer, ce sujet est dispersé, un peu comme les cendres que l'on jette au vent après la mort (au thème de l'*urne* et de la *stèle*, objets forts, fermés, instituteurs du destin, s'opposeraient les éclats du souvenir, l'érosion qui ne laisse de la vie passée que quelques plis): si j'étais écrivain, et mort, comme j'aimerais que ma vie se réduisît, par les soins d'un biographe amical et désinvolte, à quleques détails, à quelques goûts, à quelques inflexions.

> (For if, through a twisted dialectic, the Text, destroyer of all subject, contains a subject to love, that subject is dispersed, somewhat like the ashes we strew into the wind after death [the theme of the *urn* and the *stone*, strong closed objects, instructors of fate, will be contrasted with *bursts* of memory, the erosion that leaves nothing but a few furrows of a past life]: were I a writer, and dead, how I would love it if my life, through the pains of some friendly and detached biographer, were to reduce itself to a few details, a few preferences, a few inflections.) (II 1045; *SFL* 8–9)

Certain death, strewn ashes, his own imagined demise: Barthes writes the body's obituary three times over, aligning his corporeal figure with death and purifying his textual theatre of live performance's suspect, hysterical taint.

The elimination of the hysterical body and its attendant worries clears the way for the profusion of ideal corporealities that inhabit Barthes's projects of the early 1970s. *Le corps* becomes a ubiquitous figure that inflects the 'charms' of the author, the 'grain' of the voice, and the 'obtuse' meaning of photographs, among other provocative terms forged during this prolific moment in Barthes's career. The blissful pleasures of the text, the fragmented biography envisioned above, and the 'loving' body dispersed throughout writing all soon inspire book-length works: *The Pleasure of the Text* (1973), *Roland Barthes by Roland Barthes* (1975), and *A Lover's Discourse: Fragments* (1977). Barthes soon dubs the body his *mot-mana*, a portmanteau term for the elusive excesses to meaning that drive his thought.

The Pleasure of the Text in many ways marks the culmination of Barthes's break with the scientific pretences of semiology, already apparent in *S/Z* and *Empire of Signs*. Pleasure again resides in the spectacle of the text's plurality, the 'liquidation' of metalanguage (II 1509; *PT* 30), and the opening of writing's 'seam' (II 1497; *PT* 7). The text of pleasure recalls both the Roman opera and the imagined Japan where play (*le jeu*, also translated as 'acting') dissolves meaning and subject in delectable neutrality: 'que les jeux ne soit pas faits, qu'il y ait un jeu' ('the bets are not placed, there can still be a game') (II 1496; *PT* 4). The 'seam' is ephemeral, a mere *bouffée* ('puff'), a fleeting dissolve that produces a vertiginous moment when one meaning fades before another appears to take its place.

The text of pleasure is also a figurative stage, a circumscribed space of play where all meanings are possible but where none escape the textual dissolve (*le fading*) and none are secure. With distinct echoes of Artaudian dramaturgy Barthes writes: 'sur la scène du texte, pas de rampe: il n'y a pas derrière le texte quelqu'un d'actif (l'écrivain) et devant lui quelqu'un de passif (le lecteur): il n'y a pas un sujet et un objet' ('on the stage of the text, no footlights: there is not, behind the text, someone active [the writer] and out front someone passive [the reader]; there is not a subject and an object') (II 1502; *PT* 16). The textual stage does not, however, suggest any renewal of Barthes's interest in live performance practice. The ideal body he envisions is revealed in a voice, a film soundtrack, that paradoxically succeeds in revealing 'le corps anonyme de l'acteur' ('the anonymous body of the actor') (II 1529; *PT* 67) in the absence of any living body. Even though he calls on Artaud by name, Barthes defines the pleasurable textual performance against 'le théâtre de l'expression' ('the theater of expression'), 'les inflections dramatiques' ('dramatic inflections'), 'le théâtre des émotions' ('the theater of emotions'), and the expressive hysteria of the live Western performer so roundly repudiated in *Empire of Signs* (II 1528; *PT* 66).

The Pleasure of the Text is in many respects a post-structuralist revisiting of *Writing Degree Zero*. Both works are abstract meditations on writing, with few specific examples, and in both Barthes envisions a utopia of writing, a zero degree, in which an idealized corporeality (*le style* in 1953, *le corps* twenty years later) is liberated from the injunction to take on the weight of meaning. In both, the utopian vision somehow has the last word over the reminders of representation's inexorable tragedy. It is therefore not surprising that *The Pleasure of the Text* has proven less fertile ground than other texts for those who seek hints of the elusive gay signified in Barthes's work. The 'moi' whose voice utters *The Pleasure of the Text*, like the critical voice in *S/Z*, is a weightless figure who can mockingly show his 'derrière' to the 'père politique' ('political father') (II 1521; *PT* 53) and claim exemption from the demand to take a place in the ranks of the knowable, the sayable, and the nameable. There is sexuality coursing through the text of pleasure, and a reader might even ascribe a certain innuendo to Barthes's irreverent gesture, but his treatise on textual erotics carefully avoids naming specific pleasures or desires. If the reader is 'un sujet clivé, qui jouit à la fois, à travers le texte, de la constistance de son *moi* et de sa chute' ('a split subject, who simultaneously enjoys, through the text, the consistency of his selfhood and its collapse, its fall') (II 1504; *PT* 21), Barthes situates his textual subject precisely in the ephemeral, impossible moment of collapse where his sexuality is not an unspoken secret but the dissolution of truth, not the consistency of the name but its defeat.

Euphoria notwithstanding, Barthes repeatedly reminds his reader that the zero degree of meaning is not a tenable state. In the final passage of *The Pleasure of the Text* Barthes invokes the ideal voice stripped of the theatre of emotions only hypothetically: 'comme si elle existait' ('as though it existed') (II 1528; *PT* 66). The fading or dissolve from one meaning to another is a mere *bouffée* before the new image takes hold and the edges of the gap close in. The figure of the 'seam' captures the ambivalence of Barthes's ideal terms: it both separates and holds together the two pieces of cloth. In an oft-cited passage, Barthes casts the inexorable closure of representation conjoined to the utopian breach in meaning in both theatrical and corporeal imagery:

> L'endroit le plus érotique du corps, n'est-il pas *là où le vêtement bâille*? Dans la perversion (qui est le régime du plaisir textual) il n'y a pas de 'zones érogènes' (expression au reste assez casse-pieds); c'est l'intermittence, comme l'a bien dit la psychanalyse, qui est érotique: celle de la peau qui scintille entre deux pièces (le pantalon et le tricot), entre deux bords (la chemise entrouverte, le gant et la manche); c'est ce scintillement même qui séduit, ou encore: la mise en scène d'une apparition-disparition.

> (Is not the most erotic portion of the body *where the garment gapes*? In perversion [which is the realm of textual pleasure] there are no 'erogenous zones' [a foolish expression, besides]: it is the intermittence, as psychoanalysis has so rightly stated, which is erotic: the intermittence of skin flashing between two articles of clothing [trousers and sweater], between two edges [the open-necked shirt, the glove and the sleeve]; it is the flash which seduces, or rather: the staging of an appearance-as-disappearance.) (II 1498–9; *PT* 9–10)

It is neither closure of representation nor the zero degree that incites pleasure, but the staging of an intermittence that in a single gesture enacts both a utopian possibility and its failure. On Barthes's theoretical stage, the delectable mise en scène of revelation and erasure eclipses whatever is revealed or erased, namely, the body itself.

The zero degree is not an attainable state; nor, however, is it a desirable one. In *S/Z*, the pleasure of the writable resides not only in a sustained moment of meaning's breakdown but also in the production of a never-ending chain of copies that fix a meaning only to have it undermined, a cycle of rewriting and forgetting that always demands future readings and, more generally, drives artistic and literary production. By the same token, in *Empire of Signs* the weightless signifier does not entirely prevent the subtle inscription of a specific sexuality and discreet pleasures, even if it subsequently erases them. Without at least an intermittent 'hysteria,' without a meaning that takes shape however briefly, faintly, or provisionally, one hears only the dispassionate fine-tuned hum of the commentary of *S/Z*, a chaste travelogue of Barthes's Japan, or, in *The Pleasure of Text*, a surprisingly abstinent textual hedonist whose own desires never take shape. Barthes recognizes the sterility of a purely weightless signifier, and the necessity of a spectre of meaning that drives the chain of copies, determines his itinerary through the fictive Japan, and erects the meanings that pleasurably fade away, only to reconstitute themselves again:

> Certains veulent un texte (un art, une peinture) sans ombre, coupé de l'' idéologie dominante'; mais c'est vouloir un texte sans fécondité, sans productivité, un texte stérile (voyez le mythe de la Femme sans Ombre). Le texte a besoin de son ombre: cette ombre, c'est *un peu* d'idéologie, *un peu* de représentation, *un peu* de sujet: fantômes, poches, traînées, nuages nécessaires: la subversion doit produire son propre *clair-obscur*.

> (There are those who want a text [an art, a painting] without a shadow, without the 'dominant ideology': but this is to want a text without fecundity, without productivity, a sterile text [see the myth of the Woman without a Shadow]. The text needs a shadow: this shadow is *a bit* of ideology, *a bit* of representation, *a bit* of subject: ghosts, pockets, traces, necessary clouds: subversion must produce its own chiaroscuro.) (II 1510; *PT* 32)

A measure of the repudiated 'theatre of emotions,' the trace of the body in the castrato's voice, and Barthes's scattered hints about his own homosexuality – his own 'hysterical' symptoms – do not thwart the pleasures of the text; quite the contrary, they are complicit in inciting them.

The complicity of 'hysteria' in textual pleasure and the necessary failure of Barthes's pure theoretical ideals prompt a reassessment of his apparent antipathy for live performance practice. A frequently over-looked theatre scene from Barthes's post-structuralist phase suggests that live performance, precisely because it is the emblematic site where ideal theatricalities and corporealities inexorably fail, incites pleasures as an inanimate puppet never could. In the fragment of *Sade, Fourier, Loyola* entitled 'Le corps éclairé' ('The Lit Body'), Barthes again raises the question of a body whose perfect beauty, like the 'masterpiece' invoked in *Sarrasine*, eludes description: something, or somebody, is there that cannot be spoken and that demands similarly vacuous terms to fill the breach in signification. Barthes first proposes that the way to maintain a discourse on this impossible body is either through metonymy, a discussion of its clothing, for example, or through frag-menting it and describing the constituent parts. He then proposes a third way:

Ce moyen est le théâtre (ce qu'a compris l'auteur de ces lignes en assistant à un spectacle de travestis donné dans un cabaret parisien) [...] le corps sadien est en fait un corps vu de loin dans la pleine lumière de la scène; c'est seulement un corps *très bien éclairé*, et dont l'éclairement même, égal, lointain, efface l'individualité (les imperfections de la peau, les couleurs mauvaises du teint), mais laisse passer la pure vénusté; totalement désira-ble et absolument inaccessible, le corps éclairé a pour espace naturel le petit théâtre, celui du cabaret, du fantasme ou de la présentation sadienne [...] c'est finalement la théâtralité de ce corps abstrait qui est rendue par des expressions ternes (*corps parfait, corps à ravir, faite à peindre*, etc.), comme si la description du corps avait été épuisée par sa mise (implicite) en scène.

(This way is the theater [as the author of these lines understood when he attended one evening a drag performance in a Parisian nightclub] [...] the Sadian body is in fact a body seen from a distance in the full light of the stage; it is merely a *very well lit* body the very illumination of which, even, distant, effaces individuality [skin blemishes, ill-favored complexion], but allows the pure charm to come through; totally desirable and absolutely inaccessible, the lit body has as its natural arena the intimate theater, the nightclub, the fantasy, or the Sadian presentation [...] Finally, it is this abstract body's theatricality which is rendered in dull expressions [*perfect body, ravishing body, fit for a painting*, etc.], as though the description of the body had been exhausted by its [implicit] staging.) (II 1132; *SFL* 128)

The well-lit body exhausts subjectivity in a stunning theatricality that is, for once, not invoked in opposition to a pathologized live performer, but incarnated in a moment of live theatre. In this rare description of his reaction to a live performer, Barthes finds neither the endemic infirmities of Western theatre practice and specifically of the drag show decried in *Empire of Signs*, nor an interweaving of diverse signifying strands in a *combinatoire* that exhausts the body, but the inarticulate charm of a live performing body.

The well-lit body also illuminates the nature of the desires that lead Barthes to frequent a certain Parisian nightclub and of his pleasures as the delighted spectator at a drag show. In this instance, unique in his later writings, the live performing body's demand is not experienced as the crushing imposition of the Code, nor as the inexorable gluey coalescence of an oppressive name, but as the motor of pleasure. Barthes continues:

> Peut-être est-ce en somme la fonction de *ce peu d'hystérie* qui est au fond de tout théâtre (de tout éclairage) que de combattre ce peu de fétichisme qui est dans le 'découpage' même de la phrase écrite. Quoi qu'il en soit, il m'a suffi d'éprouver une vive commotion devant les corps éclairés du Cabaret parisien, pour que les allusions (apparemment fort plates) de Sade à la beauté de ses sujets cessent de m'ennuyer et éclatent à leur tour de toute la lumière et l'intelligence du désir.

> (Perhaps it is the function of *this touch of hysteria* which underlies all theater [all lighting] to combat this touch of fetishism contained in the very 'cutting' of the written sentence. However that may be, I had only to experience a vivid emotion in the presence of the lit bodies in the Parisian nightclub for the [apparently very tame] allusions Sade makes to the beauty of his subjects to cease to bore me and to glitter in their turn with all the illumination and intelligence of desire. (II 1133; *SFL* 128, my emphasis)

Barthes's 'vivid emotions' recall the pleasures of Balzac's sculptor in the Roman theatre far more than the light vertigo he experiences in Japan. Barthes himself has effectively taken Sarrasine's seat in a theatre, and it is not the elimination of the 'hysterical' live performer that pleases him. On the contrary, the 'touch of hysteria' incites his own desire for a performing body that is distinctly marked as male with a strong gay connotation. Barthes remains discreet to be sure, and his memory of the drag show falls short of an 'outing.' It nonetheless reveals that the endemically 'hysterical' live performance is not a rejected term languishing on the rubbish heap of Barthes's thought, but persists, along with his own sexuality, in a blind field within whose palpable though carefully policed boundaries his theoretically pure theatres and the ideal bodies that inhabit them necessarily fail.

By banishing live performance practice from the ideal text, the pure *combinatoire*, and even the jouissance of *The Pleasure of the Text*, Barthes paradoxically invests it with a singular power. Unlike many of his contemporaries and interlocutors, Barthes does not absorb live performance into greater theoretical projects, deconstruction and 'semanalysis,' for example, where it is but one more inflection of *l'écriture* or *le texte* that ultimately enjoys no specificity among signifying systems. Instead, the age-old conundrum of the live performer's presence shapes Barthes's discourse with the pressure of what has been displaced to secure his theoretical ideals. Barthes treads around but not over the live performing body, and allows its troubling presence to persist, to unsettle, and to elude the critical discourses of post-structuralism. Performance is located in the failure of these discourses, yet its 'celebration of the human body' continues, for it is not in the purity of the theoretical ideals but in the hysterical touch that enacts their failure that pleasure and desire reside.

4 Mourning Presence: Performance at the Crossroads

Words, Roland Barthes insists, are never innocent. They bear the weight of the meaning history invests in them and circulate in a tightly regulated economy of signification. To enter language, to write or speak, is to subjugate and be subjugated within the regime of the knowable and the sayable. Whether through a discourse of oppression or of liberation, language seizes our subjects, our voices, and our bodies in its totalizing grip. In the words of Barthes's 1977 inaugural lecture at the Collège de France, 'la langue [...] n'est ni réactionnaire ni progressiste: elle est tout simplement: fasciste' ('language [...] is neither reactionary nor progressive; it is, quite simply fascist') (III 803; *L* 461).

Language is not, however, a seamless pall that smothers its hapless victims. To write, to speak, to read, or even to think is to engage in an act of discursive production and to enter a generative field of infinite possibility. If the overthrow of language's regime remains an unattainable ideal, Barthes does not acquiesce uncritically to the selves, the bodies, the truths, and the words and images it imposes. A vigilant quest to reveal the weave, the snags, and the tears in the seductively smooth surface of signification, where language rustles and meanings shimmer, rescues Barthes from a fatalistic and joyless pessimism and for many readers constitutes the more radical reach of his criticism.[1]

One of Barthes's preferred tactics for loosening language's hold is to deploy a critical vocabulary whose multiple and contradictory definitions hold meaning in suspension. *Roland Barthes by Roland Barthes* provides a typology of these favoured terms. *Amphibologies* are words that bear two distinct meanings (*cause* for both what provokes and what one embraces, *crudité* in both its alimentary and sexual sense, etc.) (III 149–50; *RB* 72–3). Context would normally impel the reader to choose one meaning over the other, but Barthes prefers to hear both at once, 'comme si l'un d'eux clignait de l'œil à l'autre et que le sens du mot fût dans ce clin d'œil, qui fait qu'*un même mot,* dans *une même phrase*, veut dire *en même temps* deux choses différentes' ('as if one were winking at the other and as if the word's meaning were in that wink, so the *one and the same word*, in *one and the same sentence*, means *at one and the same time* two different things') (III 149–50; *RB* 72). Rare among amphibologies are those known in Arabic as *addâd*, single words that bear completely opposite meanings, as in the English word 'cleave.' The 'precious ambiguity' of these terms defies the efforts of those who would pin them down and poses a daunting challenge to Barthes's translators, who must find equivalents that similarly convey one meaning without forgetting the other.[2]

A similar predilection for *mots-valeurs* characterizes Barthes's writings, 'value words' that, like the Roman actor who proclaims *larvatus prodeo* – 'I come forward masked' – parade their ideological investment. These words often come in pairs that announce favour or displeasure in the choice of term. In Barthes's lexicon, the paradigmatic selection between structuration or structure, systematics or system, intertext or context, among other pairs, already signifies as heavily as any denotative content of the utterance (III 193; *RB* 127–9). Again, Barthes observes a second, superlatively delectable type of word, *enantiosèmes*, that the 'knife of value' carves into both a desirable and an objectionable meaning. For example, 'l'*artifice* est désiré s'il est baudelairien (opposé d'une façon franche à la Nature), déprécié comme *simili* (prétendant mimer cette meme Nature)' ('*artifice* is desired if it is Baudelairean [specifically opposed to Nature], depreciated as *ersatz* [pretending to mimic that very Nature]') (III 193; *RB* 129). In a rare reflection on the performing body Barthes also cites the word 'actor' as one of these unstable terms: 'l'*acteur* est sauvé s'il fait partie de la contre-Physis, condamné s'il appartient à la pseudo-Phsysis' ('the *actor* is saved if he participates in an anti-Physis but doomed if he belongs to pseudo-Physis') (III 193; *RB* 129).[3] The performers in Barthes's ambivalent early writings – wrestlers, Maria Casarès, and Gérard Philipe – represent such figures, desirable when they reveal their artifice in a gesture laden with signification but oppressive when they obscure the production of meaning under a cloying alibi of nature, interiority, or truth.

'Theatre' is an exceptionally fraught term in Barthes's lexicon, and the competition between its competing values continues long after he abandons his theatre criticism. Barthes's later writings mark no exception, and in the final pages of *Roland Barthes by Roland Barthes* the author makes a sweeping retrospective observation that would confirm both theatre's singular standing in his writings as well as its instability as a critical figure:

> au carrefour de toute l'œuvre, peut-être le théâtre: il n'y a aucun de ses textes, en fait, qui ne traite d'un certain théâtre, et le spectacle est la catégorie universelle sous les espèces de laquelle le monde est vu. Le théâtre tient à tous les thèmes apparemment spéciaux qui passent et reviennent dans ce qu'il écrit: la connotation, l'hystérie, la fiction, l'imaginaire, la scène, la vénusté, le tableau, l'Orient, la violence, l'idéologie (que Bacon appelait un 'fantôme de théâtre').

> (At the crossroads of the entire *œuvre*, perhaps the Theatre: there is not a single one of his texts, in fact, which fails to deal with a certain theatre, and spectacle is the universal category in whose aspect the world is seen. The theatre relates to all the apparently special themes which pass and return in what he writes: connotation, hysteria, fiction, the image-repertoire, the scene, grace, the Orient, violence, ideology [what Bacon once called the 'phantom of theatre']). (III 230; *RB* 177)

While he recognizes theatre's universality, Barthes's catalogue of 'special themes' also betrays the complexity of its widely varying inflection. On one hand, the spectacle of meaning's production is what Barthes admires in *écriture* and later in *le texte*, and so pleasurably experiences in the theatres of Japan. In the inaugural lecture he invokes theatre as a paradoxical space of lack but not of absence, void of a meaning (*un sens*) but full of meaning (*du sens*): 'le texte est l'affleurement même de la langue, et que c'est à l'intérieur de la langue que la langue doit être combattue, dévoyée: non par le message dont elle est l'instrument, mais par le jeu des mots dont elle est le théâtre' ('the text is the very outcropping of speech, and it is within speech that speech must be fought, led astray – not by the message of which it is the instrument, but by the play of words of which it is the theatre') (III 804; *L* 462). As Barthes elevates literature to the privileged status earlier reserved for *écriture* and later *le texte*, he casts it in terms of dramatic performance: 'On peut dire que la troisième force de la littérature, sa force proprement sémiotique, c'est de *jouer* les signes plutôt que de les détruire' ('We might say that literature's third force, its strictly semiotic force, is to *act* signs rather than to destroy them') (III 808; *L* 468). Theatre takes on a redemptive quality, representing nothing less than the utopia of signification that fascinates Barthes since *Writing Degree Zero*: 'Aussi ne faut-il pas s'étonner si, à l'horizon impossible de l'anarchie langagière – là où la langue tente d'échapper à son propre pouvoir, à sa propre servilité – on trouve quelque chose qui a rapport au théâtre' ('We must therefore not be surprised if on the impossible horizon of linguistic anarchy – at that point where language attempts to escape its own power, its own servility – we find something which relates to theatre') (III 808; *L* 468). Theatre is Barthes's figure of language's outer limit, what remains when there is no longer anything to say but the productive gesture of saying itself: the frontier of freedom from language's fascist empire.

Barthes's 'knife of value' slices both ways, however, and the paths that converge at his crossroad figure also lead in decidedly less euphoric directions. In his list of theatrical themes Barthes also includes ideology, the imaginary, and the loathsome domestic scene. This pejorative inflection is if anything the more prevalent, a reprise of the 'theatre of emotions' and expressive 'hysteria' that circulate as familiar epithets throughout his writings. Consider the usage in a 1976 interview:

> j'ai toujours beaucoup de mal à m'engager dans des comportements que je pourrais croire théâtralisés, dont je pourrais penser qu'ils vont être perçus comme tels, et la violence me paraît toujours théâtrale. C'est toujours ce paradoxe, ce qui est souvent dit par la société comme 'naturel,' 'impulsif,' est en réalité le plus souvent codé et très théâtralisé.

> (I always have difficulty engaging in behaviour that I think might be theatrical, that I think might be perceived as such, and violence always seems theatrical to me. It is always this paradox: what is often said by society to be 'natural,' 'impulsive,' is in reality most often coded and highly theatrical.) (III 447)

'Theatricality' here recalls Barthesian myth at its most arrogant: signification that obscures the historical and corporeal gestures that produce it under an impenetrable cloak of the natural, imbued with a common-sense necessity that further strengthens language's fascist grip.

At times Barthes more clearly signals the value invested in the theatrical figure by parsing it into opposing performance-related *mots-valeurs*. 'Mise en scène' and 'dramatization' generally signify a generative process, the gesture of production that characterizes writing (*écriture*) and incites the pleasures of the text, while the 'hysterical scene' and 'theatricality' represent the joyless and violent imposition of a product, moulded and hardened into rigid meanings (earlier, one will recall,

Barthes opposed a favoured 'theatricality' to a suspect 'theatre'). Theatrical imagery can swing in opposite directions from one passage to the next. In a 1974 article Barthes laments the theatrical and hysterical nature of public speech, linking again these two terms, while on the next page he invokes the quality that reveals the productive mise en scène of meaning as 'discrètement dramatique' (discreetly dramatic) (III 49). In a fragment of *Roland Barthes by Roland Barthes* he similarly names the domestic scene the emblem of a constraining theatricality imbued with violence and hysteria, while in the following passage he praises 'dramatization' as the staging of an enunciation, a pleasurable gesture of production quite the opposite of the scene that precedes it.[4]

The complexity of theatre in Barthes's critical vocabulary is further compounded by the scission that after 1960 severs the theatrical figure from live performance practice itself. In Barthes's later years, when interviewers recall his early interest in Vilar and Brecht and press him to comment on theatre as an art form and an institution in his contemporary France, he reiterates the importance of theatricality as a metaphor while exhibiting neither distaste nor displeasure, but apparent indifference to any moment of theatre practice itself. In 1977, in a rare remark on the subject, he acknowledges his uneasy relation to the stage, and makes explicit the displacement of his theatrical imagery from performance practice:

> J'ai des rapports compliqués avec le théâtre. Comme énergie métaphorique, il conserve encore aujourd'hui une extrême importance pour moi: je vois le théâtre partout, dans l'écriture, dans les images, etc. Mais, quant à aller au théâtre, aller voir du théâtre, ça ne m'intéresse plus guère, je n'y vais presque plus. Disons que je reste sensible à la théâtralisation.

> (My relations to the theatre are rather complicated. As a metaphorical energy, it's still very important to me: I see theatre everywhere, in writing, in images, etc. But as for going to the theatre, seeing plays, that doesn't really interest me any more, I hardly go at all now. Let's say that I'm still sensitive to theatricalization.) (III 759; *GV* 278–9).

A year later he is patently glib: 'je me sens exclu du théâtre aujourd'hui. Je n'y vais plus depuis longtemps. C'est sans doute barbare. Je dois manquer des choses' (I feel excluded from theatre today. I have not been going for a long time. This is no doubt barbarous. I'm surely missing things) (III 899).

Despite his show of offhandedness, somewhat theatrical itself, Barthes's apparent unconcern towards live theatre as performance practice is anything but disinterested. As observed in the preceding chapters of this study, the exclusion of the live and present body of the performer enables a more tidy structural analysis, secures the writerly theatres of *S/Z* and *Empire of Signs*, and more generally establishes theatre as a trope for the staging of signification unhindered by a messy uneasiness with the live performer's presence. The abstraction of performance practice, specifically the live performing body, enables the metaphorical theatres to proliferate throughout his writings. Moreover, a profound ambivalence works Barthes's rich theatrical imagery from within as well as without. Like the theatrical figure from which it is displaced, in the rare moments Barthes invokes live performance per se it too is rent by the 'knife of value.' Even in *Empire of Signs*, where Barthes decries Western theatre practice as the emblem of all that is oppressive and pleasureless in signification, the performing body nonetheless retains a trace of precious ambiguity and subtly 'winks' at its other value: the live and present body as an elusive, loving figure of fascination and impossible fulfilment that stars his writing with brief but brilliant flashes.

The question of the live performer's presence, as much through its abstraction as its rare appearances, provides a hermeneutic lens that brings new focus and perspective to Barthes's rich theatrical imagery and the thought articulated through it in his later years. The occasional refraction on this nearly transparent lens betrays the live performing body lurking silently in a blind field, a paradoxical site of both presence and absence around which Barthesian discourse and its figurative theatres circulate. In his later years, the question of a body's presence and the troubling animation of live performance continues to serve as an interpretant of what many readers consider his most enigmatic works: *Roland Barthes by Roland Barthes*, *A Lover's Discourse: Fragments*, and *Camera Lucida*. The encounter with theatre in these writings in turn offers Barthes's most illuminating insight into the place, or rather the necessary displacement, of live performance practice from the theatrical figures of theoretical and critical discourse.

Catachresis: The Performing Body as Trope

A related group of highly charged value words in Barthes's lexicon sheds revealing light on the complexity of the theatrical figure in his later writings. Rhetoric, like theatre, holds a place of both distrust and esteem in Barthes's writings.[5] Barthes's actor can either make a suspect bid for expressive realism and naturalism, or signal the artifice, the meanings, and the codes that constitute the performance – and ideally the performers themselves – as a text of loosely woven signifiers. An art of persuasion that creates discursive effects of necessity, logic, and truth similarly draws Barthes's suspicion when it hides its seductive tactics under the cloak of eloquence and abusive common sense, but wins his praise when it betrays the discursive machinery of meaning's production.

In the 1975 'Brecht and Discourse: A Contribution to the Study of Discursivity,' Barthes wields his knife of value to separate insidious rhetorical figures from those invested with more favourable value. Barthes indicts a suspect *metonymy*, or more precisely *synecdoche* (the substitution of the part for the whole), as the rhetorical vehicle through which a specious imaginary plenitude belies the plurality, discontinuity, and fragmentation on which it imposes. Language's fascism takes a literal turn when Barthes, following Brecht, notes how the Nazi leader Rudolf Hess freely invokes 'Germany' and 'the Germans' to refer solely to the interests of the country's economic elite, thereby abusing a totalizing term that obscures the diverse interests of German society under the oppressive imposition of a single name. Hess further hides his sleight of hand through a more general rhetorical 'enchaînement,' or *concatenation*: 'toute la pseudo-logique du discours – les liaisons, les transitions, le nappé de l'élocution' ('all the pseudo-logic of the discourse – links, transitions, the patina of elocution') (III 263; *RL* 216). Synecdoche and concatenating smoothness seduce the listener with a seamless veneer of common-sense truth that obscures the rhetorical ploy that imposes it.

Competing rhetorical gestures, however, discredit the meaning of an utterance by breaking apart its constituent parts, and less heighten persuasiveness with a more convincing truth than reveal the mise en scène of its enunciation. Barthes admires Brecht's tactic for defeating Hess's rhetorical bid. When rereading Hess's speech, Brecht undoes the stitches that piece it together by interspersing a sotto voce commentary after each phrase to fill in what Hess neatly elides. Brecht's fragmentation and supplementary perspectives betray the seductive concatenation and synecdochic sleight of hand that endow the apparently innocent statements with a truth effect. In other writings of the mid-1970s Barthes identifies the specific rhetorical devices Brecht so cannily deploys. The names of these favoured tropes, like Sade's surprisingly quaint provin-

cialisms or Leibnitz's delectably erudite 'horodeictic' and 'fractive' relished in *The Pleasure of the Text*, draw attention to themselves as savoury signifiers and already lend a supplementary and pleasurable 'shimmer' to the texture of writing. *Tmesis*, the unexpected splitting open of a strand of discourse, represents the reader's prerogative to read with varying intensity, to look up from the page, and even to skip passages, gestures that disrupt the smooth surface of familiar expressions and defeat authorial intent: 'un rythme s'établit, désinvolte, peu respectueux à l'égard de l'*intégrité* du texte [...] l'auteur ne peut la prévoir: il ne peut vouloir écrire *ce qu'on ne lira pas*' ('a rhythm is established, casual, unconcerned with the *integrity* of the text [...] the author cannot predict tmesis: he cannot choose to write *what will not be read*') (II 1499; *PT* 10–11). Barthes more assiduously calls on *asyndeton*, the term of ellipsis that suppresses conjunctions and other 'glue' words that lend a semblance of continuity to an otherwise fragmented discourse.[6] Classical rhetoric would demand these figures of discontinuity serve a greater argument, but in Barthes's usage asyndeton, like tmesis, signals the play of freely migrating discursive fragments loosened from the armature of dissertation. The tropes of discontinuity and combination open a proliferation of possibilities instead of enforcing obedient service to narrative logic, political positioning, or other alibis of reality and truth.

Barthes's catalogue of rhetorical tactics provides a useful conceptual frame for understanding his ambivalent theorization of live performance practice. The suspicion of synecdoche and concatenating fluidity echoes his distrust of Western theatre in *Empire of Signs*. Far from preserving a favourable fragmentation that allows productive combination and permutation, as in the admirable Bunraku, the body of Western theatre inexorably fuses the plural gestures (productive, produced, vocal) together. The body's animation leads the hapless spectator to misrecognize the performer's subjectivity and corporeality as the origin rather than the effect of the mise en scène of meaning. The Western spectators, in thrall to the semiotic dysfunction of the live and present body, cannot by Barthes's account separate the plural strands that constitute the performer's body as a text, leading him to all but repudiate live theatre and performance practice anywhere other than in his utopian Japan.

However, in 'Brecht and Discourse' a radically different, celebratory, and even redemptive value ascribed to live theatre again cuts through the anxieties that attend performance practice. Barthes hails a moment of live performance not as the vehicle of a suspect metonymy, as the reader of *Empire of Signs* might anticipate, but as a safeguard of the fragmentation and discontinuity that defeat the imaginary national unity imposed in Hess's speech:

> Comment lutter contre la métonymie? Comment, *au niveau du discours,* ramener la somme à ses parties, comment défaire le Nom abusif? C'est là un problème très brechtien. Au théâtre, la défection du Nom est facile, car il ne s'y représente, par force, que des corps [...] Brecht dit quelque part que la Raison, ce n'est jamais que ce que pense l'ensemble des gens raisonnables: le concept (toujours abusif?) est ramené à une sommation de corps historiques.

> (How to combat metonymy? How, *on the level of discourse,* to restore the sum to its parts, how to undo the abusive Name? This is a very Brechtian problem. In the theatre, the undoing of the Name is easy enough, for it is inevitably only bodies that are represented there [...] Brecht says somewhere that Reason is never what the totality of reasonable people think: the [invariably abusive?] concept is reduced to a summation of historical bodies.) (III 264; *RL* 218)

Barthes recognizes the difficulty of 'ex-nomination' and laments political discourse's rhetorical sleight of hand – 'la sujétion par violence de la partie au tout, du corps au Nom' ('subjection by violence of the part to the whole, of the body to the Name') (III 265; *RL* 219) – but again it is the presence of performing bodies that thwarts the pernicious synecdoches of political speech:

> Brecht est ici très hérétique: il résiste à toutes les métonymies; il y a une sorte d'individualisme brechtien: le 'Peuple,' c'est une collection d'individus rassemblés sur la scène; la 'Bourgeoisie,' c'est ici un propriétaire, là un riche, etc. Le théâtre oblige à défaire le Nom.

> (Brecht is very heretical: he resists all metonymies; there is a kind of Brechtian individualism: the 'People' is a collection of individuals assembled on the stage; the 'Bourgeoisie' is here a landlord, there a rich man, etc. The theatre compels undoing the Name.) (III 265; *RL* 219)

The group of individuals on stage furnishes visible evidence of diverse interests that shatter the purportedly smooth surface of German national identity. The performers, like Brecht reading Hess's speech, are not reducible to the monolithic 'nation,' which they reveal as a creaky assemblage of disparate and even competing parts whose workings, contradictions, and possibilities for further tinkering become evident to the reader/spectator.

Barthes's favourable regard for performance practice in 'Brecht and Discourse' is as ambiguous as it is uncharacteristic. The brief reference to live theatre practice remains remarkably abstract (Which play? Who is in the audience? What other aspects of theatre's 'density of signs' contribute to the effect?) and serves primarily to illustrate Brecht's exemplarity as a writer, not as a stage director. As the title of the article suggests, Brecht's cunning negotiation of discursive formations interests Barthes far more than any dynamics specific to live theatre and performance; the enquiry remains *'au niveau du discours'* (*'on the level of discourse'*) (III 264; *RL* 218, Barthes's emphasis). In the opening paragraphs of this same article Barthes asserts 'au théâtre, comme dans tout texte, l'origine de l'énonciation est irreparable' ('in the theatre, as in any text, the origin of the speech-act cannot be located') (III 260; *RL* 212), insisting deliberately that theatre enjoys no privilege among systems of representation. Barthes nonetheless grants live performance a singular power. The dissemination of meaning Barthes painstakingly labours to locate elsewhere, and which he deems virtually impossible for live Western theatre in *Empire of Signs* with no exemption for Brecht, comes 'easily' through the mere presence of the performers on stage. Unlike other media, the theatre can offer 'only bodies,' apparently cleansed of the Code, the Name, and Language that other discursive systems, a written text, for example, cannot so easily elude. In 'Brecht and Discourse' Barthes suggests that theatre, specifically theatre practice, is *not* a text like any other, and the performing body's presence implies not the production of discourse but its horizon, the 'thing itself' that eludes language's fascist reach. The performers' presence thwarts the language that would exhaust their bodies in a hardened meaning.

Even as he names theatre the universal figure of his thought and suggests the singular power of live performance, Barthes shows little inclination to resume his role as a theatre critic. 'Brecht and Discourse' represents a rare mention of any moment of performance practice, and metaphorical theatres and figurative bodies continue to displace live performance from the theoretical theatres of Barthes's final writings. In his closing comments at the 1977 colloquium held in his honour at Cérisy-la-Salle, Barthes invokes another favoured trope: *catachresis* displaces literal designation with a metaphor so completely that there is no longer a literal designation at all. Barthes delights in catachresis's demand for exhaustive rhetorical figuration, 'a conjunction of the image and nothingness' that neatly abstracts the literal thing itself, the referent, from the signifer: 'il n'y a aucun mot dans la langue qui permette de dénoter le référent de la figure; pour désigner les bras d'un fauteuil il n'y a pas d'autres mots que ... les bras du fauteuil' (there is no word in the language that permits a denotation of the figure's referent: to designate the arms of a chair there are no other words than ... the arms of a chair) (III 878). His choice of a corporeal figure displaced from any reference to the human body (the literality of the arms reduced to 'nothingness') more broadly characterizes the ideal theatricality that flourishes in the absence of any moment of live performance practice. More than synecdoche, asyndeton, or tmesis, catachresis is the emblematic trope of theatre in Barthes's later writings: the moment of live performance is the 'thing itself' displaced by metaphorical theatres and figurative corporealities.[7]

A live performing body makes rare appearances in Barthes's final writings, but it doesn't so much open a theoretical space for a new theatre practice as trace the unattainable limit of writing, language, image, and the discursive existence Barthes is constrained to live. On the threshold of nothingness, a live and present body lingers nonetheless to haunt *Roland Barthes by Roland Barthes*, *A Lover's Discourse: Fragments*, and *Camera Lucida*. The later Barthes openly contemplates the abstraction of a live and present body: the beloved's, his mother's, and his own disappearance from the stage of discourse. The mood of his writing changes markedly, and the euphoric jouissance of the early 1970s cedes to more melancholy introspection on the discourse of the self, of a person in love, and of loss and death: Proustian topoi, but for Barthes they hold little promise the past will be regained. Instead, in considerations of his own life, of love, and finally of the medium of photography, Barthes offers a sustained meditation on a live and present body as both a utopian ideal and a painful reminder of all that is proscribed in the 'logosphere' he inhabits. He comes to realize that a 'present' body beyond the grip of language is also an absence, and that the elusive 'life itself,' when contemplated from the shores of an existence constituted through discourse and language, is all but indistinguishable from death.

Staging the Self

The opening page of *Roland Barthes by Roland Barthes* provides a single handwritten instruction for the reader: 'Tout ceci doit être considéré comme dit par un personnage de roman' ('it all must be considered as if spoken by a character in a novel') (III 81; *RB* 1). The 'as if' is the key to understanding Barthes's directive, for the text that follows fails to produce the portrait of a psychological or historical subject, 'retenu, assuré, justifié par la représentation d'un individu civil' ('hampered, validated, justified by the representation of an individual with a private life and a civil status') (III 86; *RB* 4), nor does it offer a linear account of an author's life and career that one might expect from a book in the *Ecrivains de toujours* series.[8] Instead, the 'Roland Barthes' in question is a series of short entries, most a single paragraph, that constitute a compendium of textual poses taken by Barthes's writing subject over the years: fragments of a Barthesian discourse, of Barthes *as* discourse.

Roland Barthes by Roland Barthes stages the author's encounter with *l'imaginaire*, another heavily charged term in Barthes's lexicon. The word (often translated as 'the image repertoire' or 'the image system') has a rich history, but in this case the dominant inflection is Lacan's, filtered through Barthes's typically unorthodox appropriation of psychoanalytical terms and notions.[9] Unlike the baby in Lacan's 'mirror stage' who finds satisfaction in an *imago* that belies the plurality and discontinuity on which it imposes, Barthes chafes under the image of a discrete self and strives instead to suspend its coalescence. Instead of erecting a consistent 'I,' in *Roland Barthes by Roland Barthes* the system of fragments appears in no way complete or exhaustive; to add or subtract passages, or to rearrange them differently (they are in alphabetical order in the text) does not create a more accurate likeness, or a more convincing fiction of a unified self. Lest the usage of the pronoun 'I' itself suggest an image of subjective totality to the reader, Barthes refers to his 'character in a novel' in the first, second, and third persons, often shifting pronouns from one passage to the next. As both a work and the image of the man who is its author and its subject, 'Roland Barthes' is (to use Barthes's value terms) more a systematics than a closed system, more a structuration of the self than a stable structure, an unassembled mosaic of pieces that, when taken together, however one might order them, do not form the neat shape of a discernible whole. The final passage of the book is an appropriate bookend to the opening instruction: a denunciation of the 'monster of totality' in favour of the boundless text.[10]

Barthes casts his arrangement of discontinuous textual passages in theatrical terms: 'L'effort vital de ce livre est de mettre en scène un imaginaire. "Mettre en scène" veut dire: échelonner des portants, disperser des rôles, établir des niveaux et, à la limite: faire de la rampe une barre incertaine' ('The vital effort of this book is to stage an image-system. 'To stage' means: to arrange the flats one in front of the other, to distribute the roles, to establish levels, and, at the limit: to make the footlights a kind of uncertain barrier') (III 175; *RB* 105). The mask again serves as the figure for the mise en scène of the subject: 'l'imaginaire est pris en charge par plusieurs masques (*personae*), échelonnés selon la profondeur de la scène (et cependant *personne* derrière)' ('The image-repertoire is taken over by several masks [*personae*], distributed according to the depth of the stage [and yet *no one – personne*, as we say in French – is behind them]') (III 186; *RB* 120). Barthes's ideal staging again evacuates any subject or body under the mask and draws everything and everybody – his body – into a productive act of distribution and combination.

The stratification of signifying gestures in a richly layered mise en scène echoes the terms of Barthes's earliest theatre criticism. In 1954 Barthes invokes the 'cybernetic machine' of theatre's multiple elements that produces meaning through the careful and pleasurable combination and alternation of the plural parts in a signifying system – the 'density of signs' (sound, lights, costumes, set, etc.) – and not through the 'realistic' qualities of any given element. The computer metaphor further informs Barthes's earlier criticism through his fascination with the binary digital code, based on the single difference between zero and one, which in itself resembles nothing, imitates nothing, mirrors nothing, but in combination is infinitely generative. The consummately arbitrary digital code takes structuralist aspirations to their ascetic extreme: all knowledge, and reality itself, can be captured in a single difference whose possibilities for combination proliferate infinitely (one can only imagine what Barthes would have had to say, with both favour and dismay, about virtual realities and other computer-generated representations of recent years).

In *Roland Barthes by Roland Barthes* the appeal of the cybernetic system and the digital code accompanies a concomitant suspicion of analogue reproduction: the likeness of proportions that purports to be the decidedly non-arbitrary imprint or mirror of nature. Barthes acknowledges his long struggle with the 'demon of analogy':

La bête noire de Saussure, c'était l'*arbitraire* (du signe). La sienne, c'est l'*analogie*. Les arts 'analogiques' (cinéma, photographie), les méthodes 'analogiques' (la critique universitaire, par exemple) sont discrédités. Pourquoi? Parce que l'analogie implique un effet de Nature: elle constitue le 'naturel' en source de vérité; et ce qui ajoute à la malédiction de l'analogie, c'est qu'elle est irrépressible [...] dès qu'une forme est vue, *il faut* qu'elle ressemble à quelque chose.

(Saussure's *bête noire* was the *arbitrary* [nature of the sign]. His is *analogy.* The 'analogical' arts [cinema, photography], the 'analogical' methods [academic criticism] are discredited. Why? Because analogy implies an effect of Nature: it constitutes the 'natural' as a source of truth; and what adds to the curse of analogy is the fact that it is irrepressible: no sooner is a form seen than it *must* resemble something.) (III 128; *RB* 44)

Barthes's distaste for analogy drives him to divine the system in even the most apparently direct impressions of reality. In his early writings on photography, for example, he locates the plural codes that reveal the seemingly objective analogue imprint of nature as a rich text of interwoven meanings. However, even in his high structuralist mode of the early 1960s Barthes recognizes a resistant and decidedly non-arbitrary 'message without a code' in the photographic image. Cinema is even more suspect when it hypnotizes the spectator with a seductive illusion of life and movement. In 1975 Barthes observes:

L'image est là, devant moi, pour moi: coalescente (son signifiant et son signifié bien fondus), analogique, globale [...] l'image me captive, me capture: je *colle* à la représentation, et c'est cette colle qui fonde la *naturalité* (la pseudo-nature) de la scène filmée.

(The image is there, in front of me, for me: coalescent [its signified and its signifier melted together], analogical, total [...] the image captivates me, captures me: I am *glued* to the representation, and it is this glue which established the *naturalness* [the pseudo-nature] of the filmed scene.) (III 258; *RL* 348)

Cinema's illusion is so powerful that it nearly defies analysis. Barthes can only avert his eyes, and his resistance to a film's lure is reduced to noting the beam of light that flickers through the room, watching it glance off the bodies of other spectators, and listening to the texture of the soundtrack to 'loosen the glue' of the hypnotic image. In 'The Third Meaning' (1973) he analyses film stills instead of moving pictures, for cinema's phantoms – 'animation, flux, mobilité, "vie," copie' ('animation, flux, mobility, 'life,' copy') (II 883; *IMT* 66–7) – are too distracting and impede his pursuit of 'the filmic.'

Semiologists have observed two modes of representation that surpass even cinema and photography in laying claim to truth outside a system of signification, and appear even more undeniably analogue, more secure in the alibi of nature, and more resistant to a semiological analysis. The first we know: if cinema sits on the threshold of the analysable, live performance, where the evidence of animation and life is even stronger, seems hopelessly doomed to invoke a source of truth and thereby defies semiological analysis. Ann Ubersfeld succinctly summarizes the unease of theatre semiotics with the live performing body's animation in terms that echo the ambivalence of theorists, past and present, over the live performing body's unsure status as a sign:

> Le comédien est le tout du théâtre. On peut se passer de tout dans la représentation, excepté de lui [...] Mais le saisir en fonction des signes qu'il produit n'est pas chose simple. Paradoxalement il est à la fois producteur et produit dans le domaine des signes: il est le peintre et sa toile, le sculpteur, son modèle et son œuvre [...] La tentation est grande de tenir le travail comme inanalysable, et de se replier sur une vue subjectiviste et mystique.

> (The actor is the entirety of theatre. One can do without everything except him [...] But to grasp him as a function of the signs he produces is not a simple thing. Paradoxically he is at once producer and product in the domain of signs: he is the painter and the canvas, the sculptor, his model, and his work [...] the temptation is great to consider the work impossible to analyze, and to fall back on a subjectivist and mystical view.)[11]

Patrice Pavis notes a similar corporeal resistance to semiosis in live performance, a body without a code: 'l'acteur ne peut transformer son propre corps jusqu'à en nier la nature [...] il y a donc, semble-t-il, une part d'incodifiable au théâtre' (the actor cannot transform his own body so far as to deny its nature [...] there is, it would seem, an uncoded part in theatre).[12] The mystifying confusion of signification's producer and the produced sign in the live performing body is precisely what spurs Barthes's repudiation of Western theatre in *Empire of Signs*. Live performance does not reveal a productive mise en scène, a hollow mask with nobody underneath, or a text of intertwining codes whose weaving and unravelling constitute the true spectacle, but rather enacts the gluey coalescence of an expressive 'hysterical' subject: a person adheres inexorably to the *persona*, a *somebody* animates the body.

A second, apparently irredeemable form of analogue reproduction also thwarts a semiological approach. In his *Theory of Semiotics*, Umberto Eco lists the mirror image among certain 'embarrassing phenomena' that defy analysis: 'Not only can [a specular image] not properly be called an image [...] but even granted the existence of the image it must be admitted that it does not stand for something else; on the contrary it stands in front of something else, it exists not instead of but because of the presence of that something.'[13] In Eco's mirror 'source and addressee coincide; [...] receiver and transmitter coincide; expression and content coincide,'[14] terms that reproduce Barthes's phraseology as he demonizes analogy and that echo Ubersfeld's caveat for a semiotic account of live performance. Barthes notes his own distaste for a mirror of distinct Lacanian resonance: 'Lorsque je résiste à l'analogie, c'est en fait à l'imaginaire que je résiste: à savoir: la coalescence du signe, la similitude du significant et du signifié, l'homéomorphisme des images, le Miroir, le leurre captivant' ('When I resist analogy, it is actually the imaginary I am resisting: which is to say: the coalescence of the sign, the similitude of signifier and signified, the homeomorphism of images, the Mirror, the captivating bait') (III 128; *RB* 44). In the semiological aberrations of both mirror and theatre, the image is conjoined to a body, demands its presence, and thereby stakes claim to the truth of what, and who, the body is.

A similar semiotic shortcircuit characterizes Eco's specular image, the subject in the throes of Lacan's mirror stage, and what Ubersfeld, the Prague Schoolers, Barthes, and others in the field of theatre semiotics observe in live theatre practice: the performing body is inexorably conjoined to the image of a *somebody*. The semiotician, like the psychoanalyst, strives to pry the corporeal image/sign loose from an apparently 'natural' body, and then track the image's coalescence and circulation within a discursive and symbolic system. However, the spectre of something that systems and images cannot exhaust – Barthes's demon, Eco's embarrassment, Lacan's real – shadows these analytical discourses. A body that discursively does not exist nonetheless stubbornly persists as the horizon of language, of the system, and of discourse.

Barthes stages his *imaginaire* in *Roland Barthes by Roland Barthes* through the catachresis that evacuates the live performing body and its attendant anxieties from a theoretical theatricality. The strictly metaphorical stage allows the imaginary 'Roland Barthes' to emerge as an ideal mise en scène of multiple masks – 'Quel corps? Nous en avons plusieurs' ('Which body? We have several') (III 141; *RB* 60) – with no one, *no body*, behind them. However, on the few occasions when he continues to invoke a live performance specifically, the displacement of a persistent corporeality to some degree fails. Three detailed 'scenes' stand out as rare instances in which Barthes reflects on a body engaged in a theatrical act and broaches the troubled question of the separation, or lack thereof, between a body and an imaginary *somebody* in live performance practice. Each offers a telling glimpse of the irresolution between unease and fascination that attends live performance, and confirms its ambivalent situation as both the tragedy of representation and a utopian horizon in Barthes's critical discourse.

The Trap of Theatre

A remarkable performance follows directly on Barthes's situation of theatre at the crossroads of his work in *Roland Barthes by Roland Barthes*. In the entry titled 'le théâtre,' Barthes begins by reprising his admiration for clear and intelligible gestures similar to those the wrestlers of *Mythologies* so admirably execute. Such acts enable the spectator to see the productive gesture of performance under 'true' emotions and to unhinge the sign from the affect, unlike a naturalist or realist theatre, which would confuse the two in expressive outbursts that draw the charge of 'hysteria.' With regret Barthes believes himself incapable of enacting this separation himself, hence his frequent show of emotionless boredom when he is photographed (which he admits elsewhere is a mask like any other: his own 'hysteria'). He nonetheless admires such conviction in others: 'la conviction même de l'autre qui en fait à ses yeux un être de théâtre et le fascine' ('the very conviction of others which in his eyes makes them into creatures of theatre and fascinates him') (III 250–1; *RB* 177). He then cites the 'best theatre he has ever seen,' a scene that takes place in the dining car of a Belgian train:

> Des employés (douane, police) se sont attablés dans un coin; ils ont mangé avec tant d'appétit, de confort et de soin (choisissant les épices, les morceaux, les couverts appropriés, préférant à coup d'œil sûr le steak au vieux poulet fade), avec des manières si bien appliqués à la nourriture (nettoyant soigneusement leur poisson de la douteuse sauce gribiche, tapotant leur yaourt pour en soulever la capsule, grattant leur fromage au

lieu de le peler, se servant de leur couteau à pomme comme d'un scalp), que tout le service Cook s'en est trouvé subverti: ils ont mangé la même chose que nous, mais ce n'était pas le même menu. Tout avait changé d'un bout du wagon à l'autre, par le seul effet d'une *conviction* (rapport du corps, non à la passion ou à l'âme, mais à la jouissance).

(Certain employees [customs officer, policemen] were sitting at a corner table; they ate their meal with so much appetite, comfort, and care [choosing the spices, the pieces, the appropriate tableware, preferring at a knowing glance the steak to the insipid chicken], with manners so perfectly applied to the food [carefully scraping off their fish the suspect cream sauce, tapping their yogurt in order to remove the seal, scratching their cheese instead of peeling it, using their fruit knife as if it were a scalpel], that the whole Cook service was subverted: they were eating the same things as we were, but it was not the same menu. Everything had changed, from one end of the car to the other, by the single effect of a *conviction* [relation of the body not to passion or to the soul but to pleasure, to bliss].) (III 231; *RB* 178)

Barthes relishes the scene at the other end of the car, if not his own dinner, as the employees' meal becomes a text in its own right, and one whose production unfolds before his eyes. The broad, resolute gestures of choosing and combining recall the experience eating in his idealized Japan, where the diner deploys chopsticks that both designate and displace the desired food item in a meal whose production is similarly intelligible and whose product (a finished dish, a set menu) never coalesces into a discrete whole. The railway employees also resemble the wrestlers of *Mythologies* and the puppeteers of Bunraku theatre, whose visible acts of producing theatre constitute the true spectacle for Barthes. The Cook service meal itself, which most travellers consume as a fixed product concocted in some hidden kitchen and imposed in all its institutional mediocrity, is for Barthes as uninteresting and inconsequential as the outcome of the wrestling match or the content of Bunraku's dramatic narrative, which he confesses he does not follow. The intelligibility of the dinner's composition eclipses what is composed, and the gesture of production, driven by pleasure (here gastronomical), outshines both the consumed product and the employees themselves as producers or agents behind the deed.

The employees' memorable corporeal conviction produces a forgettable meal, but if live performance, like the mirror, inexorably conjoins a somebody to the body and establishes this *persona* as the origin and not the effect of bodily gestures, as Barthes elsewhere contends, would it not also constitute the employees, as well as the spectator who takes delight in watching them, as 'individuals with a private life and a civil status?'[15] Barthes names the nationality and professions of the employees, and draws a distinction between them and 'us' (presumably Barthes and his dinner companions), but in his view the crucial difference from one end of the car to the other remains one of intelligibility and 'conviction,' not of class (for example) or position in the state apparatus. One can only imagine what Brecht might have made of the divisions in 'civil' status in the car and how they shape the employees' show of pleasure as they eat; in his *Life of Galileo*, for example, the title character's pleasure in taking a meal is laden with gestic meaning. Barthes neglects to explore the implications of the body executing these gestures as the index of a subject situated in a social situation, hence the Brechtian reproach he imagines in another passage of *Roland Barthes by Roland Barthes*: Barthes avows his inability to engage in political speech that reduces any utterance 'jusqu'a son résidu de réel' ('to its residue of reality') (III 135; *RB* 53), preferring instead to discredit and at the limit discard reality as the residue of the utterance. This evacuation is precisely what he deems impossible in live theatre, but in the dining car the 'best theatre he has seen' exempts the performing body of the responsibility, or obligation, of being *somebody*.

A second theatre scene in *Roland Barthes by Roland Barthes* confirms Barthes's enduring fascination with live performance specifically, and again signals its confluence with the unnamed homosexuality that similarly lingers in the interstices of his writings. In a passage entitled 'Eros and the Theater,' Barthes recognizes *presence* as live theatre's singularity among media:

> La fonction érotique du théâtre n'est pas accessoire, parce que lui seul, de tous les arts figuratifs (cinéma, peinture), donne les corps, et non leur représentation. Le corps de théâtre est à la fois contingent et essentiel: essentiel, vous ne pouvez le posséder (il est magnifié par le prestige du désir nostalgique); contingent, vous le pourriez, car il vous suffirait d'être fou un moment (ce qui est en votre pouvoir) pour sauter sur la scène et toucher ce que vous désirez. Le cinéma, au contraire, exclut, par une fatalité de nature, tout passage à l'acte: l'image y est l'absence *irrémédiable* du corps représenté. (Le cinéma serait semblable à ces corps qui vont, l'été, la chemise largement ouverte: *voyez mais ne touchez pas*, disent ces corps et le cinéma, tous deux, à la lettre, *factices*.)

(The erotic function of the theatre is not accessory, for the theatre alone of all the figurative arts [cinema, painting] presents the bodies and not their representation. The body in the theatre is at once contingent and essential: essential, you cannot possess it [it is magnified by the prestige of nostalgic desire]: contingent, you might, for you would merely need to be momentarily crazy [which is within your power] in order to jump onto the stage and touch what you desire. The cinema, on the contrary, excludes by a fatality of Nature all transition to the act: here the image is the *irremediable* absence of the represented body. [The cinema would be like those bodies which pass by, in summer, with shirts unbuttoned to the waist: *Look but don't touch,* say these bodies and the cinema, both of them, literally, *factitious*.]) (III 157–8; *RB* 83–4)

Barthes's short reflection on the ontology of live theatre grants the performing body a surprising immediacy even beyond that of the captivating cinema image. Barthes discriminates between arts that represent the body – literally factitious: made by humans and therefore mediated by consciousness, language, technology, history, etc. – and an enticing presence that distinguishes live theatre among media.

In his readings of Artaud, Derrida contends that the apparent presence of live performance is already a repetition, always deferred by representation.[16] Barthes's fascination with presence would appear to revise his earlier subscription to this 'decisive' tenet of deconstruction. However, even as Barthes acknowledges something, or somebody, that distinguishes performance among systems of signification, a familiar deconstructive caution qualifies his observations. Representation's closure is not so easily defeated, and Barthes defers the 'possession' of presence to a future contingency, a moment of *folie* that might or might not come to pass. It is an unresolved tension between essential and contingent bodies that enthrals the spectator, not the mad gesture of the spectator who jumps on the stage. Indeed, if executed, such a transgressive gesture would doubtless meet with a swift censure that robs the performance of its erotic duality. The passerby's bare-chested body that Barthes admires, no less live than the stage performer but as inaccessible as the cinematic image, illustrates the pressures that keep the spectators in their seats on the far side of the footlights. Were Barthes to jump up and touch one of these desirable bodies, he would not dissolve the barrier that separates the spectator and the stage but find himself on its other side, plunging his own body and his own desires – desires he so carefully shelters from his reader's view – into the spotlight of the public's knowing gaze, where they will be subject to the epithets, censure, and brutal policing of the dreaded Name. The spectator who climbs onto the stage to satisfy a thirst for an unmasked presence underneath or behind representation does not liberate the body from the hold of signification, subjectivity, and language, but submits to the inexorable and punishing reimposition of meaning.[17] The singular pleasures of live performance instead flow through an eroticism that, as Lawrence Schehr observes, must remain 'the hidden interpretant, the operator of personal liberation in writing, the sign that has no name, but which must proceed masked.'[18] Theatre's erotic charge, like Barthes's homosexuality, resides not in the act of a madman crossing the border of the footlights, but in the unresolved realm of possibility, in a temptation, in a question: the dangling 'what if?' whose thrill endures only so long as any answer is deferred.

The third theatre scene in *Roland Barthes by Roland Barthes* is Barthes's most intimate, explicit, and perhaps most telling encounter with live performance practice: the image and account of his own experience as an actor in the 1936 production of *The Persians* at the Sorbonne (cited in the opening pages of this study). The masked and costumed Barthes declaims the lines of Darius as he looms powerfully over the cowering chorus framed against the neoclassical architecture of the Sorbonne. This striking image contrasts starkly with his own perspective on the experience. He sees only fragments of the scene through the small holes in the mask: 'une fenêtre, un encorbellement, un coin du ciel' ('a window, a cornice, a piece of the sky') (III 117; *RB* 33). Aeschylus's text, his character, the theatre, and the Sorbonne itself, along with the logic, reason, eloquence, and knowledge it historically represents, become a kaleidescopic and incomplete combination of parts. 'Je m'en voulais de m'être laissé prendre dans ce piège inconfortable – tandis que ma voix continuait son debit égal, rétive aux *expressions* que j'aurais dû lui donner' ('I excoriated myself for getting caught in this uncomfortable trap – while my voice continued its smooth delivery, resisting the *expressions* I should have given it') (III 117; *RB* 33). Barthes's voice, his body, and the character he performs are unhinged from each other, not unlike the polyphonic weave of signifying gestures he idealizes in Bunraku. Barthes teeters on the brink of failing, of dropping his mask and piercing the barrier of the footlights as surely as the spectator who jumps onto the stage, though in the opposite direction. However, the spectators at the 1936 production, like the reader of *Roland Barthes by Roland Barthes,* see only a masked performer acting in a play against a harmonious façade. Desire, fascination, and anxious fragmentation on the mask's 'dark underside' remain hidden from view and cut off from expression. Only Barthes can ascertain what lies on both sides of the mask, yet he does not delight in his unique double vision. Instead, fear overtakes him in the anxious 'trap' of theatre.

The Darius photograph and its accompanying caption appear in the collection of forty-three images, mostly of Barthes's family and childhood years, that 'figure the prehistory' of the textual Barthes, the Barthes as *écriture*, that follows. In the photograph section Barthes wilfully indulges the reader's desire for the image of a biographical subject with a past and a family, 'un individu civil' ('an individual with a private life and civil status') (III 86; *RB* 4), yet even here he does not acquiesce passively to the meanings that would lay hold of his body, his image, and his self. Like the text that follows, the photograph section stages *l'imaginaire* as a site of productive possibility and contest, and amply cautions a reader who would consume these photographs as the reflection of a more true or real Barthes. In the brief introduction to the photograph section Barthes explains that he has chosen images not that reflect who he is, but that fascinate him precisely when they fail to coalesce into the image of a unitary subject:

> L'imagerie agit comme un médium et me met en rapport avec le 'ça' de mon corps; elle suscite en moi une sorte de rêve obtus, dont les unités sont des dents, des cheveux, un nez, une maigreur, des jambes à longs bas, qui ne m'appartiennent pas, sans pourtant appartenir à personne d'autre qu'à moi: me voici dès lors en état d'inquiétante familiarité: je *vois* la fissure du sujet (cela même dont il ne peut rien dire). Il s'ensuit que la photographie de jeunesse est à la fois très indiscrète (c'est mon corps du dessous qui s'y donne à lire) et très discrète (ce n'est pas de 'moi' qu'elle parle).
>
> (Such imagery acts as a medium and puts me in a relation with my body's *id*: it provokes in me a kind of obtuse dream, whose units are teeth, hair, a nose, skinniness, long legs in knee-length socks which don't belong to me, though to no one else: here I am henceforth in a state of disturbing familiarity: I *see* the fissure in the subject [the very thing about which he can say nothing]. It follows that the childhood photograph is both highly indiscreet [it is my body *from underneath* which is presented] and quite discreet [the photograph is not of 'me'].) (III 85; *RB* 3)

Barthes contemplates a body that is more 'organic' than 'morphological,' paradoxically both an individual being and a lack, a 'fissure,' a gap between fragments. He sees this body from underneath in all its discontinuity, a compendium and a *combinatoire,* alongside the composed exterior persona it reflects in representation's mirror and shows to the world.

The Lacanian resonance of an author contemplating his own image is made explicit in the photograph situated at the centre of the opening section. Infant Barthes sits propped in his mother's arms, staring at the camera. The caption, culled from the closing passages of Lacan's mirror stage essay, reads simply 'That's you' ('tu es cela'). The photograph, with its pose and the baby's confused and transfixed gaze, could plausibly serve as a textbook illustration to accompany Lacan's text. However, as in the textual fragments that follow, Barthes resists 'normal' movement through the mirror stage and the coalescence of a fictive subject under the blazon of a unified 'I.' A preceding photograph of Barthes and his mother casts an ironic gloss over the invocation of Lacan. In this startling image, one of the first in the book, Barthes hangs from his mother's neck like an infant, while the length of his dangling legs and his mother's strained stance betray that he is quite a bit older, too old to assume with ease this infantile pose (were he standing on his own feet, by all appearances he would be nearly as tall as his mother). The image of the mother mediates the photograph section, and indeed, all of *Roland Barthes by Roland Barthes*: her captionless, blurred image is the frontispiece of the book, a primary image at once connected and exterior to what follows. As both a book and its subject, 'Roland Barthes' cleaves to his mother, demands her love, and refuses to separate from her, as if caught in a chronically incomplete mirror stage that continues to a perversely advanced age.

The subject, from a psychoanalytical perspective, is a house of cards erected out of necessity, a smoke and mirrors act performed under duress. Barthes sees both the illusion and the fragmented 'reverse side' that betrays its instability, but the tension between the image-repertoire and the *imago*, between the scattered field of *cela* and the coalescent *tu*, inspires little of the euphoria that the reader of *The Pleasure of the Text*, written only two years before, might expect from the 'fading' between the subject and its vertiginous collapse. A change of tone distinguishes *Roland Barthes by Roland Barthes* from earlier works of the 1970s. As with the theatre image, Barthes's double vision incites more a brooding anxiety and ennui than the ecstasy of subjective loss. Commenting on an image of himself as a very young child that follows immediately on the mirror stage image, Barthes elaborates on his discomfort as he gazes into the 'mirror' of the photograph:

Car ce n'est pas l'irréversible que je découvre en elle, c'est l'irréductible: tout ce qui est encore en moi, par accès; dans l'enfant, je lis à corps découvert l'envers noir de moi-même, l'ennui, la vulnérabilité, l'aptitude aux désespoirs (heureusement pluriels), l'émoi interne, coupé pour son malheur de toute expression.

(For it is not the irreversible I discover in my childhood, it is the irreducible: everything which is still in me, by fits and starts; in the child I read quite openly the dark underside of myself – boredom, vulnerability, disposition to despairs [in the plural, fortunately], inward excitement, cut off [unfortunately] from all expression.) (III 106; *RB* 22)

Barthes has a face, a body, and an individuality 'à corps découvert' that he will never be able to show, a body of pleasures ('excitements') but more prevalently of unease.[19] Moreover, the body from underneath, in excess to the image, about which he can say nothing, will remain for the readers of *Roland Barthes,* as for the spectators at the Sorbonne, and for all but Barthes himself, precisely that: nothing. The irreducible body has no place or existence within discourse and representation.

Barthes's predicament playing Darius succinctly illustrates his struggle with the images and words that would seize him with a stereotype, a reductive adjective, or the dreaded Name. The photograph on the page immediately following the Darius image, taken the following year (1937), adds a familiar inflection to what is both sheltered and imprisoned on the reverse side of the mask Barthes outwardly presents to the world. Barthes as a young man sits next to a smiling woman on a lawn. Why this photograph, which to an unknowing eye would seem an entirely banal image of apparent heterosexual coupledom (a date?) unremarkable other than for clothing that seems unduly formal for the occasion? The caption reads: 'D'où vient donc cet air-là? La Nature? le Code?' ('Where does this expression come from? Nature? Code?') (III 118; *RB* 34). The removal of the literal mask from one image to the next does not liberate the irreducible desires and fears, pleasures and anxieties, discontinuity and plurality that lurk on its dark underside in the performance of *The Persians.* Barthes's laconic questions and the stiffness of the pose suggest a certain bemusement over a mask, no less opaque than the one he wears at the Sorbonne, that fails in its bid for a credible 'pseudo-physis.' Intelligibility, if not conviction, seizes his image, here rewritten as heterosexual, though by all accounts Barthes would suffer as much (if not more) under the imposition of a readable homosexual 'mask.'

Barthes's performance, be it of Darius or a heterosexual (or homosexual) man, conjures the memory of another theatrical body that suffers the repeated imposition of imaginary identities. In the courtyard of the Sorbonne, and generally throughout the staging of the image repertoire in *Roland Barthes by Roland Barthes*, Barthes effectively assumes the place of La Zambinella, the castrato in *S/Z*, on the stage of representation. Both are condemned to wear a factitious mask, but also have an irreducible 'reverse side' that is at once an excess and a lack, both that which exceeds discourse and the demand that discourse fill the gap. Where the castrato represents the symbolic breakdown of the gender binary, in the image of the couple sexuality again acts as Barthes's emblematic 'joker' in the epistemological deck: not *a* homosexuality, be it open or closeted, but a question, a realm of production and possibility palpable 'under the mask' that does not congeal into a tidy image, a reductive Name, Nature, the Code, or a secret truth.

In the memorable performance on the Roman stage La Zambinella, briefly, annihilates the subject and liquidates the codes that would seize the body before meanings rush in to smooth over any fissures in the subjective mask. In the photograph section of *Roland Barthes by Roland Barthes*, Barthes, too, provides a utopian moment, at least for one notable reader. In another image, Barthes as a pensive adolescent reclines barefoot on the same beach in the Landes where his mother walks in the frontispiece image, wearing a trace of a smile and lounging in the ethereal haze of the camera's soft focus. The resemblance of the young Barthes to Girodet's *Sleep of Endymion*, the alleged portrait of La Zambinella in *Sarrasine*, is striking: heavy eyelids, gender ambiguity, and most notably the recumbent body. The languid pose contrasts with the stiffness of his body at the picnic. The caption, a citation of Diderot, is an elliptic '"Nous, toujours nous" ...' ('Ourselves, always ourselves ...') (III 112; *RB* 28). Pierre Saint-Amand, a critic who recognizes his own love for Barthes in this photo, observes a sensuality that is 'full of intentions but keeps its secret. It is caught in a voluptuous suspension.'[20] Barthes invites the reader, *challenges* the reader, to write the meaning of the body he offers to our gaze, or, even more perversely, to leave it unwritten.

Exile from the oppressive realms of the knowable and the sayable is a refuge, but it nonetheless remains a trap. The reader of *Sarrasine* will recall that the castrato, the incarnation of the neutral and the textual, is also the jittery and frightened plaything of more powerful men, manipulated, exploited, held prisoner, kidnapped, and very nearly killed. Readers, narrators, observers, and artists seize, manipulate, and coerce this body according to their own desires. To enter society, to become visible, be it at the Parisian ball, a Roman orgy, or on the stage, is to suffer the imposition of a mask of identity, however factitious. The alternative – withdrawal from the public's knowing and desiring eyes – is hardly more appealing. La Zambinella ends up a frightening and pathetic spectre shunned by society and sequestered in the secret chambers of a Parisian mansion that both shelter and imprison a body that is nobody, neither man nor woman, neither live nor dead, cut off from both the world and language. For Barthes, too, the underside of the mask is a lonely and anxious place, and the spectre of La Zambinella casts doubt on whether one can exempt his youthful image from meaning any more than the writers, sculptors, spectators, painters, and narrators of *Sarrasine* can view the castrato without ascribing a gender. Saint-Amand's transport might serve as a cautionary example: even as he delights in the suspension of meaning, he too rewrites the body and creates a Barthes in the image of his own desire when he admires the 'luminous nudity' of the adolescent Barthes's torso – in the photograph Barthes is wearing a shirt, and a shadow all but obscures Barthes's upper body except the arms and face.[21]

The unmasked, undressed Barthes remains a fantasy. The irreducible body under the figurative or literal mask is cut off from expression, denied a place in language and representation; discursively, *it does not exist*. Nonetheless, Barthes does not altogether relinquish the idea that something, or rather, somebody, *persists*, an important distinction he draws a few years later in the inaugural lecture. Barthes develops the crossroads image to define literature as a resistant discursive practice:

> *S'entêter* veut dire affirmer l'Irréductible de la littérature: ce qui, en elle, résiste et survit aux discours typés qui l'entourent: les philosophies, les sciences, les psychologies; agir comme si elle était incomparable et immortelle. Un écrivain – j'entends par là, non le tenant d'une fonction ou le servant d'un art, mais le sujet d'une pratique – doit avoir l'entêtement du guetteur qui est à la croisée de tous les autres discours, en position *triviale* par rapport à la pureté des doctrines (*trivialis*, c'est l'attribut étymologique de la prostituée qui attend à l'intersection de trois voies).

> (*To persist* means to affirm the Irreducible of literature, that which resists and survives the typified discourses, the philosophies, sciences, psychologies which surround it, to act as if literature were incomparable and immortal. A writer – by which I mean not the possessor of a function or the servant of an art, but the subject of a praxis – must have the persistence

of the watcher who stands at the crossroads of all other discourses, in a position that is *trivial* in relation to the purity of doctrine [*trivialis* is the etymological attribute of the prostitute who waits at the intersection of three roads].) (III 807; *L* 467)

The author as a persona, a 'mask,' remains dead, an effect of literature, just as Barthes himself remains a character in the text of *Roland Barthes by Roland Barthes*. However, Barthes also proposes somebody else, a writer-cum-cruiser who loiters where the truths and selves erected within discourse pass by. The persistent and desirable body, moreover, is a performing body: 'Tout à la fois de s'entêter et se déplacer relève en somme d'une méthode de jeu' ('to persist, and at the same time, to shift ground relates, in short, to a kind of acting'), and then, as cited above, 'à l'horizon impossible de l'anarchie langagière [...] on trouve quelque chose qui a rapport au théâtre' ('on the impossible horizon of linguistic anarchy [...] we find something which relates to theatre') (III 808; *L* 468). This performance is not, however, the ideal inanimate theatre Barthes so frequently invokes elsewhere: the coded and hollow body-as-mask that circulates freely as a sign. It is instead the boundary where the persistent body and discourse touch, where the mask and the body that wears it are conjoined: a confluence of the irreducible body and the pure signifier that compromises both ideals. It is neither a utopian 'performance degree zero' nor a disembodied ideal nor a corporeal presence cleansed of meaning, but the live performing body in all its unsettled complexity that Barthes locates at the crossroads of discourse and of his oeuvre.

As a young performer at the Sorbonne or an aging viewer contemplating family photographs, Barthes considers his own image with a disturbing split vision: he sees both his irreducible body *from underneath*, which he still experiences in his present time, about which he can say nothing, and the masks of meaning that face outward on the world, circulate in a system of meaning, and cut the reverse side off from expression. He is both mute and gregarious, present in the image and absent, irreducible and iterable, and most nightmarishly both alive and dead. Barthes witnesses nothing less than a premonition of his death, the death of all authors but also the future erasure of his own irreducibility after he, the only one who can apprehend it, will exist no more. With a nod to Freud one might add that Barthes, as he contemplates his own image in the mirror, in the image, or on the stage, is also both *fort* and *da*. Barthes does not mention *Beyond the Pleasure Principle* directly in

Roland Barthes by Roland Barthes, but he embarks on this project by imagining his own withdrawal as a desiring subject or a desiring body from the scene of representation. The last passage included in *Roland Barthes by Roland Barthes,* written the day Barthes begins work on the book, reads:

> Autre discours: ce 6 août, à la campagne, c'est le matin d'un jour splendide: soleil, chaleur, fleurs, silence, calme, rayonnement. Rien ne rôde, ni le désir ni l'agression; seul le travail est là, devant moi, comme une sorte d'être universel: tout est plein. Ce serait donc cela, la Nature? Une absence ... du reste? La *Totalité*?

> (Different discourse: this August 6, the countryside, the morning of a splendid day: sun, warmth, flowers, silence, calm, radiance. Nothing stirs, neither desire nor aggression; only the task is there, the work before me, like a kind of universal being: everything is full. Then that would be Nature? An absence ... of the rest? Totality?) (III 232; *RB* 180)

Barthes's rhetoric of quiescence, laden with asyndeton, ellipsis, and unanswered questions, evokes a liminal moment where the peaceful fulfilment he enjoys is already (as he is already writing) being disturbed by a plunge into the imaginary. Yet the splendid moment he destroys is also 'nothing,' an 'absence,' secured by bringing the motors of language and discourse, desire and aggression, to a standstill. Barthes's *heure exquise* is also a subtraction, a silencing, an emptying, not only a before but an after. A romantic poet asks if, when experiencing the infinite and annihilating calm of a radiant sunset, he is contemplating death itself.[22] In his celebration of fullness – or rather fullness as emptiness – Barthes does not so directly pose the question in *Roland Barthes by Roland Barthes,* but it will haunt *A Lover's Discourse* and *Camera Lucida* as, again through the displacement of the body's presence, he openly ponders the confluence of life and death, of presence and absence, and of the irreducible and the iterable in the final, mournful years of his life.

Liebestod

Barthes's 1977 *A Lover's Discourse: Fragments* is a best-seller and draws a wider immediate readership than any of his previous books. The success contributes to Barthes's new role as a figure of national prominence, not only as the newly appointed Chair of Literary Semiology at the Collège de France who lectures to standing-room-only crowds, but also through television and radio appearances, newspaper and magazine coverage (including an interview in *Playboy*), and a theatre production based on *A Lover's Discourse.* Barthes's status as a radical outsider who assails the cultures of the entrenched university and the media cedes to that of an eminent leader in the world of arts and letters, revered among the educated bourgeoisie and belletrists he so pointedly criticizes in his earlier years.[23]

Barthes is nonetheless surprised at the mass appeal of a book that is not a celebration or even a study of love per se, certainly not physical or sexual love, but the interior discursive ramblings of a lonely figure who worries, waits, and weeps his way through fits of jealousy, anxiety, anger, fatigue, loss, and despair. *A Lover's Discourse: Fragments* is, according to Barthes, a dramatic work, but the drama is without character, plot, audience, or performer.[24] Neither a biographical person, nor an individual subject, the lover is a discursive site that Barthes traces through an encyclopedic series of figures, poses, and gestures. Barthes gleans these amorous outbursts of language in canonical literary works (Goethe's *Sorrows of Young Werther* is the most cited), psychoanalysis, philosophy, conversations with friends, and his own emotional experience. The fragments are again arranged in alphabetical order, 'sans plus d'ordre qu'un vol de moustiques' ('with no more order than a flight of mosquitoes') (III 463; *LD* 7), and follow no narrative trajectory that would constitute anything resembling a love story. Love is a catalogue of discursive positions, not an emotion for which language is merely the instrument of expression. The amorous discourse is also a soliloquy, and it rarely demands the response of a loved other who remains generally silent and oblivious to the torrent of the amorous monologue.

The mother is ubiquitous in *A Lover's Discourse* as the figure of a primary fulfilment that satisfies and silences the subject's demand for love. The lover is therefore infantile: 'seuls l'amoureux et l'enfant ont le cœur gros' ('only the lover and the child have a heavy heart') (*LD* 53). Unlike the benign figure who watches over *Roland Barthes by Roland Barthes,* however, no radiant maternal image embraces the subject who performs on love's discursive stage. In *A Lover's Discourse* the mother is the figure of inexorable absence, of an unanswered demand. Here the autobiographical thread woven throughout *A Lover's Discourse* is perhaps at its most salient. Barthes's mother, with whom he lived most of his life, is dying while he composes the *Lover's Discourse*, and he later writes of his panic at the thought of her imminent death and the devastating significance of this loss.[25] Although Barthes draws the discourse of love from varied sources, at times it is openly himself who speaks, and The Mother is clearly his own mother: 'j'allais, le soir, attendre son retour à l'arrêt de l'autobus U^bis, à Sèvres-Babylone; les autobus passaient plusieurs fois de suite, elle n'était dans aucun' ('I would go, evenings, to wait for her at the U^bis bus stop, Sèvres-Babylone; the buses would pass one after the other, she wasn't in any of them') (III 472; *LD* 14–15). The lover's soliloquy floods in to fill her absence, displacing the demand for love with a discourse of desire: 'J'agis en sujet bien sevré; je sais me nourrir, *en attendant*, d'autres choses que du sein maternel' ('I behave as a well-weaned subject; I can feed myself, *meanwhile*, on other things besides the maternal breast') (III 472; *LD* 14). The confluence of the infantile love with sexual desire leads to one of Barthes's more surprising observations: 'L'amoureux pourrait se définir: un enfant qui bande' ('The lover might be defined as a child getting an erection') (III 553; *LD* 105). The mother's absence, while painful, is also productive, starts up the motor of desire, and provides Barthes's lover – and Barthes as lover – the stage for his existence as a site of discourse.

It is neither sex nor any other fulfilment of desire that sustains the lover's existence, but the flow of the discourse of desire itself. The lover's discourse, like the 'internal recitation' that for Derrida constitutes the phenomenological subject of Western metaphysics (the cogito), grants the lover his 'being': the lover speaks, therefore he is.[26] The silencing of discourse that represents the lover's ultimate fulfilment therefore also marks the end of his existence. As discourse, however, love conquers all, even its own fulfilment, and the supplement to all knowledge and language about which the lover can say *nothing* – the uniquely desirable presence of the beloved (or the mother) that stills the drone of desire – demands to be spoken nonetheless. Barthes identifies several figures for the 'nothing-to-say.' The irreducible occurs under the rubric of *adorable* (an inane word that describes nothing, but signals the absence of any description), *atopos* ('without place,' 'unqualifiable'), and the *tel* ('thus,' 'so,' or 'such'). The loved object transcends the stereotype, the name, or the adjective as a unique being, a category of which the beloved alone is the sign. 'S'il n'était qu'une place, je pourrais bien, un jour, le remplacer, mais le supplément de sa place, son *tel*, je ne puis rien lui substituer' ('if he were only a site, I might well, someday, replace him, but I can substitute nothing for the supplement of his site, his *thus*') (III 666; *LD* 221): nothing, of course, except the word 'thus' itself, a stopgap term like the 'masterpiece' of *S/Z* that effectively marks even the unmarkable as a site of discourse.

The theatre returns again in *A Lover's Discourse* as the metaphorical arena of anxious tension between the irreducible and the iterable, between the refuge of the mask's dark underside and the outward image caught in a knowing spotlight:

> Le rideau s'ouvre à l'envers, non sur une scène intime, mais sur une salle publique. Quoi qu'elle dise, l'information m'est douloureuse: un morceau mat, ingrat, de la réalité me tombe dessus. Pour la délicatesse amoureuse, tout à fait quelque chose d'agressif: un bout de 'science,' fût-elle vulgaire, fait irruption dans l'Imaginaire.

> (The curtain rises the wrong way round – not on an intimate stage, but on the crowded theatre. Whatever it tells me, the information is painful: a dull, ungrateful fragment of reality lands on me. For the lover's delicacy, every fact has something aggressive about it: a bit of 'science,' however commonplace, invades the Image-repertoire.) (III 591; *LD* 139)

Much as the aging Barthes contemplating the photographs in *Roland Barthes by Roland Barthes* witnesses both the irreducible and its theft, the lover wants to hold the beloved with himself on the mask's 'reverse' side but cannot avoid seeing the social face imposed on the unique being from without. A third party – an informer, a gossip – whispers in the lover's ear, forcing him to see the lover not as *the* unique other, but merely as one among others, classified within language. The beloved himself, 'maintenu longtemps dans le cocon de mon propre discours' ('long maintained in the cocoon of my own discourse') (III 484; *LD* 27), can at times utter a word or make a gesture so stereotypical and theatrical that he defeats his own 'thusness.' Confronted with the beloved's image seized in the mirror of representation, framed and frozen by the proscenium of the *imaginaire,* the lover effectively witnesses a death: 'Le troisième pronom est un pronom méchant: c'est le pronom de la non-personne, il absente, il annule [...] c'est comme si je le [mon autre] voyais mort, réduit, rangé dans une urne au mur du grand mausolée du langage' ('The third person pronoun is a wicked pronoun: it is the pronoun of the non-person, it absents, it annuls [...] it is as if I saw my other dead, reduced, shelved in an urn upon the wall of the great mausoleum of language') (III 630; *LD* 185). The triumph of language is at its most noisome in the 'scene,' the domestic squabble or lover's spat that, for Barthes, exemplifies the violence of language. Reeking of arrogance, myth, and common sense, the scene, which incites 'hysterical' claims to truth in discourse and in which the feuding parties strive to have 'la dernière réplique' ('the last word') (III 652; *LD* 208), represents the most pejorative inflection of Barthes's theatrical metaphor.

If theatre serves as a trope for love, the stage of love in turn leads Barthes directly to confront the anxieties of presence and the necessary, though mournful, evacuation of the live and present body of the other – be it performer, mother, or lover – from his analysis of language and discourse. Barthes is condemned to consider the other with a nightmarish double vision: the other is, impossibly, both present and absent, both behind the curtain and in front of it, both alive and dead, both an irreducible being and the inexorably absent referent of a fixed and frigid iterable sign:

> Situation en somme inouïe; l'autre est absent comme référent, présent comme allocutaire. De cette distortion singulière, naît une sorte de présent insoutenable; je suis coincé entre deux temps, le temps de la référence et le temps de l'allocution: tu es parti (de quoi je me plains), tu es là (puisque je m'adresse à toi). Je sais alors ce qu'est le présent, ce temps difficile: un pur morceau d'angoisse. L'absence dure, il me faut la supporter. Je vais donc la *manipuler* [...] Cette mise en scène langagière éloigne la mort de l'autre: un moment très bref, dit-on, sépare le temps où l'enfant croit encore sa mère absente et celui où il la croit déjà morte. Manipuler l'absence, c'est allonger ce moment.

> (A preposterous situation; the other is absent as referent, present as allocutory. This singular distortion generates a kind of insupportable present; I am wedged between two tenses, that of reference and that of the allocution: you have gone [which I lament], you are here [since I am addressing you]. Whereupon I know what the present, that difficult tense is: pure portion of anxiety. Absence persists – I must endure it. Hence I will *manipulate* it. [...] This staging of language postpones the other's death: a very short interval, we are told, separates the time during which the child still believes his mother to be absent and the time during which he believes her to be already dead. To manipulate absence is to extend this interval.) (III 473; *LD* 15–16)

Barthes mourns the present as what the lover must sacrifice to carry on the discourse of love, as well as what he himself must relegate beyond the horizon of his own analysis of this discourse. At the uneasy confluence of the childish demand for love and desire for the beloved, the theatre of love is an anxious place, a painful interval that Barthes, like the lover, dispiritedly fills with the flow of discourse.

There are two exits from the unhappy stage of love. The first is nostalgic: to bathe in the beloved's pure presence, cleansed of representation's adulterating taint. Barthes offers a few rare figures for this ultimate fulfilment of desire. In the calm of the lover's (or mother's) arms, 'tout est alors suspendu: le temps, la loi, l'interdit: rien ne s'épuise, rien ne se veut: tous les désirs sont abolis, parce qu'ils paraissent définitivement comblés' ('everything is suspended: time, law, prohibition: nothing is exhausted, nothing is wanted: all desires are abolished, for they seem definitively fulfilled') (III 553; *LD* 105). This moment also occurs in a 'tender' gesture, a distant echo of the 'tender and lovable' performing bodies he admired in his early theatre criticism: 'ce geste, n'est-il pas comme un condensé miraculeux de la présence?' ('is this gesture not a kind of miraculous cystallization of presence?') (III 669; *LD* 224–5). The lover also delights in the elimination of all distance between him and his beloved: 'rêve d'union totale avec l'être aimé' ('dream of total union with the loved being') (III 671; *LD* 226). Lover and beloved bask in each other's inimitable presence unseized in any image, locked in embrace on the dark side of the mask, behind the closed curtains of representation's stage.

Presence regained, however, remains a dream forever deferred. Barthes's wording cautions the reader that the blissful union is unsustainable, that the desires only seem fulfilled, and that only a 'miracle' can satisfy the infantile demand for love. The motor of desire might briefly idle but it never shuts down entirely. 'Comblements: on ne les dit pas' ('Fulfillments: they are not spoken') (III 511; *LD* 55), but speak the lover must, for the production of this discourse of suffering constitutes his very existence. A more definitive halt to the discursive machine therefore demands the lover's own disappearance from the troubled theatre of love: 'ce n'est pas parce qu'il est mort que Werther a cessé d'être amoureux, bien au contraire' ('it is not because he is dead that Werther has stopped being in love, quite the contrary') (III 594; *LD* 143). The end of the lover's soliloquy is not union with the beloved but the end of the lover, a purely discursive subject for whom restful silence does indeed equal death.

Kleist's suspicion of the phenomenological subject's 'disorders of consciousness' and the two routes towards the silencing of its internal recitation illuminate Barthes's theatres of love with their uneasy light. Barthes's lover and Kleist's spectator suffer, caught between nostalgia for pure presence before representation and the evacuation of life itself from an economy of discursive figures and inanimate signs. Kleist ultimately could not endure the interval between original innocence and inanimate perfection. Barthes's lover also owes a painful existence to the duration of the internal recitation that drones on the stage of love. Through his discourse, the lover, like the surface of the mask, both lies between and conjoins the irreducible and the repeatable, the beloved's body and its image. The lover sees both sides of the proscenium, and witnesses both the beloved's 'thusness' and his frozen, framed image. Meanwhile, the flood of discourse that constitutes the lover as a discursive subject flows inexorably towards a silence that both fulfils him and robs him of his very existence. The lover's discourse springs from a tension, a painful irresolution of fulfilment deferred, a plaintive *'what if?'* that as a question, more than any answer, generates the script recited on the discursive stage of love.

Mourning the 'Live'

Although an unforeseen accident leads to Barthes's death shortly after the 1980 publication of *Camera Lucida: Reflections on Photography*, it is nonetheless tempting to read his last book as the capstone of his long and prolific career. Barthes himself envisions the moment during which he writes *Camera Lucida*, after his mother's death and his appointment to the Collège de France, as a time of both culmination and renewal, the end of one life and the beginning of another. Upon his death Barthes leaves us the outline of his *Vita Nova*, or 'new life.'[27] The sparse surviving notes for this project offer little grasp of the form it might eventually have taken, but they locate the beginning of this new life precisely on 15 April 1978, and appear to include parts of two other projects in progress at this time: the 'Soirées de Paris' section included in *Incidents* – a series of journal entries in which he sadly renounces his amorous liaisons with younger men – and a reference to the 'narrative' form and an intellectual quest in his as-yet-untitled book on photography.[28]

The chapter number that opens *Camera Lucida* signals a departure from Barthes's other writings of the 1970s. Gone, apparently, are the arbitrarily ordered fragments liberated from the armature of narrative and dissertation that offer multiple entries for the reader's pleasurable navigation. In the place of an invitation to skip passages (tmesis) in pursuit of textual pleasure, Barthes makes a show of embarking on a methodical analysis more reminiscent of Descartes's measured reasoning in *The Discourse on the Method*. Like his predecessor, Barthes chafes under current received ideas, and writes of his uneasiness, suffering, dissatisfaction, and even desperation as the discourses of knowledge he wields over his lifetime with virtuoso flair – sociological, semiological, psychoanalytical – harden into rigid systems that fail to account for his irreducibility (III 1114; *CL* 8). In a gesture similar to Descartes's clearing of a tabula rasa, Barthes embarks on a logical phenomenological deduction by becoming 'primitive': 'je congédie tout savoir, toute culture, je m'abstiens d'hériter d'un autre regard' ('I dismiss all knowledge, all culture, I refuse to inherit anything from another eye than my own') (III 1144; *CL* 51). Barthes proceeds from the radical singularity of his own existence by bracketing the received knowledge, science, technique, and aesthetics that would tell him what photography is. He goes further than Descartes, however, when he circumvents the cogito by departing from rare photographs that exist *for him* not as a rational subject, but as 'quelques mouvements personnels' ('a few personal impulses') (III 1114; *CL* 8–9) that confirm his irreducible existence as a unique individual and a singular body that has not assumed a place as a *somebody* within a system of meaning.

There is something distinctly theatrical about the deliberate and methodical reasoning in *Camera Lucida*, whose discourse is coated in a smooth veneer of the same concatenating rhetoric (repetition of 'first,' 'and then,' 'thus,' 'and so,' etc.) Barthes roundly denounces only a few years earlier. Even a cursory familiarity with the lessons of Barthes's prior work, in which he radically questions the innocence of any writing, will raise a reader's suspicions about the sudden appeal to the lived experience of an individual who steps out from under the masks of discourse, *écriture*, and the image repertoire to find the essence of photography. 'Il n'existe aucun discours qui ne soit une fiction' (There exists no discourse that is not fiction), announces the title of a 1976 article (III 385–6). It follows that there is no subject of discourse who is not a fictive character, and the instruction that opens *Roland Barthes by Roland Barthes*, 'tout ceci doit étre considéré comme dit par un personnage de roman' (it all must be considered as if spoken by a character in a novel), would be the motto of all discourse. The device Barthes earlier borrows from Descartes – *larvatus prodeo* (I come forward signalling my mask) – bids the reader pause before taking his 'primitive' logic at face value: despite protest to the contrary Barthes might not be a discursively nude primitive at all, but instead poses for the reader in period Cartesian costume.

Barthes soon loosens the mask of the logical and deliberate method that opens his study. After the first chapters, the fussy narrative linearity of his logical argument relaxes somewhat into more discrete passages that, chapter numbers nothwithstanding, lend *Camera Lucida* some of the fragmented and 'textual' quality typical of Barthes's other writings in the 1970s. Nancy M. Shawcross observes the 'mosaic' quality of *Camera Lucida*, which consists of 'pieces whose existence appears to precede the larger work in which they currently reside.'[29] Moreover, Barthes clothes his logical deduction in the very discourses he claims to strip away. Barthes repudiates sociology, but a certain sociological impulse drives what could be considered a *mythologie* of the photographic image. As for psychoanalysis, the quest of *Camera Lucida* follows a line of thought, articulated through the terms of an unorthodox but unmistakable psychoanalytic discourse, that already runs through *Roland Barthes by Roland Barthes* and dominates *A Lover's Discourse: Fragments*. Within a few pages of his claim to primitiveness Barthes freely invokes 'l'imaginaire' (the image-repertoire), and the mother reappears as the only possible satisfaction of the child's demand for love (III 1116; *CL* 12). The mother and her absence will by the second half of the study constitute the primary term for Barthes's pursuit of the photographic essence, and although he seeks to rescue her individuality from the generalizations of psychoanalysis, he articulates his efforts through its terms.

The claim to evade the discourse of semiology most markedly betrays Barthes's purportedly primitive reasonings. Fascination with photography and its analogue 'demon' is not new to Barthes, and as his work spirals through its successive phases he offers numerous accounts of a photographic excess to the coded system of representation. In *Mythologies* Barthes divines the ideological investment in tabloid photographs of royalty and movie stars, yet even at the most *engagé* moment of his criticism he exempts certain images that defy predication, transcend cultural and semiological systems, and give rise to 'mystical feelings of perdition' (Garbo's face) or to trauma (shock photos). The structuralist Barthes of the following years reads the photograph as a system of signification ridden with linguistic, syntactic, aesthetic, and rhetorical codes that make it 'la plus sociale des institutions' ('the most social of institutions') (I 948; *IMT* 31). However, Barthes again provides for an analogue remainder in photography that bypasses systems of meaning, the 'message without a code,' and recognizes traumatic elements whose power follows from a simple incontrovertible fact: '*il fallait que le photographe fût là*' ('*the photographer had to be there*') (I 948; *IMT* 30, emphasis in original). In *Empire of Signs* he remarks on the ghostly power of the photographic image to defeat the passage of time. After 1970, when the closed systems of structuralism break apart and give freer rein to the signifier, Barthes notes an 'obtuse' meaning in photographs that exceeds the code as a 'scandal' in signification. In language that both echoes his early remarks on the performing body and foreshadows later projects, he refers to the obtuse meaning as 'touchant' (touching) and 'aimable' (lovable): one can only affirm that it exists, for to say what it is would be to eliminate it, to draw it into the same codes and systems it baffles (II 873; *IMT* 59).[30] The fundamental opposition that Barthes 'discovers' in *Camera Lucida* therefore does not spring ex nihilo from a primitive deduction, but marks the latest inflection of an opposition developed over decades of semiological rumination. Photography is again saturated with meanings drawn from the well of knowledge accessible to any number of educated viewers, the *studium*, and once more, on rare occasions something uncoded punctures the smooth surface of meaning. Barthes names this inarticulate supplement to knowledge the *punctum*: a personal impulse that stems not from what the photograph represents but from the mournful recognition that *this thing was* and the inexorable deferral of the photographed subject's 'being there' or 'presence' to a lost past.

A crucial difference nonetheless distinguishes *Camera Lucida* from Barthes's previous thought on photography. In his earlier writings, he locates the 'message without a code, ' the 'obtuse meaning,' or the 'lovable' quality in the photograph itself. In the study of Eisenstein film stills in 'The Third Meaning,' for example, he implies that there is something inherently touching about the angle of an old woman's headscarf or the contrast between two men's faces. The novelty of the *punctum* is that the touching quality of the photograph depends on the viewer as much as anything in the image. In the brief reflections on photography in *Roland Barthes by Roland Barthes*, Barthes already observes qualities that no other reader will see: the apprehension of his individuality and irreducibility constitutes his particular interest of the image, an interest whose singularity no other viewer can share. In *Camera Lucida* he more explicitly displaces the poignant power of the photograph itself to his own highly personal encounter with the image. Barthes does not ask what photography is for a viewing public in general (and a fortiori for the photographer, the chemist, the physicist, the semiologist, the psychoanalyst, or even the person being photographed), but, rather, what is photography *for him* as a singular individual, which raises a much larger existential question: 'Je suis le repère de toute photographie, et c'est en cela qu'elle m'induit à m'étonner, en m'adressant la question fondamentale: pourquoi est-ce que je vis *ici et maintenant*?' ('I am the reference of every photograph, and this is what generates my astonishment in addressing myself to the fundamental question: why is it that I am alive *here and now*?') (III 1167; *CL* 84). Photography leads Barthes to discover his own life, his own singular presence *hic et nunc*.

By naming his own irreducible existence the touchstone of photography's essence, Barthes opens himself up to the charge of 'subjectivism' from critics who lament his retreat from the more radical unseating of an individual subject in his structuralist years. Annette Lavers suggests that Barthes deploys a 'god-like self-justifying discourse' in *Camera Lucida*.[31] In making such an indictment, however, she fails to observe that Barthes invokes an 'intractable' individuality only to recount its evacuation from the scene of representation. Barthes's appeal to a unique 'life itself' beyond representation does not erect a triumphant subject, but instead enacts the mournful displacement of the irreducible being from discourse that, not without sad irony, coincidentally heralds the imminent disappearance of his own existence.

Throughout *Camera Lucida* the body mediates Barthes's reflections on life and death, presence and absence, and animation and immobilization. The first images Barthes discusses are of himself, though he does not include them for the reader's consideration. Barthes laments the painful necessity of assuming a pose for the lens, of 'being somebody,' and deplores photographs that efface any trace of his singular being. Even when he attempts to drop the artifice and 'be himself' photography seizes him, freezes him, robs him of life, eliminates him as an individual, and replaces him with an effigy:

> c'est 'moi' qui ne coïncide jamais avec mon image; car c'est l'image qui est lourde, immobile, entêtée (ce pour quoi la société s'y appuie), et c'est «moi» qui suis léger, divisé, dispersé et qui, tel un ludion, ne tiens pas en place, tout en m'agitant dans mon bocal: ah, si au moins la Photographie pouvait me donner un corps neutre, anatomique, un corps qui ne signifie rien. Hélas, je suis condamné.

('myself' never coincides with my image; for it is the image which is heavy, motionless, stubborn [which is why society sustains it], and 'myself' which is light, divided, dispersed; like a bottle-imp, 'myself' doesn't hold still, giggling in my jar: if only Photography could give me a neutral, anatomic body, a body which signifies nothing! Alas, I am doomed.) (III 1116; *CL* 12)

Here he finds none of the startling irreducibility he saw in the images of his childhood in *Roland Barthes by Roland Barthes*, nor is he in a position similar to that of the actor in the courtyard of the Sorbonne: a fragmented, mischievous individual trapped under a frozen mask who might 'giggle' but who is also imprisoned, cut off from representation and expression. Instead, these photographs evacuate the imp and save only the jar; the image immobilizes him despite the photographer's vain attempts to breathe life into the effigy through spontaneous poses or outdoor settings. The photographer's task is little different from that of an embalmer painting a corpse's face: 'Au fond, ce que je vise dans la photo qu'on prend de moi (l'"intention" selon laquelle je la regarde), c'est la Mort: la Mort est *l'eïdos* de cette Photo-là' ('Ultimately, what I am seeking in the photograph taken of me [the "intention" according to which I look at it] is Death: Death is the *eidos* of that Photograph') (III 1118; *CL* 15).

Between unspeakable presence *hic et nunc* and death by image lies the act of being photographed itself: 'ce moment très subtil où, à vrai dire, je ne suis ni un sujet ni un objet, mais plutôt un sujet qui se sent devenir objet' ('that very subtle moment when, to tell the truth, I am neither subject nor object but a subject who feels he is becoming an object') (III 1116; *CL* 14). The act of photography that 'kills' Barthes is also, for the split second of its duration, a delectable moment of fading between a subject and an object, a blurring of the membrane between life and death before the mask hardens and definitively separates body from image. Barthes savours the 'voluptuous' quality of the mechanical click that succeeds in breaking through 'la nappe mortifère de la Pose' ('the mortiferous layer of the Pose') (III 1118; *CL* 15). Neither the utopian before nor the tragic afterwards, the click marks the fleeting *present* of the image's becoming that Barthes identifies with life itself: 'peut-être en moi, quelqu'un de très ancien entend encore dans l'appareil photographique le bruit vivant du bois' ('perhaps in me someone very old still hears in the photographic mechanism the living sound of the wood') (III 1118; *CL* 15). The duration of the shutter's opening is the sole moment when the image's production eclipses the product: the photographic gesture of *écriture*, what one might call the 'geno-image' (after Kristeva's 'genotext').[32] However, the utopian generative moment of becoming remains conjoined to the tragedy of its closure. The camera's click represents less an interval in which one can pleasurably linger than a fold in time, and the 'present' moment is reduced to a split second so short one cannot grasp it. The English term 'snapshot,' originally a hunting term, captures the conjunction of the pleasurably resonant snap of the closing shutter and the violent shot that robs the subject of life and freezes it into an image.[33] Barthes's brief reflection on the shutter's click is little more than an aside to the rest of *Camera Lucida*, in which he contemplates images that have already been produced, many before his lifetime, and whose 'subtle moment' is always already deferred to a lost past. The act of photographing demands that the thing itself be present, but the photographs themselves can attest only that *this thing was* ('cela a été'), never that *this thing is*.

Having opened with his own death by image, Barthes seeks photographs that nonetheless confirm he lives, if not in the image then as a viewer of images: 'La photo elle-même n'est en rien animée (je ne crois pas aux photos "vivantes") mais elle m'anime' ('The photograph is in no way animated [I do not believe in "lifelike" photographs], but it animates me') (III 1121; *CL* 20). These images are rare, but in the flood of photographs that pass before his eyes Barthes notes those that provoke 'de menus jubilations, comme si celles-là renvoyaient à un centre tu, un bien érotique ou déchirant, enfoui en moi-même' ('tiny jubilations, as if they referred to a stilled center, an erotic or lacerating value buried in myself') (III 1119; *CL* 16). Barthes's kernel of individuality and its diminutive pleasures are as far from a confident cogito's triumphant rationality as from the ecstatic jouissance of *The Pleasure of the Text*, yet these small and obliquely invoked 'impulses' lie at the heart of Barthes's project, for they, like the click of the camera, represent the way, however narrow, of conceiving an individual existence that neither erases nor crushes him.

The first half of *Camera Lucida* charts Barthes's progression away from the image itself towards the intractable supplement of his own existence as a viewer. Observing the *punctum* as it animates him, he gradually realizes that it is not what is in the photograph that is so moving as much as something he brings to the image himself. James Van der Zee's portrait of a family touches him. Why? Barthes initially posits that it has something to do with the out-of-date fashion worn by one of the figures, yet will the banal details of the woman's outfit strike any other viewer mute with fascination? Derek Attridge dryly notes: 'I do not find the low belt and strapped pumps piercing me with inexplicable force.'[34] When Barthes later revisits this image he attributes its powerful attraction to something more personal: the woman's necklace resembles that of his aunt, who lived a sad and lonely life. The force of the photograph is no longer attributable to general science or common knowledge, but to an individual reaction to which the general reader of *Camera Lucida* would be impervious without Barthes's explanation. A photograph of Robert Wilson and a suggestive self-portrait, both by Robert Mapplethorpe, also pique Barthes interest and desire by betraying a whole existence external to the image, hence an erotic quality that, far from the full-frontal compositions of pornography, emanates from a 'subtle beyond' on which no knowing light will shine: 'comme si l'image lançait le désir au-delà de ce qu'elle donne à voir: pas seulement vers "le reste" de la nudité, pas seulement vers le fantasme d'une pratique, mais vers l'excellence absolu d'un être, âme et corps' ('as if the image launched desire beyond what it permits us to see: not only toward "the rest" of the nakedness, not only toward the fantasy of *praxis,* but toward the absolute excellence of being, body and soul together') (III 1148; *CL* 59). Here again, however, Barthes's search for the essence of photography leads to a blind field within himself: the unnamed desires and sexual praxis he carefully defends against the knowing grip of discourse and that retain their 'absolute excellence' by staying off the stage of representation.

If the opening section of *Camera Lucida* becomes a journey of self-discovery, in the second half Barthes's finds what he has been seeking in the much-discussed 'Winter Garden' image, a photograph of his mother as a small child that he comes across while sorting through her possessions after her death. Sociological, psychoanalytical, and semiological discourses fail to account for Barthes's response to the image: it is not The Mother as a universal figure in the psychoanalytical family romance that touches him, but *his* mother, not a sign or meaning that circulates in any system of knowledge or discourse but a *mathesis singularis,* 'the impossible science of the unique being.' He finds his mother's irreducibility in the image, something that only he can ascertain. The image moves Barthes so deeply that he believes finally to have found a photograph that not only animates him with a *punctum,* but that exists only for him and therefore answers the question that drives his study: not to produce a new discourse of knowledge by asking 'what is photography' but to discover an irreducible individuality that exceeds such discourses by asking 'what is photography *for me*?' He does not reproduce the image for his readers, who will only see the *studium* of fin-de-siècle culture, photographic aesthetics, or perhaps, through the depth of his reaction to the image, the mother of psychoanalytic resonance. Even if viewers experience a *punctum* of their own in some detail of the photograph they will not experience Barthes's singularly powerful relation to this image.

Barthes attributes the *punctum*'s power specifically to both a body's 'presence' and its 'liveness': 'Dans la Photographie, la présence de la chose (à un certain moment passé) n'est jamais métaphorique; et pour ce qui est des êtres animés, sa vie non plus' ('In Photography, the presence of the thing [at a certain moment] is never metaphoric; and in the case of animated beings, their life as well') (III 1164; *CL* 78). Barthes appears, at last, to make peace with his analogical demons, but he still does not catch up to the zero degree of meaning and corporeality that has been eluding him since the rhapsodic invocation of 'style' in *Writing Degree Zero*. The intractable photographed subject and its living presence remain always already displaced. The *noeme* of photography lies in the past, in the *this thing has been,* not in life and presence but in death twice over, for it not only situates the little girl in the Winter Garden image in a lost past (his mother has died), but the irreducible being of which she bears the evidence also testifies to a future death: 'Devant la photo de ma mère enfant, je me dis: elle va mourir' ('In front of the photograph of my mother as a child, I tell myself: she is going to die') (III 1175; *CL* 96). The photographed subject both has died and will die, its death is both *what was* and *what will be,* but the present, life itself, the *what is,* has been evacuated from the image. Photography is at one and the same time a testimony to *presence* and *liveness* and to their inexorable theft.

A live and present body, namely, Barthes's own as the viewer of the images, nonetheless persists in his mournful encounter with photography. Barthes's title provocatively situates the viewer's body as the mediator of the photographic image. The camera lucida is an optical device that trains one of the operator's eyes on a piece of paper and the other on a subject, allowing both to be seen at once as if superimposed; the operator may then trace the outlines of the subject on the paper to create a likeness of analogue proportions. A very different principle governs the function of the camera obscura, a dark chamber into which light enters through a small hole and projects an inverted image on the opposite surface. Though the camera obscura is more akin to modern photography, Barthes takes the title of his book from the camera lucida, whose operator alone sees at one and the same time both object and image. As the narrator of *Camera Lucida*, Barthes similarly situates himself and his body at the juncture where the 'thing itself' still lingers in the image that would supplant it:

> Je vis la Photographie et le monde dont elle fait partie selon deux régions: d'un côté les Images, de l'autre mes photos; d'un côté, la nonchalance, le glissement, le bruit, l'inessentiel (même si j'en suis abusivement assourdi); de l'autre, le brûlant, le blessé.

> (I experience the Photograph and the world in which it participates according to two regions: on one side the Images, on the other my photographs; on one side, unconcern, shifting, noise, the inessential [even if I am abusively deafened by it], on the other the burning, the wounded.) (III 1177–8; *CL* 98)

The body of the camera lucida's operator, as well as Barthes's own as the viewer of photographs, effectively dwells in the moment of the camera shutter's click, in the impossible, unspeakable time and place, *hic et nunc*, where 'real' and image are conjoined, presence and absence meet, and the 'exorbitant thing' has not yet been evacuated from the image.

Presence is not easily regained, however, and the interval Barthes inhabits as the viewer of photography remains less a space than a volumeless border, less a moment of pleasure than one of loss. Viewing the Winter Garden photograph he does not experience jouissance in a delectable moment of becoming, but rather a nightmarish prolongation of the theft of the 'thing itself' and a premonition of death. The *punctum* proves to Barthes that he exists in the here and now, but no one other than he can see this evidence, and the poignant trace of an inexpressible something or *somebody* will for all others be the 'inessential noise' of nothing, of *nobody*. The absent Winter Garden image itself indicates a void as much as the grail at the end of Barthes's quest; it has been suggested that Barthes refuses to show the image not because it would fail to illustrate the *punctum* he alone so mournfully feels but because the Winter Garden image itself does not exist.[35] Regardless of whether this photograph exists or for that matter whether Barthes includes the image in the book, the intractable *punctum* of the image, its testimonial to lost presence, the proof of photography's existence *for him* and thereby of his own irreducible existence, will be imperceptible to the reader of

Camera Lucida. Barthes writes that photography is death inscribed twice over – the photographed subject both has died and will die – but he foresees a third death as well. In the image of his mother, Barthes writes, 'ma propre mort est inscrite' ('my own death is inscribed') (III 1174; *CL* 93). Barthes's own body is the singular 'medium' that conjoins the Winter Garden image to his mother's irreducible being, and his own future disappearance will mark a loss of her singular existence even more definitive than her death itself.

Theatre returns in *Camera Lucida*, but far from offering sanctuary to the live, the theatrical performances Barthes invokes enact the primal scene of the theft of a body's 'liveness' and 'presence' that photography repeats in the age of mechanical reproduction. As distant forerunners of the *punctum*, Barthes cites ancient and 'primitive' theatres that join life to death, presence to absence, and an irreducible supplement to an immobilized image: 'les premiers acteurs se détachaient de la communauté en jouant le rôle des Morts: se grimer, c'était se designer comme un corps à la fois vivant et mort' ('the first actors separated themselves from the community by playing the role of the Dead: to make oneself up was to designate oneself as a body both living and dead') (III 1129; *CL* 31). These performers, however, are more dead than living, and such theatre ultimately evacuates life in favour of the inanimate, hollow effigy. Reprising his earlier remarks on Bunraku and Kabuki, in *Camera Lucida* Barthes lists No, Kathakali, Chinese theatre, and the masked tragedy of antiquity as theatres that separate production from product, the gesture of performance from the performed gesture, life from the image:

> Si vivante qu'on s'efforce de la concevoir (et cette rage de 'faire vivant' ne peut être que la dénégation mythique d'un malaise de mort), la Photo est comme un théâtre primitif, comme un Tableau Vivant, la figuration de la face immobile et fardée sous laquelle nous voyons les morts.

> (however 'lifelike' we strive to make it [and this frenzy to be lifelike can only be our mythic denial of an apprehension of death], Photography is a kind of primitive theatre, a kind of *Tableau Vivant*, a figuration of the motionless and made-up face beneath which we see the dead.) (III 1129; *CL* 31–2)

The photograph *qua* theatre realizes the void of interiority Barthes admires in the wrestlers of *Mythologies*, Maria Casarès, and the ancient tragedians, and that reaches its most extreme expression in his praise for the Bunraku puppet in *Empire of Signs*. The frozen bodies of primitive theatre dispel any immediate presence of Artaudian resonance, and guarantee instead the conversion of the *this is*, the illusory 'life' that in performance as well as photography palliates our fear of death, to the mournful *this has been* that defines photography in *Camera Lucida*. Barthes's originary theatre represents not 'liveness,' but the same death from which photography derives its grievous force.

The distracting chimera of life, however, is precisely what Barthes elsewhere deems endemic in Western performance practice. A consideration of Barthes's earlier unease with live theatre complicates the theatrical figure in *Camera Lucida*, which emerges through a familiar displacement. Indeed, one might wonder if Barthes is invoking a live performance at all when he once again takes great care to cite theatres that immobilize, obscure, or replace the body, or those that exist in ancient or distant utopias of the sign far removed from the 'here and now' of his own contemporary France.

In his brief remarks on cinema in *Camera Lucida* Barthes shows similar circumspection. Like live theatre, for which it often acts as a surrogate in his writing, cinema's narrative flow, illusion of life, and inexorable movement forward exasperates Barthes and denies film the mournful power of photography. However, in a striking passage redolent of Kleist's marionettes, Barthes describes a filmed scene that redeems pleasure in Fellini's otherwise tedious *Casanova*. Casanova's dance with an automaton achieves 'une sorte d'acuité atroce et délicieuse' ('a kind of painful and delicious intensity') that has a *punctum*-like effect on Barthes as spectator:

> chaque détail [...] me bouleversait: la minceur, la ténuité de la silhouette, comme s'il n'y avait qu'*un peu* de corps sous sa robe aplatie; les gants fripés de filoselle blanche; le léger ridicule (mais qui me touchait) du plumet de la coiffure, ce visage peint et cependant individuel, innocent: quelque chose de désespérement inerte et cependant disponible, d'offert, d'aimant, selon un mouvement angélique de 'bonne volonté.' Je pensais alors irrésistiblement à la Photographie: car tout cela, je pouvais le dire des photos qui me touchaient (dont j'avais fait, par méthode, la Photographie même).

> (each detail [...] overwhelmed me: the figure's slenderness, its tenuity – as if there were only a trifling body under the flattened gown; the frayed gloves of white floss silk; the faint [though touching] absurdity of the

ostrich feathers in the hair, that painted yet individual, innocent face: something desperately inert and yet available, offered, affectionate, according to an angelic impulse of 'good will' ... At which moment I could not help thinking about Photography: for I could say all this about the photographs which touched me [and out of which I had methodically constituted Photography itself].) (III 1190; *CL* 116)

Despite Barthes's insistence on similarities, the automaton differs fundamentally from the photographed body. Never having lived, the automaton spares Barthes the encounter with past and future death that weighs on the Winter Garden image, or, to cite one of many other examples, on a Kertész photograph entitled 'Ernest. Paris, 1931' in which a young schoolboy looks directly into the camera: 'Il est possible qu'Ernest vive encore aujourd'hui: mais où? comment? Quel roman!' ('It is possible that Ernest is alive today: but where? How? What a novel!') (III 1168; *CL* 83). The questions of Ernest's life and death, and Barthes's astonishment over the fact that what he sees has indeed existed and might still exist, would be absurd if brought to an automaton that had never had any life to lose. Where Barthes deplores the lifeless effigy that the photographed subject (himself) becomes, here the lifeless puppet inversely exhibits the 'touching' qualities denied to the photographed Barthes and the actors in the film (and a fortiori a live performer), and inspires pleasures unmitigated with the mournful theft of life that attends photographs of an animate body.

The inert automaton briefly suspends the impossible quest of Barthes's 'note' on photography, namely, the impossible charge of trying to say the unsayable, to cast in language something that exceeds language's grasp. Like the lover of *A Lover's Discourse* who utters 'adorable' or 'thus' to mark within discourse the unqualifiable beloved, Barthes writes: 'Je n'ai d'autre ressource que cette *ironie*: parler du "rien à dire"' ('I have no other resource than this *irony*: to speak of the "nothing to say"') (III 1174; *CL* 93). Barthes can only invoke the effect and not its cause: 'la pression de l'indicible qui veut se dire' ('the pressure of the unspeakable which wants to be spoken') (III 1119; *CL* 19). However, like the soliloquizing lover, Barthes speaks nonetheless and forges discursive terms for that which exceeds discourse. The *punctum* acts as a cenotaph to what cannot be spoken, and Barthes's term fills the gap in language with a signifier robbed of a signified, a valueless token that marks the breach where discourses fail.

Meaning, Barthes reminds us, abhors a vacuum, and as a theoretical figure, a discursive term, and the object of a critical enquiry even the *punctum* cannot escape the investment of a signified. By describing and analysing the *punctum*, ascribing to it certain properties, bringing to light when and where it wounds him, or merely by granting it an erudite name, Barthes cannot keep the dust of meaning and value from collecting on his purportedly weightless term. Derek Attridge observes that 'the more successful he is in conveying to the reader in language the special quality of the features that have moved him, the more he shifts them [...] to the realm of the coded and cultural.'[36] The maternal image, Barthes's attraction to certain eroticized male bodies, or his own biographical subject endowed with a history and a lineage inflect the *punctum* of *Camera Lucida* with the sociological and psychoanalytical discourses from which he seeks to shelter it. As with other zero-degree terms, a faint voice whispers into the discursive breach the *punctum* ostensibly designates.

In *Camera Lucida* Barthes mourns a body's singular presence that within the terms of discourse is manifest as nothingness, loss, absence, and death. The theatrical figure in which Barthes locates the origin of photography's essence – *tableau vivant*, more aptly named *tableau mort* in Barthes's assessment – emblematically enacts the theft of a living and present body. Through this displacement, however, live performance itself is again sheltered from the fascist reach of language, including Barthes's own, and in this respect surpasses even his most carefully theorized zero-degree terms as the horizon of discourse. Denied even a word such as the *punctum* to designate it, spirited from the theatrical trope by a systematic catachresis, divined only by the the imprint its absence leaves on his discursive figures, it is the *present* body – his own, the performer's, the loved other's, the mother's – that more radically brings the pressure of the unspeakable to bear Barthes's reflection, in *Camera Lucida* and throughout his later writings.

Conclusion

Barthes's richest comment on performance lies not in his theatre criticism of the 1950s, nor in the few remarks he ventures on live performance specifically in his later years. Nor will one find it in the ideal modes of signification and representation articulated through metaphorical theatres that displace live performance practice from a theoretical trope. It resides in Barthes's withdrawal from the theatre and his subsequent neglect – be it refusal or failure – to forge a critical discourse on live performance in its specificity. Barthes celebrates live performance in the most eloquent and respectful manner he knows by carving out a discursive blind field in which the repudiated performance paradoxically realizes his ideal: the unattainable horizon of the unspeakable on whose near side, where he lives and writes, the meanings and terms of an oppressive epistemological regime rob him and those he loves of their bodies, of their singularity, and of life itself.

Barthes locates performance in neither the political nor the personal, neither the social nor the individual, neither the theft of repetition nor a singular being. It is neither the nauseous theatre of hysteria nor a searing and unmediated presence, neither the tragedy nor the utopia of representation. It is, rather, the unspeakable moment of their conjunction where neither term definitively prevails. Performance is like a coin whose visible face conceals while it girds its reverse side: a toss will bring one or the other into a knowing light, yet neither stamp accounts for the coin. Barthes's systematic willingness to unload live performance and its troubling presence from his theatrical figures invites those who produce discourse on performance to realize that the place of performance lies not in one winning account, nor in any resolution of the bid, but in the uncertain duration of the toss itself. To use another metaphor of play, one of Barthes's own, performance is a wild card in the deck of contemporary theoretical and critical discourse, ascribed different values but the guarantor of none.

By leaving performance an unanswered (and often unasked) question, Barthes provides a critical perspective on the efforts of theorists of theatre and performance to define, harness, or explain away live performance's singularity. Barthes's virtual abstention from such accounts reveals how those who generate knowing discourses on the nature of live theatre and performance, be they actors, directors, theorists, or critics, enter an arena of political and ethical choices, take up a mask, and themselves become players in the tragedy of representation, as caught in the 'trap' of a discursive theatre as the young Barthes playing his role at the Sorbonne. Barthes's theatrical tropes prompt us to ask if similar catachrestic displacements secure accounts that dismiss or deconstruct the distinction between live performance and technologically mediated modes of representation, and if they similarly stake out a blind field over their discursive horizon for something, or somebody, excluded from their terms. Barthes's experience also issues a caveat to those who would hail live performance's singularity as an oppositional site of resistance to an oppressive symbolic order:

unspeakability comes at a price, and exemption from the sayable also demands abstention from the social, political, and cultural struggles for which discourse is the necessary arena. To bestow on an 'unmarked' performance a purpose, a strategic resistance, or a future goal, however noble the intention, is to enact once again its inexorable subjection to the empire of discourse. The tempting horizon traced by performance recedes as one approaches it and permits no access to an oppositional outside, no hopeful glimpse of a promised land beyond language's reach. The performing body cannot *resist*, but only *persists* (to use Barthes's term) as the index of discourse's limit, be it a discourse of oppression or liberation. *Larvatus prodeo.* Barthes's finger designates the 'mask' of theoretical discourse on theatre and performance, but testifies to no deeper truth underneath.

The encounter relayed in 'Visages et figures' very early in Barthes's career stands as a fitting bookend to the thoughts on photography that close his *œuvre*.[37] The woman Barthes observes on the opposite seat of the train resists signs of social and class identity and does not 'hysterically' parade the codes of myth: she wears no readable 'mask.' Although her simple and quiet individuality is denied expression within theoretical discourses – Marxist, semiological, psychoanalytical – the woman on the train somehow stubbornly persists, and Barthes apprehends the singularity of her 'mute' existence even as it is obscured for society at large. One might anticipate that the woman's imperviousness to mythic posing would appeal to Barthes as the horizon where meanings fail, yet the opposite is true. Her silent, living presence does not bring Barthes any closer to a blissful utopia of signification. On the contrary, she attains the 'zero degree' at a price he find grievous: her silent presence testifies not to 'pure' life but to its theft. She is the meeting of a body and nobody, both a presence and a void, a boundary that separates mute flesh from its theft by a frozen, lifeless effigy. Barthes experiences the failure of discourse that she represents as a loss, not a liberation: though live and present, she has been 'robbed of all expression' and ceases, discursively, to exist.

The poignancy of the woman's plight is enhanced by certain similarities to Barthes's own mother. One might recall, for example, the passage in *A Lover's Discourse* where Barthes remembers his mother returning on the U^{bis} bus after a long day of work during the financially unsteady years of his youth; 'les fins de mois difficiles' (difficult ends of the month) continue to plague the Barthes household well into the early years of his career as a published writer. More importantly, the woman on the train, like his still living mother in 1953, is not deferred to a past moment by photography's mournful *this thing was*; she is there in front of him, *this thing is,* yet her 'liveness' and 'presence' in no way free her from the crushing exigencies of language and meaning. On the contrary, she inspires a feeling of loss that heralds, at a distance of more than twenty-five years, the mournful, inarticulate *punctum* that wounds Barthes as he contemplates the little girl in the Winter Garden image who both has died and will die, but who has no present existence. To apprehend a singular presence, even of a living being sitting directly in front of a viewer/spectator, is to witness its inexorable theft. At the crossroads of life and death, of being and nothingness, of the zero degree and language's closure, the woman on the train illustrates with exemplary clarity the displacement of the live body from a language, including critical discourse on theatre and performance, that at once obliterates and preserves the impossible, unspeakable present in which Barthes, like his alter ego Orpheus, gazes on what he loves and loses it forever.

Notes

Introduction

1 Retrospectives include a conference at Yale University in December 2000
and a major exhibition at the Centre Georges Pompidou in the winter
of 2003. The catalogue of the exhibition has been published. Marianne
Alphant and Nathalie Léger, eds., *R/B; Roland Barthes* (Paris: Seuil, Centre
Pompidou, and Imec, 2002).

2 See, for example, the recent attempt to reclaim Balzac from Barthes, nearly
thirty years after *S/Z*'s critical dismantling of the realist illusion, in Claude
Brémond and Thomas Pavel, *De Barthes à Balzac: Fictions d'une critique,
critiques d'une fiction* (Paris: Albin Michel, 1998).

3 Most monographs on Barthes's life and career offer only a passing nod to
his work on theater, if it draws mention at all. These include Philip Thody,
Roland Barthes: A Conservative Estimate (London: Macmillan, 1977); Annette
Lavers, *Roland Barthes: Structuralism and After* (Cambridge: Harvard Uni-
versity Press, 1982); Jonathan Culler, *Roland Barthes* (New York: Oxford
University Press, 1983); Steven Ungar, *Roland Barthes: The Professor of Desire*
(Lincoln: University of Nebraska Press, 1983); Philipe Roger, *Roland
Barthes, roman* (Paris: Bernard Grasset, 1986); Michael Moriarty, *Roland
Barthes* (Stanford, CA: Stanford University Press, 1991); and Rick Rylance,
Roland Barthes (Hemel Hempstead: Harvester Wheatsheaf, 1994). Moriarty's
study and Louis-Jean Calvet's biography *Roland Barthes: A Biography*
(Bloomington: University of Indiana Press, 1994) both contain chapters
ostensibly dedicated to Barthes's theatre years and offer brief discussions
of his discovery of Brecht and its implications, but include little discussion
of contemporary French theatre (with the exception of Sartre's *Nekrassov*),
Vilar's *Théâtre National Populaire*, and other topics frequently addressed in
Barthes's theatre criticism. Moriarty and Roger have revisited Barthes's

theatre years in short articles. See Michael Moriarty, 'Barthes's Theatrical Aesthetic,' *Nottingham French Studies* 36, no. 1 (spring 1997): 3–13; and Philipe Roger, 'Barthes with Marx,' in *Writing the Image after Roland Barthes,* ed. Jean-Michel Rabaté (Philadelphia: University of Pennsylvania Press, 1997), 174–86. Two more recent studies offer broader, though still not comprehensive, accounts of Barthes's activities as theatre critic. See Claude Coste, *Roland Barthes moraliste* (Lille: Presses Universitaires du Septentrion, 1998); and Andy Stafford, *Roland Barthes: Phenomenon and Myth* (Edinburgh: Edinburgh University Press, 1998).

4 At the time of his death Barthes was preparing, with the assistance of Jean-Loup Rivière, a volume in which his writings on theatre would have been collected. The subsequent control of others over his intellectual estate prevented the project from coming to fruition. See Calvet, *Roland Barthes,* 260–1. A recent volume edited by Rivière, without any new contribution by Barthes, gathers many of his writings on theatre under one cover. See Roland Barthes, *Ecrits sur le théâtre,* ed. Jean-Loup Rivière (Paris: Seuil, 2002). This body of work, also included in the *Œuvres complètes,* remains in great part inaccessible to an anglophone readership as most of the articles have not been translated into English.

5 Andy Stafford makes this observation in 'Constructing a Radical Popular Theatre: Roland Barthes, Brecht, and *Théâtre populaire,*' *French Cultural Studies* 7 (1996): 33–48. It should be noted that Barthes also addresses theatre in many of the *Mythologies.*

6 See Roland Barthes, 'Témoignage sur le théâtre' (1965), I 1530–2.

7 Heinrich von Kleist, 'On the Marionette Theater,' 1810, trans. Roman Paska, in *Zone 3: Fragments for a History of the Human Body, Part One,* ed. Michel Feher, Ramona Nadaff, and Nadia Tazi (Cambridge, MA: MIT Press, 1989), 417.

8 See Jacques Derrida, 'La Parole Soufflée' and 'The Theater of Cruelty and the Closure of Representation,' in *Writing and Difference,* trans. Alan Bass (Chicago: University of Chicago Press, 1978). For more on Derrida's reading of Artaud, see chapter 3.

9 In a seminal article, Josette Féral writes: 'Performance does not aim at *a* meaning, but rather *makes* meaning insofar as it works right in those extremely blurred junctures out of which the subject eventually emerges. And performance conscripts this subject both as a constituted subject and as a social subject in order to dislocate and demystify it. Performance is the death of the subject.' Josette Féral, 'Performance and Theatricality: The Subject Demystified' (1982), in *Mimesis, Masochism, and Mime: The Politics of Theatricality in Contemporary French Thought,* ed. Timothy Murray (Ann Arbor: University of Michigan Press, 1997), 292.

10 Peggy Phelan, *Unmarked: The Politics of Performance* (New York: Routledge, 1993).

11 Janelle Reinelt, 'The Politics of Discourse: Performance Meets Theatricality,' *Substance* 31 (2002): 202.

12 Phelan, *Unmarked*, 148.

13 Ibid.

14 See Philip Auslander, *Presence and Resistance* (Ann Arbor: University of Michigan Press, 1997); *Liveness* (New York: Routledge, 1999); and 'Liveness: Performance and the Anxiety of Simulation,' in *Performance and Cultural Politics*, ed. Elin Diamond (London and New York: Routledge, 1996), 196–213.

15 Auslander, *Liveness*, 159.

16 Phelan, *Unmarked: The Politics of Performance*, 148. Auslander notes that 'although Phelan discusses performance artist Angelika Festa's *Untitled Dance (with fish and others)* (1987) in the context of her argument on the ontology of performance, she does not specifically address the encroachment of technologies of reproduction on this piece, in which Festa made extensive use of video technology to construct the image Phelan analyses.' Auslander, 'Liveness: Performance and the Anxiety of Simulation,' 197.

17 Sue-Ellen Case, 'The Naked Body and Theories of Performance,' *Substance* 31 (2002): 193.

18 One could therefore imagine a deconstruction of the apparently irreconcilable differences between Phelan and Auslander. This impasse turned polemical in the pages of *TDR* after Auslander reviewed *Unmarked*. See Auslander's review in the *Drama Review* 38 (1994): 185–7; and Jill Falzoi's response with Auslander's rebuttal in the *Drama Review* 38 (1994): 13–17. See also Auslander's reviews of four books on avant-garde theatre in the *Drama Review* 37 (1993): 196–201.

19 Auslander, *Liveness*, 32.

20 Marvin Carlson, *Performance: An Introduction* (London and New York: Routledge, 1996), 6–7.

21 Judith Butler, *Gender Trouble: Feminism and the Subversion of Identity* (London and New York: Routledge, 1990), 140.

22 Judith Butler, 'Performative Acts and Gender Constitution: An Essay in Phenomenology and Feminist Theory,' in *Performing Feminisms: Feminist Critical Theory and Theatre*, ed. Sue-Ellen Case (Baltimore: Johns Hopkins University Press, 1990), 278.

23 Butler, *Gender Trouble*, 137.

24 Judith Butler, *Bodies That Matter: On the Discursive Limits of 'Sex'* (New York and London: Routledge, 1993), introduction, x. For further examination of the dissonance between Butler's performativity and theatre practice, see

Timothy Scheie, 'Body Trouble: Corporeal "Presence" and Performative Identity in Cixous's and Mnouchkine's *L'Indiade ou l'Inde de leurs rêves*,' *Theatre Journal* 46 (March 1994): 31–44; and '"Questionable Terms": Shylock, Céline's *L'Eglise*, and the Performative,' *Text and Performance Quarterly* 17 (April 1997): 153–69.

25 Emily Apter, 'Acting Out Orientalism: Sapphic Theatricality in Turn-of-the-Century Paris,' in Diamond, *Performance and Cultural Politics*, 16.

26 Féral, 'Theatricality: The Specificity of Theatrical Language,' passim.

27 'Despite all I know theoretically about the ideological dangers and misuses of performative presence, and its implication in structures of power and authority, I continue to find women's presence onstage seductive.' Jill Dolan, *Presence and Desire* (Ann Arbor: University of Michigan Press, 1993), 1.

28 Ibid., 151.

29 Jill Dolan, 'Geographies of Learning: Theatre Studies, Performance, and the Performative,' *Theatre Journal* 45 (1993): 440–1.

30 Herbert Blau, *Take Up the Bodies: Theatre at the Vanishing Point* (Chicago: University of Illinois Press, 1982), 285.

31 'There are as many Barthes as projects on which he embarked, each one giving way to the next.' Antoine Compagnon, 'Who Is the Real One?' *in Writing the Image after Roland Barthes*, ed. Jean-Michel Rabaté (Philadelphia: University of Pennsylvania Press, 1997), 197.

32 Jonathan Culler (1983), in one of the first books on Roland Barthes after his death, already asks this question. In the proceedings of a recent symposium at Yale University entitled 'Back to Barthes,' co-organizers Peter Brooks and Naomi Schor note that 'his "lesson" remains elusive,' and remark that the diverse papers 'challenge any consensus of Barthes's work in voices that are resolutely plural, open, non-conclusive, yet wholly engaged with this elusive figure and his multiple lessons.' Peter Brooks and Naomi Schor, 'Roland Barthes: Twenty Years After,' *Yale Journal of Criticism* 14, no. 2 (2001): 435.

33 For a study of the poetics of fragmentation and Barthes's style as an essayist, see Reda Bensmaïa, *The Barthes Effect: The Essay As Reflective Text*, trans. Pat Fedkiew (Minneapolis: University of Minnesota Press, 1987).

Chapter One

1 Bernard Dort observes the paradoxical co-existence of Barthes's discomfort with an 'affirmation' of 'tranquility' in the Sorbonne performance. Bernard Dort, 'Le 'piège' du théâtre,' *Critique* 423–4 (August–September 1982): 689.

2 I do not wish to suggest that such investigations do not exist at all. The numerous books on Barthes's career include useful and detailed critical accounts of *Writing Degree Zero* and of Barthes's theoretical dance on the periphery of more orthodox Marxist and existentialist thought. These include Annette Lavers, *Roland Barthes: Structuralism and After* (Cambridge, MA: Harvard University Press, 1982); Philippe Roger, *Roland Barthes, roman* (Paris: Bernard Grasset, 1986); and Michael Moriarty, *Roland Barthes* (Stanford, CA: Stanford University Press, 1991).

3 Ten years later, in the preface to *On Racine*, Barthes writes: 'C'est qu'en fait la transparance est une valeur ambiguë: elle est à la fois ce dont il n'y a rien à dire et ce dont il y a le plus à dire' ('As a matter of fact, transparence is an ambiguous value; it is both what cannot be discussed and what there is most to say about') (I 986; *OR*, foreword viii).

4 One could infer that the socialist realism Barthes derided, revolutionary in content but rooted in a stultifying aesthetic, also profoundly reveals a historical moment, although not in the manner its authors would likely have wished. Moriarty notes the irony lost on post-war socialist realism that Barthes brings to light: the stereotyped realist conventions endorsed and enforced by Andrej Aleksandrovich Zhdanov, Stalin's cultural authority, speak volumes less through representing the horrors of bourgeois industrialism or the heroism of workers and peasants than through the narrow range of an orthodox and outdated 'bourgeois' mode of expression that makes palpable the contradictions and brutal constraints of communist orthodoxy in the time of Stalin. Michael Moriarty, *Roland Barthes*, 40.

5 Philippe Roger's investigation of the revisions Barthes makes in the articles that constitute *Writing Degree Zero*, from their initial publication to their more familiar form in the collected volume, reveals that Barthes later substitutes the word 'utopia' for 'tragedy' in some cases, including in the title of the final essay 'The Utopia of Language.' The optimistic vision that closes the book is a late editorial revision. The two terms, 'tragedy' and 'utopia,' can be considered opposite sides of a single coin: literature's utopia, forever deferred into the future, is the present's tragedy. See the chapter entitled 'Le Degré zéro de l'engagement' in Roger, *Roland Barthes, roman*, 245–61.

6 Kristin Ross explores the interwoven trajectories of modernization and decolonization in *Fast Cars, Clean Bodies: Decolonization and the Reordering of French Culture* (Cambridge, MA: MIT Press, 1995).

7 Jean Duvignaud, one of Barthes's collaborators at *Théâtre populaire*, asks: 'peut-on concevoir, aujourd'hui, l'importance qu'avait le théâtre dans ces

années-là? Le théâtre avait gardé cette préséance littéraire et intellectuelle qu'il avait en Europe et surtout en France depuis le XVIIe siècle' (Can one conceive today of the importance of theatre in those years? Theatre had maintained the literary and intellectual precedence it had in Europe and especially in France since the seventeenth century). Jean Duvignaud, '"Théâtre populaire": histoire d'une revue,' *Magazine littéraire* 314 (October 1993): 63.

8 For an account of popular theatre initiatives in France, see Loren Kruger, *The National Stage: Theatre and Cultural Legitimation in England, France, and America* (Chicago: University of Chicago Press, 1992); and Emile Copfermann, *Le théâtre populaire, pourquoi?* (Paris: François Maspero, 1965). See also Guy Leclerc, *Le T.N.P. de Jean Vilar* (Paris: 10/18, 1971).

9 Kruger offers a summation of the arguments put forth by proponents of a popular theatre, including Barthes: bourgeois theatre 'owes its legitimacy in large part to the persistence [...] of the flawed, sympathetic, and usually private protagonist, with whom the bourgeois audience can identify, the dramaturgical articulation of the contradiction within bourgeois society between public relations of apparently inescapable domination and suffering that is identified as essentially private and thus not the province of public social action, as well as to the determination of the theatre as industry by capitalist relations of production, working to maximize profit through the commodity of the star and the star role.' Kruger, *The National Stage*, 18.

10 For a discussion of the rise and fall of the Fédération nationale des amis du théâtre populaire, see Copfermann, *Le théâtre populaire, pourquoi?* 61–72.

11 '[L]e sport ne suscite qu'une morale de la force, alors que le théâtre d'Eschyle (*L'Orestie*) ou de Sophocle (*Antigone*) provoquait son public à une véritable émotion *politique*, l'engagement à pleurer l'homme englué dans la tyrannie d'une religion barbare ou d'une loi civique inhumaine' (Sports only give rise to a moral of force, while the theatre of Aeschylus [*The Oresteia*] or of Sophocles [*Antigone*] inspires in the public a truly *political* emotion, the commitment to weep for man mired in the tyranny of a barbaric religion or an inhuman civil law) (I 217).

12 Here Barthes again situates himself in opposition to Sartre, who the next year in *Théâtre populaire* will claim that such canonical works appeal to a petit-bourgeois sensibility more than a proletarian one, and that new plays written specifically for the working classes are needed: 'Jean-Paul Sartre nous parle du théâtre,' interview with Bernard Dort, *Théâtre populaire* 15 (September–October 1955), reprinted as 'People's Theater and Bourgeois

Theater' in *Sartre on Theater*, ed. Michel Contat and Michel Rybalka, trans.
Frank Jellinek (New York: Pantheon, 1976).

13 See Roland Barthes, 'Ruy Blas' (1954), (I 404–6); his comments on *Marie
Tudor* in '"L'Etourdi" ou le nouveau contremps' (1955), (I 524); the mythology 'La Dame aux Camélias,' (I 673–5; *M* 103–5); 'Le soulier de satin'
(1959), (I 819–20); and the impatient remarks on both Racine and Claudel
in 'Tragédie et hauteur' (1959), (I 814–15).

14 Barthes makes no direct reference to any Brechtian production before the
Berliner Ensemble's 1954 Paris performance of *Mother Courage*, still several
months away at the time of 'Pouvoirs de la tragédie antique' and 'The
World of Wrestling.' The extent of Barthes's familiarity with Brecht in 1953
is unclear, though he was no doubt aware of such an influential figure.
Vilar had already directed a controversial production of *Mother Courage* at
the TNP Barthes later writes: 'J'ai une grande reconnaissance envers le
Festival international d'art dramatique de Paris: je lui dois une découverte
qui a pris beaucoup d'importance dans ma vie d'amateur de théâtre: la
découverte, non de Brecht, que je connaissais déjà partiellement par le
texte, par Vilar, par Serreau, mais du Berliner Ensemble et de ses techniques de représentation' (I am grateful to the Paris International Festival
of Dramatic Arts: I am indebted to it for a discovery that assumed great
importance in my life as a theatre-goer: the discovery not of Brecht, whom
I already partially knew through his texts, through Vilar, through Serreau,
but of the Berliner Ensemble and its performance techniques) (I 728).

15 In his 'Petit manifeste de Suresnes,' written in 1951 at the refounding of
the TNP, Vilar offers a brief explanation of his stage aesthetic: 'pour [le
public], où que ce soit, notre scène s'offrira dans sa nudité formelle. Nul
colifichet, nulle tricherie adroite, nul décor. Seuls, l'amour et l'honneur de
Rodrigue pareront ce plancher de sapin que demain éclabousseront les
ivresses et les gras jurons de Falstaff ou de Mère Courage.' (For [the
public], wherever it may be, our stage will offer itself in its formal nudity.
No trinkets, no clever trickery, no décor. Only the love and honour of
Rodrigue will adorn these pine planks that tomorrow will be splashed
with the drunkenness and curses of Falstaff or Mother Courage.) Jean
Vilar, *Le théâtre: service public* (Paris: Gallimard, 1975), 145.

16 See Roland Barthes, 'A l'avant-garde de quel théâtre?' ('Whose Theater?
Whose *Avant-Garde*?'), (I 1224–26; *CE* 67–70).

17 See Roland Barthes, 'Fin de Richard II' (1954), (I 389–92). It should be
noted that Barthes earlier praises Philipe's performance in *The Prince of
Homburg*.

18 The Amis du théâtre populaire were engaged in a similar broadening of

interests, which led to tensions with the TNP. See Copfermann, *Le théâtre populaire, pourquoi?*

19 See Roland Barthes, 'Une tragédienne sans public' (1954), (I 410–12). Barthes will not always assess Casarès's acting so favourably. In the 'Racine Spoken' section of *On Racine* her 'hysterical' excesses emblematize less a distancing stylization than a mystifying display of psychological upheaval.

20 A collection of Vilar's writings on these and other topics spanning the years 1938–71 can be found in *Le théâtre, service public* (Paris: Gallimard, 1975). Some of Vilar's earlier interviews, writings, and letters are collected in *De la tradition théâtrale* (Paris: Gallimard, 1955). See also Jean Vilar, *Jean Vilar par lui-même* (Avignon: Maison Jean Vilar, 1991).

21 I am here disagreeing with Moriarty, who maintains that Barthes's 'popular' theatre was a primarily negative notion, opposed to 'bourgeois' aesthetics.

22 Roland Barthes, 'L'éblouissement' (1971), (II 1181–2).

23 Stafford suggests the editors' politicization and unconditional praise of Brecht precipitates Vilar's fall from grace in the pages of *Théâtre populaire*. Andy Stafford, 'Constructing a Radical Popular Theatre: Roland Barthes, Brecht, and *Théâtre populaire*,' *French Cultural Studies* 7 (1996): 39.

24 Bertolt Brecht, 'Short Description of a New Technique of Acting Which Produces an Alienation Effect,' in *Brecht on Theatre*, trans. John Willett (New York: Hill & Wang, 1964), 143.

25 Barthes refers to the very different 'historical complex' of East Germany in 'La revolution brechtienne' ('The Brechtian Revolution'), (I 1203; *CE* 38).

26 See Roland Barthes, '"Ubu roi"' (1955), (I 522–3).

27 Reviews of *The Cherry Orchard, Oedipus Rex*, Jean Duvignaud's *Marée Basse*, and Goldoni's *La Locandiera* between 1954 and 1956 all betray Barthes's impatience with the contemporary French stage. Reviews in following years show even less restrained scorn.

28 Camus's letter is included in the edition of Barthes's complete works. Albert Camus, 'Lettre d'Albert Camus à Roland Barthes sur "La Peste"' (I 457–458).

29 See Roger, *Roland Barthes, roman*, 175.

30 When Victor Kravchenko's exposé of Soviet prison camps, *I Chose Freedom*, was first published in a French translation, the French Communist Party and various left-leaning intellectuals, including Sartre, denounced it as unsubstantiated anti-communist propaganda and even questioned whether Kravchenko was the author. Kravchenko, a former Soviet official, sued *Les lettres françaises* for libel, and after calling survivors of Soviet

prison camps as witnesses won his case and received monetary damages. The Communist Party's vicious campaign against him participated in a broader refusal to recognize the brutality of Stalin's regime in the face of mounting evidence, and precipitated a crisis of confidence for many communist sympathizers.

31 Roger, 'Barthes with Marx,' 174.

32 In 1955, Jean Paulhan, under the pseudonym 'Jean Guérin,' asks why, if Barthes is Marxist, he does not come out and say so. In his terse response Barthes accuses his inquisitor of McCarthyism and refuses to answer the question. See Roland Barthes, 'Suis-je marxiste?' (1955), (I 499).

33 In addition to the 'aesthetically traditional' qualities of *Nekrassov*, Andy Stafford also notes another irony in Barthes's defense: the play ran in a boulevard theatre for an audience that was anything but popular. Stafford, 'Constructing a Radical Popular Theatre,' 42.

34 Barthes provides a schema of the four phases of his career and names the corresponding intertexts: the 'social mythology' phase in dialogue with Sartre, Marx, and Brecht; the 'semiology' phase with the intertext of Saussure; the 'textuality' phase with Sollers, Kristeva, Derrida, and Lacan; and the 'morality' phase with the intertext of Nietzsche placed in parentheses (I 205; *RB* 145).

35 Philip Thody, *Roland Barthes: A Conservative Estimate* (London: Macmillan, 1977).

36 For a detailed account of Barthes's appropriation of Brecht's dramaturgy, see Ellis Shookman, 'Barthes's Semiological Myth of Brecht's Epic Theater,' *Monatshefte* 18, no. 4 (1989): 459–75.

37 Stafford notes Barthes's 'rather indolent drama critic's cynicism.' Stafford, 'Constructing a Radical Popular Theatre,' 44.

38 For his remarks on Vinaver, see Roland Barthes, '"Aujourd'hui ou les Coréens" (1956), (I 556–7). Barthes's assessment of Planchon is usually positive, but as he nears the end of his tenure at *Théâtre populaire* he levels a familiar complaint against a Planchon production insofar as it fails to attain the exemplary semiosis of Brecht. As was often the case with Vilar, the choice of repertoire is in great part to blame: 'Ce qu'on demande? Qu'un tel exercice signifie quelque chose [...] est-ce qu'on pouvait raisonnablement espérer donner un sens aux *Trois Mousquetaires*?' (What do we demand? That such an exercise signify something [...] can one reasonably hope to give meaning to *The Three Musketeers*?) (I 848–9).

39 Roland Barthes, 'Commentaire: Préface à Brecht, "Mère Courage et ses enfants"' (1960), (I 889–905).

40 Stafford, 'Constructing a Radical Popular Theatre,' 47–8.

41 Philippe Roger, 'Barthes with Marx,' in *Writing the Image after Roland Barthes*, ed. Jean-Michel Rasaté (Philadelphia: University of Pennsylvania Press, 1997), 174–86.

42 Ross, *Fast Cars, Clean Bodies*, 161.

43 Vilar, *Le théatre, service public*, 165.

44 Ibid., 147.

45 Ibid., 153

46 The point here is not to suggest that Vilar is a wilful accomplice of the xenophobic far right. It is, rather, that by raising the question of his audience's national character without adequately acknowledging the tensions that inhere within invocations of the nation, as he does so thoroughly when pondering the 'people,' Vilar relinquishes control over the meanings that rush in to complete his thoughts with seductively simple 'common sense' answers, including those that insidiously 'go without saying' in the service of an ideology he might abhor. In the absence of further reflection on the national inflection of the TNP's spectators, one is left to extrapolate the distinction between Vilar's invocation of the good folk of France and similar phraseology when it circulates in different contexts, including that of the nationalist far-right discourse of Pierre Poujade and his followers in the 1950s and of the Front National today.

47 Dort suggests that Barthes's ambivalence towards theatre derives from 'quelque chose de la force et de l'évidence du corps' (something from the force and evidence of the body), and unlike most commentators of Barthes's writings on theatre entertains the possibility that his relative silence on performance practice after 1960 is paradoxically due as much to excessive love for performance as exasperation over bourgeois conventions. See Bernard Dort, 'Le "piège" du théâtre,' 689 and 703.

Chapter Two

1 Artaudian cruelty can manifest itself in varied and sometimes unexpected ways. In a surprising passage, Artaud identifies with Plato and aligns his theatre with an essential beauty, offering a rare glimpse of a euphoric and less violent cruelty. In his 'Alchemical theatre' Artaud imagines Plato as an enrapt spectator: '[The Mysteries of Eleusis] must have brought to a climax that nostalgia for pure beauty of which Plato, at least once in this world, must have found the complete, sonorous, streaming naked realization: to resolve by conjunctions unimaginably strange to our waking minds, to resolve or even annihilate every conflict produced by the antagonism of matter and mind, idea and form, concrete and abstract, and to

dissolve all appearances into one unique expression which must have been the equivalent of spiritualized gold.' Antonin Artaud, 'The Alchemical Theater,' *The Theater and Its Double*, trans. Mary Caroline Richard (Grove Press: New York, 1958), 52.

2 Jiří Veltruský, 'Man and Object in Theater' (1940), *A Prague School Reader on Esthetics, Literary Structure and Style*, ed. and trans. Paul L. Garvin (Washington: Georgetown University Press, 1964), 84.

3 Petr Bogatyrev, 'Semiotics in the Folk Theater' (1938), in *Semiotics of Art: Prague School Contributions*, ed. Ladislav Matejka and Irwin R. Titunik (Cambridge, MA: MIT Press, 1976), 34. Bogatyrev's conception of the 'material thing's' status in relation to the sign is somewhat ambiguous: at times the sign of the sign seems to supplant the material object altogether, and at other moments the materiality accompanies the signs. Freddie Rokem argues that this ambiguity does not weaken Bogatyrev's analysis, but makes it more complex than is appreciated by those who too quickly dismiss the particular dynamics of the decidedly unarbitrary sign on stage. See Freddie Rokem, 'A chair is a Chair is a CHAIR: The Object as Sign in the Theatrical Performance,' *The Prague School and Its Legacy*, ed. Yishai Tobin, *Linguistic & Literary Studies in Eastern Europe* 27 (Amsterdam and Philadelphia: John Benjamins Publishing Company, 1988), 275–88.

4 Jindřich Honzl, 'Dynamics of the Sign in the Theater' (1940), in Matejka and Titunik, *Semiotics of Art*, 75.

5 Ibid.

6 Veltruský, 'Man and Object in Theater,' 86. In a later observation, Veltruský writes: 'the stage figure and the stage action have only such qualities as are needed to fulfill their semiotic function; in other terms, the puppet is a pure sign because all its components are intentional.' Jiří Veltruský, 'Puppetry and Acting,' *Semiotica* 47 (1983): 69–122; quoted in Michael Quinn, *The Semiotic Stage: Prague School Theater Theory* (New York: Peter Lang, 1995), 92.

7 Artaud, 'Metaphysics and the Mise en Scene,' in *The Theater and Its Double*, 44. Artaud calls for such staging strategies throughout the essays in *The Theater and Its Double*. For example: 'Every spectacle will contain a physical and objective element [...] concrete appearances of new and surprising objects, masks, effigies yards high' (93); and 'ten thousand and one expressions of the face caught in the form of masks can be labeled and catalogued so they may eventually participate directly and symbolically in this concrete language of the stage, independently of their particular psychological use' (94).

8 Quinn, *The Semiotic Stage*, 75.

9 Veltruský, 'Puppetry and Acting,' 69.

10 Bogatyrev, 'Semiotics in the Folk Theater,' 48.

11 'In the puppet theater an actor does not exist as a live person; there the movements of the puppet actor are pure sign of sign.' Bogatyrev, 'Semiotics in the Folk Theater,' 48.

12 These early mythologies, written for *Esprit*, are longer than the many that would follow once the mythology became a regular rubric in *Les lettres nouvelles*. Of the three, only 'The World of Wrestling' appears in its entirety in the 1957 French edition. Even in its shorter form 'Visages et figures' counts among several mythologies that, for unstated reasons, are not included in the English translation of *Mythologies*.

13 For a more complete discussion of Barthes and the photographic image's *punctum*, see chapter 4.

14 The Baudelaire article predates, by a matter of weeks, Barthes's epiphanic discovery of Brecht.

15 Roland Barthes, 'Histoire et sociologie du vêtement: quelques observations méthologiques' (1957), I 741–52.

16 Roland Barthes, 'Préface à Brecht, 'Mère Courage et ses enfants' (1960), I 889–905.

17 Jean-Pierre Sarrazac locates the 'present-ness' of theater at the meeting point of Artaud and Brecht for critics and playwrights in 1950s France, and relates this notion to Barthes's own 'literalness' or 'literality.' Sarrazac suggests that the impossible ideal of a raw *hic et nunc* in performance leads to Barthes's disillusionment with the stage. However, Sarrazac does not draw a clear distinction between a live performer's 'presence' and the literality of an object described in a text, and he invokes a 'theatricality' whose broad figurative sweep obscures the singular anxiety that attends the live performing body. See Jean-Pierre Sarrazac, 'The Invention of "Theatricality": Rereading Bernard Dort and Roland Barthes,' *Substance* 31 (2002): 57–72.

18 François Dosse offers a helpful history of structuralism's inflection through different disciplines, personalities, and institutions. See François Dosse, *History of Structuralism*, 2 vols., trans. Deborah Glassman (Minneapolis: University of Minnesota Press, 1997).

19 Dosse writes that 'structural linguistics provided a method and a common language for bringing about a scientific renewal of the social sciences. Linguistics appeared as the model for a whole series of sciences lacking in formalism, and it penetrated ever more deeply into anthropology, literary criticism, and psychoanalysis and profoundly changed the mode of philosophical questioning.' Dosse, *History of Structuralism* I, 388.

20 This passage appears in a paragraph omitted in the *Œuvres complètes* edition.

21 Roland Barthes, 'Sur le système de la mode' (1967), II 462.

22 Kristen Ross notes the 'disembodied' aspect of structural man. Ross, *Fast Cars, Clean Bodies*, 161.

23 See chap. 1.

24 It is not an exaggeration to refer to the structuralist enterprise as an ambitious revolutionary coup. Lévi-Strauss, Lacan, and Barthes himself all had rather grandiose visions of uniting the 'human' sciences under the banner of a single interdisciplinary domain that would subsume the old academic disciplines of philosophy, history, and literature. See Dosse, *History of Structuralism* I, 316–48.

25 See the chapter entitled 'Africa: The Continental Divide of Structuralism' in Dosse, I, 264–72.

26 Ross, *Fast Cars, Clean Bodies*, 163.

Chapter Three

1 Timothy Murray, 'Introduction,' in *Mimesis, Masochism, and Mime: The Politics of Theatricality in Contemporary French Thought*, ed. Timothy Murray (Ann Arbor: University of Michigan Press, 1997), 2–3.

2 Antonin Artaud, *The Theater and Its Double*, trans. Mary Caroline Richards (New York: Grove Press, 1958), 8.

3 Jacques Derrida, 'La Parole soufflée,' *Writing and Difference*, trans. Alan Bass (Chicago: University of Chicago Press, 1978), 194.

4 Artaud, *The Theater and Its Double*, 51.

5 Jacques Derrida, 'The Theater of Cruelty and the Closure of Representation,' *Writing and Difference*, 250.

6 Lawrence Schehr, *The Shock of Men: Homosexual Hermeneutics in French Writing* (Stanford, CA: Stanford University Press, 1995), 97.

7 Julia Kristeva, 'The Subject in Process,' in *The Tel Quel Reader*, ed. Patrick ffrench and Roland-François Lack (London and New York: Routledge, 1998), 134.

8 Ibid., 166.

9 Kristeva's terms draw scepticism from those who question to what extent the *sémiotique* evades the compromised terms of a patriarchal symbolic order. Judith Butler traces two points of critique. First, the subversive *sémiotique* 'appears to depend on the stability and reproduction of precisely the paternal law that she [Kristeva] seeks to displace'; and second, it inflects this purportedly pure generative impulse with a meaning of its

own: 'Kristeva describes the maternal body as bearing a set of meanings that are prior to culture itself [...] her naturalistic descriptions of the maternal body effectively reify motherhood and preclude an analysis of its cultural construction and variability.' Judith Butler, *Gender Trouble: Feminism and the Subversion of Identity* (New York and London: Routledge, 1990), 80.

10 Julia Kristeva, 'Modern Theater Does Not Take (a) Place,' in *Mimesis, Masochism, and Mime*, Timothy Murray, ed., 280.

11 In *Roland Barthes by Roland Barthes*, Barthes compares his thought process to a fickle butterfly's trajectory ('La papillonne') (III 149; *RB*: 71–2).

12 D.A. Miller, *Bringing Out Roland Barthes* (Berkeley: University of California Press, 1992). Miller also locates a gay resonance even in Barthes's earliest writings. See D.A. Miller, 'Foutre! Bougre! Ecriture!' *Yale Journal of Criticism* 14 (2001): 503–11.

13 Ross Chambers, 'Pointless Stories, Storyless Points: Roland Barthes between "Soirées de Paris" and "Incidents,"' *L'Esprit Créateur* 34 (summer 1994): 12–30. For a tempered comment on the confluence of homosexuality and post-colonial privilege, see also Lawrence Schehr, 'Roland Barthes's Semioerotics,' *Canadian Review of Comparative Literature / Revue canadienne de littérature comparée* (March–June 1994): 65–77.

14 Murray Pratt, 'From "Incident" to "Texte": Homosexuality and Autobiography in Barthes's Later Writing,' *French Forum* 22 (May 1997): 231.

15 Pierre Saint-Amand, 'The Secretive Body: Roland Barthes's Gay Erotics,' *Yale French Studies* 90 (1996): 153–71.

16 Barbara Johnson, 'Bringing Out D.A. Miller,' *Narrative* 10:1 (2002): 7.

17 *Tel Quel* is a frequent forum for Barthes and many of his interlocutors. The journal's eclectic and mercurial editorial direction well suits the rapid changes and reversals of the theoretical climate of the 1960s and 1970s. Barthes is never an orthodox *Tel Quelien*, but he greatly admires Philip Sollers, the journal's chief editor and his close friend, and eventually publishes a collection of articles on Sollers's literary experiment in *Writer Sollers* (1979), trans. Philip Thody (Minneapolis: University of Minnesota Press, 1987). For a survey of the journal and successive positions staked out by its editors, see Danielle Marx-Scouras, *The Cultural Politics of Tel Quel: Literature and the Left in the Wake of Engagement* (University Park: Pennsylvania State University Press, 1996).

18 Even an apparently gratuitous detail for which no connotation seems to account has its meaning: that of 'reality' itself. See Barthes's 'L'effet du réel' ('The Reality Effect'), (II 479–84; *RL* 141–8).

19 Barthes uses the term 'symbolic' in an idiosyncratic manner that, as is typical, drifts somewhat even in a single work. For a useful situation of

the symbolic in *S/Z* against its Lacanian and stucturalist meanings, see
Schehr, *The Shock of Men*, 89.

20. Honoré de Balzac, 'Sarrasine,' reprinted in Barthes, Roland, *S/Z*: 238.

21 Ibid.

22 Ibid., 244.

23 For a study of Barthes's utopian places, see Diana Knight, *Barthes and
Utopia: Space Travel, Writing* (New York: Oxford University Press), 1997.

24 Balzac, 'Sarrasine,' 239.

25 Ibid., 237.

26 See chapter 2.

27 Balzac, 'Sarrasine,' 239.

28 Chambers, 'Pointless Stories, Storyless Points,' 19.

29 Joke Dame, 'Unveiled Voices: Sexual Difference and the Castrato,' in
Queering the Pitch: The New Gay and Lesbian Musicology, ed. Philip Brett,
Elizabeth Wood, and Gary C. Thomas (London and New York: Routledge,
1994), 139–53. Philip Stewart also observes Barthes's systematic ellipsis of
homosexual connotations in *S/Z*, most notably in Barthes's 'methodically
selective' reading of the cardinal/protector of La Zambinella and the
prince whose interest in the castrato dates to the singer's pre-operative
boyhood. Philip Stewart, 'What Barthes Couldn't Say: On the Curious
Occultation of Homoeroticism in *S/Z*,' *Paragraph* 24 (2002): 1–16.

30 Kaja Silverman, *The Acoustic Mirror: The Female Voice in Psychoanalysis and
Cinema* (Bloomington: Indiana University Press, 1988), 191.

31 Naomi Schor critically evaluates how Barthes's displacement of sexual
difference from ideal 'neutral' figures also entails the erasure of femininity,
and proposes the need to 'salvage the usable relics and refuse of patriar-
chy' rather than obliterate gender difference. Naomi Schor, 'Dreaming
Dissymmetry: Barthes, Foucault, and Sexual Difference,' in *Men in Feminism*, ed. Alice Jardine and Paul Smith (New York: Methuen, 1987): 110.
Jane Gallop, in her account of a feminist ambivalence towards Barthesian
pleasure, bluntly states her concerns: 'Women have historically been
associated with sexual difference, have been sexually differentiated from
the generic so-called mankind. The wish to escape sexual difference might
be but another mode of denying women. I distrust male homosexuals
because they choose men over women just as do our social and political
institutions, but they too share in the struggle against bipolar gender
constraints, against the compulsory choice of masculine or feminine.' Jane
Gallop, 'Feminist Criticism and the Pleasure of the Text,' *North Dakota
Quarterly* 54 (spring 1986): 131.

32 Silverman, *The Acoustic Mirror*, 193.

33 Carolyn Abbate, *Unsung Voices: Opera and Musical Narrative in the Nine-teenth Century* (Princeton, NJ: Princeton University Press, 1991), preface, xv.

34 Ibid.

35 It is significant that in this article, 'Le troisième sens: notes de recherche sur quelques photogrammes de S.M. Eisenstein' ('The Third Meaning: Research Notes on Some Eisenstein Stills'), Barthes propaedeutically excludes the body of live performance practice from his discussion of this 'useless' expenditure: 'quelque chose, dans les deux visages, excède la psychologie, l'anecdote, la fonction et pour tout dire le sens, sans pourtant se réduire à l'entêtement que tout corps humain met à être là' ('something in the two faces exceeds psychology, anecdote, function, exceeds meaning without, however, coming down to the obstinacy in presence shown by any human body') (II 868; *IMT* 54). Once again, Barthes recognizes the phenomenon of a stubborn corporeal presence only to quickly dismiss it from consideration.

36 See again Chambers, 'Pointless Stories, Storyless Points.'

37 Miller, *Bringing Out Roland Barthes*, 5.

38 Diana Knight, *Barthes and Utopia*, 153.

39 Barthes's blithe ignorance of the Japanese language and apparent disre-gard for the historical, ideological, and social investment in Japanese theatre, its traditions, and its narratives, recall Artaud's selective admira-tion for Balinese drama at the 1931 Colonial Exposition. In words that might also characterize Barthes's account of Bunraku, Patricia Clancy writes that there is no reason to believe that Artaud, when writing 'On Balinese Theater,' 'based it on anything other than his own reactions to the experience.' Patricia A. Clancy, 'Artaud and the Balinese Theatre,' *Modern Drama* 28, no. 3 (September 1985): 409.

40. The images of the two sons, as well as numerous other photographs, do not appear in the English translation of *Empire of Signs*.

41 Miller, *Bringing Out Roland Barthes*, 39.

42 Elin Diamond, *Unmaking Mimesis* (London and New York: Routledge, 1997), 20.

43 In Barthes's hand-corrected manuscripts, held at the Institut Mémoires de l'Edition Contemporaine (IMEC), one can observe where he replaces the less evocative 'expression' with 'hysteria.'

Chapter Four

1 Not all readers share the high regard for Barthes's later work. Jane Gallop notes the disagreement that characterizes accounts of Barthes's later

writings, and cites Steven Ungar's approving *Roland Barthes: The Professor of Desire* (Lincoln: University of Nebraska Press, 1983) and Annette Lavers's sceptical *Roland Barthes: Structuralism and After* (Cambridge: Harvard University Press, 1982) as emblematically polar assessments his post-structuralist work. Jane Gallop, 'Feminist Criticism and the Pleasure of the Text,' *North Dakota Quarterly* (spring 1986), 120–5.

2 In a 1978 article for *El País* Barthes acknowledges the demands of his writing on his translators: 'Pour moi, je dirais qu'il s'agit d'un style classique par la facture de la phrase, la syntaxe, et moderne par l'ambiguïté des mots, le poids des connotations – ce qui doit le rendre difficile à traduire dans une langue étrangère et fait que l'auteur a beaucoup de gratitude pour ses traducteurs' (For me, I would say it is a matter of classical style in the crafting of the sentence and the syntax, and modern by the ambiguity of the words and the weight of connotations – which must make it difficult to translate into a foreign language and makes the author very grateful to his translators) (III 848).

3 *Physis* is Barthes's word for the suspect 'natural.'

4 See the fragments entitled 'La scène' ('Scenes') and 'La science dramatisée' ('Science Dramatized') (III 216–19; *RB* 159–61).

5 Critics have observed that both of these tendencies and their opposing conclusions evince the ambivalence towards rhetoric and rhetorical figures that is found in Barthes's later writing. Commenting on *Roland Barthes by Roland Barthes* Michel Beaujour observes a hostility towards rhetoric, while Philippe Roger, refuting Beaujour's claim, remarks that rhetoric, unlike fascist language, is not what coerces us to speak but what permits us to speak, and notes rhetoric's 'triumphant return' in *Roland Barthes by Roland Barthes*. See Michel Beaujour, *Miroirs d'encre* (Paris: Seuil, 1980): 267–8; and Philippe Roger, *Roland Barthes, roman* (Paris: Bernard Grasset, 1986): 179.

6 A frequently cited example of asyndeton is '*Veni. Vedi. Vici.*' The logic of cause and effect that links these propositions is left unsaid. It is not, for example, 'First I came, but then I saw, so therefore I conquered.'

7 As early as 1954, when still active as a theatre critic and clearly impassioned with the theatre, in 'Baudelaire's Theater' Barthes already distinguishes between a favourable theatricality and a suspect theatre. Michael Moriarty suggests that while Baudelaire, according to Barthes, achieved an ideal theatricality only in his non-dramatic texts, Barthes effectively does the inverse: 'he was henceforth to make contact with theatricality everywhere else except in the theatre.' Michael Moriarty, 'Barthes's Theatrical Aesthetic,' *Nottingham French Studies* 36, no. 1 (spring 1997), 13.

8 The books in the *Ecrivains de toujours* series usually include passages of a well-known writer's own texts, organized around key themes or by chronology, and interspersed with the commentary of the editor. Barthes makes an earlier contribution to this series with his *Michelet par lui-même*, published in 1954. The irony of Barthes writing his own volume for this series blurs the line between writer and commentator, author and editor, object and subject, language and metalanguage, and further contributes to the multiple and fragmented images of Barthes that emerge in *Roland Barthes by Roland Barthes*.

9 Even as its terms proliferate in Barthes's texts, psychoanalysis, as a discourse that often stakes scientific and empirical truth claims of its own, is held at a distance. In *Roland Barthes by Roland Barthes* he writes: 'Son rapport à la psychanalyse n'est pas scrupuleux (sans qu'il puisse pourtant se prévaloir d'aucune contestation, d'aucun refus). C'est un rapport *indécis*' ('His relationship to psychoanalysis is not scrupulous (though without being able to pride himself on any constestation, any rejection). It is an *undecided* relation') (III 209; *RB* 150). In a 1977 interview he characterizes his relation to psychoanalysis in *A Lover's Discourse: Fragments*: 'le rapport que j'ai dans ce livre avec le psychanalyse est très ambigu; c'est un rapport qui, comme toujours, utilise des descriptions, des notions psychanalytiques, mais qui les utilise un peu comme les éléments d'une fiction, qui n'est pas forcément crédible' ('my relation to psychoanalysis in this book is quite ambiguous; it's a relation that uses psychoanalytical descriptions and ideas, as usual, but uses them a bit like the elements of fiction, which is not necessarily credible') (III 778; *GV* 288).

10 One might question the purported arbitrariness of Barthes's alphabetical ordering. *Roland Barthes by Roland Barthes* went through several editorial drafts, and many fragments were in the end not chosen to be included in the book. The titles of some changed throughout the process, which would explain why some entries appear out of order, but there also seems to be some thematic grouping and connections between successive fragments that seem more than felicitous accident: 'La jeune fille bourgeois' (The Middle-Class Maiden) is apparently out of alphabetical order and followed by the closely related 'l'amateur' (The Amateur), and the entry on 'Le corps' (The Body) is followed immediately by a reflection on Barthes's own body in 'La côtelette' (The Rib Chop). Occasionally one can detect an overarching structure, such as the placing of the fragment 'Le monstre de la totalité' (The Monster of Totality), which Barthes identifies as the first fragment to be written for *Roland Barthes by Roland Barthes*, at the end of the book.

11 Ann Ubersfeld, *L'école du spectateur: Lire le théâtre II* (Paris: Editions Sociales, 1977), 165–6. Author's translation.

12 Patrice Pavis, *Problèmes de sémiologie théâtrale* (Montreal: Presses de l'Université du Québec, 1976), 23. Pavis ultimately claims that the iconic quality of theatre nonetheless participates in a coded system, but he does not revisit the question of the performer's body and its exceptional resistance. Keir Elam also encounters resistance in the body, and although he offers several layers of signs to account for it, culminating in an individual 'idiolect,' it remains unclear whether even his complex account exhausts corporeality. Would not two performer's 'speaking' the same idiolect with their bodies each do so with an individual 'accent' of their own? Elam concedes that 'it is difficult to identify general and stable kinesic codes and subcodes in our theater.' Keir Elam, *The Semiotics of Theatre and Drama* (London: Routledge, 1980), 77.

13 Umberto Eco, *A Theory of Semiotics* (Bloomington: Indiana University Press, 1976), 202.

14 Ibid.

15 The same could be asked of the Bunraku manipulators: the wooden puppet might be the inanimate excess to their gestures, dispelling the illusion of originary life or presence in the represented character, but what of their own distinctly *animate* presence?

16 See chapter 3.

17 Bernard Dort, in his brief commentary on this passage, writes that performer and spectator alike gain nothing by crossing the footlights. Theatre is a barrier, a horizon, not what lies on either side: 'le théâtre dessine toujours une frontière' (theatre always traces a border). Bernard Dort, 'Le "piège" du théâtre,' *Critique* 423–4 (August–September 1982), 702.

18 Lawrence Schehr, *The Shock of Men: Homosexual Hermeneutics in French Writing* (Stanford, CA: Stanford University Press, 1995), 121.

19 The English translation's 'openly' fails to capture the significance and resonance of Barthes's choice of words in this passage.

20 Pierre Saint-Amand, 'The Secretive Body: Roland Barthes's Gay Erotics,' *Yale French Studies* 90 (1996): 171.

21 Elin Diamond cites other cases of 'hysterical hallucination' in the male spectator. Elin Diamond, *Unmaking Mimesis* (London and New York: Routledge, 1997), 37. It is possible that Saint-Amand is referring to another photo included in *Roland Barthes by Roland Barthes*, apparently taken the same day as the one he describes, in which Barthes kneels next to his mother and half-brother and possibly reveals some 'luminous nudity,' though much of Barthes's torso remains covered.

22 Joseph von Eichendorff captures this typically romantic sentiment in the final verse of 'Im Abendrot.'

23 Lavers observes: 'Barthes sacrificed his aggression in order to gain acceptance of all the aspects of himself which had for so long been repressed.' Lavers, *Roland Barthes*, 210.

24 In this respect the English translation of the title, which attributes the discourse to a subject (the lover), is infelicitous. It is not, however, an easy title to translate. More accurate renderings would be *Fragments of an Amorous Discourse* or *Fragments of a Discourse of Being in Love*, which do not inscribe a proprietary subject as the origin of the discourse but define love as a discursive site. The translation of the substantive 'l'amoureux' poses a similar problem. The common English rendering is 'lover' (in French 'l'amant'), while a more accurate translation would be 'one who is in love.'

25 Barthes expresses his feelings of this time, at moments nearing panic, in the journal entries included in the 1979 article 'Déliberation' (III 1004–14; *RL* 362–9).

26 Barthes's lover is marked as male, leading Naomi Schor, Barthes's suggestions notwithstanding, to challenge the neutrality of the lover's sexual indifference. Schor locates passages of *A Lover's Discourse: Fragments* that fall 'into a paradoxical reinscription of the very difference the strategy was designed to denaturalize.' Naomi Schor, 'Dreaming Dyssymmetry: Barthes, Foucault, and Sexual Difference,' in *Men in Feminism*, ed. Alice Jardine and Paul Smith (New York: Methuen, 1987), 100.

27 Facsimile reproductions of Barthes's notes for his *Vita Nova*, along with annotated transcriptions, are included in his collected works (III 1287–94, 1299–1307).

28 The date in one of Barthes's outlines for the *Vita Nova* is exactly a year later, 15 April 1979, which is also the day Barthes claims to begin composing the text of *Camera Lucida*. The coincidence raises the question of whether he alters the date in the other drafts, and if so, why he deems this necessary.

29 Nancy M. Shawcross relates *Camera Lucida* to earlier theorizations of text, music, 'play,' and writing in *Roland Barthes on Photography: The Critical Tradition in Perspective* (Gainesville: University Press of Florida, 1997), 73. One can, however, overstate the 'writerly' aspect of *Camera Lucida*. In an earlier remark Shawcross observes that Barthes's book 'unfolds like a mystery novel,' a genre characterized less by writerly textuality that linear readerliness.

30 Shawcross, *Roland Barthes on Photography*, 1–24 passim. Shawcross's

opening chapter offers a useful survey of Barthes's lifelong engagement with the photographic image.

31 Lavers, *Roland Barthes*, 215. Lavers counts among the critics who consider Barthes's later career as a time of decadence. Her study of Barthes's writings is almost entirely devoted to 1960s structuralism and all but ends with *S/Z*; the final decade of his life, and the discussion of *The Pleasure of the Text, Roland Barthes by Roland Barthes*, and *A Lover's Discourse: Fragments* (*Camera Lucida* had only just appeared) are confined to a single chapter. In a brief coda on the newly published *Camera Lucida* and more generally on Barthes's later career, Lavers tempers the admiration that suffuses her account of semiology and structuralism and registers palpable disapproval of a theoretical fiction 'whose attendant risks of subjectivism are obvious.'

32 'The genotext is thus the only transfer of drive energies that organizes a space in which the subject is not *yet* a split unity that will become blurred, giving rise to the symbolic. Instead, the space it organizes is one in which the subject will be *generated* as such by a process of faciliations and marks within the constraints of the biological and social structure.' Julia Kristeva, *Revolution in Poetic Language* (1974), trans. Margaret Waller (New York: Columbia University Press, 1984), 86.

33 Susan Sontag, an avid reader of Barthes, suggests the violent nature of photography. See Susan Sontag, *On Photography* (New York: Farrar, Strauss & Giroux), 1977. I would like to thank Cat Zuromskis for her insight into the phenomenon of the snapshot.

34 Derek Attridge, 'Roland Barthes's Obtuse, Sharp Meaning,' in *Writing the Image after Roland Barthes*, ed. Jean-Michel Rabaté (Philadelphia: University of Philadelphia Press, 1997), 80.

35 See Diana Knight, 'The Woman without a Shadow,' in *Writing the Image after Roland Barthes*, ed. Jean-Michel Rabaté (Philadelphia: University of Pennsylvania Press, 1997), 138. Knight observes that the mother's pose, as Barthes describes it in the Winter Garden image, is remarkably similar to that of his mother as a young girl in another photograph entitled 'La Souche,' reproduced near the end of *Camera Lucida*.

36 Attridge, 'Roland Barthes's Obtuse, Sharp Meaning,' 81.

37 See chapter 2.

Works Cited

Abbate, Carolyn. *Unsung Voices: Opera and Musical Narrative in the Nineteenth Century*. Princeton, NJ: Princeton University Press, 1991.

Alphant, Marianne, and Nathalie Léger, eds. *R/B; Roland Barthes*. Paris: Seuil, Centre Pompidou and IMEC, 2002.

Apter, Emily. 'Acting Out Orientalism: Sapphic Theatricality in Turn-of-the-Century Paris.' In *Performance and Cultural Politics*, ed. Elin Diamond, 15–34. London and New York: Routledge, 1996.

Artaud, Antonin. *The Theater and Its Double*, trans. Mary Caroline Richard. New York: Grove Press, 1958.

Attridge, Derek. 'Roland Barthes's Obtuse, Sharp Meaning,' in *Writing the Image after Roland Barthes*, ed. Jean-Michel Rabaté, 77–89. Philadelphia: University of Pennsylvania Press, 1997.

Auslander, Philip. *Liveness*. New York: Routledge, 1999.

– 'Liveness: Performance and the Anxiety of Simulation.' *Performance and Cultural Politics*. In *Performance and Cultural Politics*, ed. Elin Diamond, 196–213. London and New York: Routledge, 1996.

– *Presence and Resistance*. Ann Arbor: University of Michigan Press, 1997.

– Rebuttal. *Drama Review* 38 (1994): 185–7.

– Review of *The Theory-Death of the Avant-Garde* by Paul Mann, *The Object of Performance: The American Avant-Garde since 1970* by Henry M. Sayre, *Performing Drama/Dramatizing Performance: Alternative Theatre and the Dramatic Text* by Michael Vanden Heuvel, and *Theatre, Theory, Postmodernism* by Johannes Birringer. *Drama Review* 37 (1993): 196–201.

– Review of *Unmarked: The Politics of Performance* by Peggy Phelan. *Drama Review* 38 (1994): 185–7.

Barthes, Roland. *A Barthes Reader*, ed. Susan Sontag. New York: Hill & Wang, 1982.

– *Camera Lucida*, trans. Richard Howard. New York: Hill & Wang (Noonday Press), 1981.
– *Critical Essays*, trans. Richard Howard. Evanston, IL: Northwestern University Press, 1972.
– *Criticism and Truth*, trans. Katrine Pilcher Keuneman. London: Athlone, 1987.
– *Ecrits sur le théâtre*, ed. Jean-Loup Rivière. Paris: Seuil, 2002.
– *Elements of Semiology*, trans. Annette Lavers and Colin Smith. New York: Hill & Wang, 1967.
– *Empire of Signs*, trans. Richard Howard. New York: Hill & Wang, 1982.
– *The Fashion System*, trans. Matthew Ward and Richard Howard. New York: Hill & Wang, 1983.
– *Image Music Text*, trans. Stephen Heath. New York: Hill & Wang, 1977.
– *Incidents*, trans. Richard Howard. Berkeley: University of California Press, 1992.
– *A Lover's Discourse: Fragments*, trans. Richard Howard. New York: Hill & Wang, 1978.
– ed. *Michelet par lui-même*, trans. Richard Howard. New York: Hill & Wang, 1987.
– *Mythologies*, trans. Annette Lavers. New York: Hill & Wang, 1972.
– *Œuvres complètes*, vols. 1–3, ed. Eric Marty. Paris: Seuil, 1993.
– *On Racine*, trans. Richard Howard. New York: Performing Arts Journal Publications, 1983.
– *The Pleasure of the Text*, trans. Richard Miller. New York: Hill & Wang, 1975.
– *Roland Barthes*, trans. Richard Howard. New York: Hill & Wang, 1977.
– *The Rustle of Language*, trans. Richard Howard. Berkeley and Los Angeles: University of California Press, 1986.
– *Sade, Fourier, Loyola*, trans. Richard Miller. New York: Hill & Wang, 1976.
– *S/Z*, trans. Richard Miller. New York: Hill & Wang, 1974.
– *Writer Sollers*, trans. Philip Thody. Minneapolis: University of Minnesota Press, 1987.
– *Writing Degree Zero*, trans. Annette Lavers and Colin Smith. New York: Hill & Wang, 1968.
Beaujour, Michel. *Miroirs d'encre*. Paris: Seuil, 1980.
Bensmaïa, Reda. *The Barthes Effect: The Essay as Reflective Text*, trans. Pat Fedkiew. Minneapolis: University of Minnesota Press, 1987.
Blau, Herbert. *Take Up the Bodies: Theatre at the Vanishing Point*. Chicago: University of Illinois Press, 1982.
Bogatyrev, Petr. 'Semiotics in the Folk Theater.' In *Semiotics of Art: Prague School Contributions*, ed. Ladislav Matejka and Irwin R. Titunik, 33–50. Cambridge, MA: MIT Press, 1976.

Brecht, Bertolt. *Brecht on Theatre,* trans. John Willett. New York: Hill & Wang, 1964.

Brémond, Claude, and Thomas Pavel. *De Barthes à Balzac: Fictions d'une critique, critiques d'une fiction.* Paris: Albin Michel, 1998.

Brett, Phillip, Elizabeth Wood, and Gary C. Thomas, eds. *Queering the Pitch: The New Gay and Lesbian Musicology.* London and New York: Routledge, 1994.

Brooks, Peter, and Naomi Schor. 'Roland Barthes: Twenty Years After,' *Yale Journal of Criticism* 14, no. 2 (2001): 433–7.

Butler, Judith. *Bodies That Matter: On the Discursive Limits of 'Sex.'* New York and London: Routledge, 1993.

– *Gender Trouble: Feminism and the Subversion of Identity.* London and New York: Routledge, 1990.

– 'Performative Acts and Gender Constitution: An Essay in Phenomenology and Feminist Theory.' In *Performing Feminisms: Feminist Critical Theory and Theatre,* ed. Sue-Ellen Case, 270–82. Baltimore: Johns Hopkins University Press, 1990.

Calvet, Louis-Jean. *Roland Barthes: A Biography.* Bloomington: University of Indiana Press, 1994.

Camus, Albert. 'Lettre à Roland Barthes sur "la Peste."' In Roland Barthes, *Œuvres complètes,* vol. 1, ed. Eric Marty, 457–8. Paris: Seuil, 1993.

Carlson, Marvin. *Performance: An Introduction.* London and New York: Routledge, 1996.

Case, Sue-Ellen, 'The Naked Body and Theories of Performance.' *Substance* 31 (2002): 186–200.

– ed. *Performing Feminisms: Feminist Critical Theory and Theatre.* Baltimore: Johns Hopkins University Press, 1990.

Chambers, Ross. 'Pointless Stories, Storyless Points: Roland Barthes between "Soirées de Paris" and "Incidents."' *L'Esprit Créateur* 34 (summer 1994): 12–30.

Clancy, Patricia A. 'Artaud and the Balinese Theatre.' *Modern Drama* 28, no. 3 (September 1985): 397–412.

Compagnon, Antoine. 'Who Is the Real One?' In *Writing the Image after Roland Barthes,* ed. Jean-Michel Rabaté, 196–200. Philadelphia: University of Pennsylvania Press, 1997.

Copfermann, Emile. *Le théâtre populaire, pourquoi?* Paris: François Maspero, 1965.

Coste, Claude. *Roland Barthes moraliste.* Lille: Presses Universitaires du Septentrion, 1998.

Culler, Jonathan. *Roland Barthes.* New York: Oxford University Press, 1983.

Dame, Joke. 'Unveiled Voices: Sexual Difference and the Castrato.' In *Queering the Pitch: The New Gay and Lesbian Musicology*, ed. Phillip Brett, Elizabeth Wood, and Gary C. Thomas, 139–53. London and New York: Routledge, 1994.

Derrida, Jacques. *Writing and Difference*, trans. Alan Bass. Chicago: University of Chicago Press, 1978.

Diamond, Elin, ed. *Performance and Cultural Politics*. London and New York: Routledge, 1996.

– *Unmaking Mimesis*. London and New York: Routledge, 1997.

Dolan, Jill. 'Geographies of Learning: Theatre Studies, Performance, and the Performative.' *Theatre Journal* 45 (1993): 417–41.

– *Presence and Desire*. Ann Arbor: University of Michigan Press, 1993.

Dort, Bernard. 'Jean-Paul Sartre nous parle du théâtre.' *Théâtre populaire* 15 (September–October 1955). Reprinted as 'People's Theater and Bourgeois Theater.' In *Sartre on Theater,* ed. Michel Contat and Michel Rybalka, trans. Frank Jellinek. New York: Pantheon, 1976.

– 'Le "piège" du théâtre.' *Critique* 423–4 (August-September 1982): 688–703.

Dosse, François. *History of Structuralism*, vols. 1 and 2, trans. Deborah Glassman. Minneapolis: University of Minnesota Press, 1997.

Duvignaud, Jean. 'Théâtre populaire: histoire d'une revue.' *Magazine littéraire* 314 (October 1993): 63–4.

Eco, Umberto. *A Theory of Semiotics*. Bloomington: Indiana University Press, 1976.

Elam, Keir. *The Semiotics of Theatre and Drama*. London: Routledge, 1980.

Falzoi, Jill. Letter to the editor. *Drama Review* 38 (1994): 13–17.

Féral, Josette. 'Performance and Theatricality: The Subject Demystified.' In *Mimesis, Masochism, and Mime: The Politics of Theatricality in Contemporary French Thought*, ed. Timothy Murray, 289–300. Ann Arbor: University of Michigan Press, 1997.

– 'Theatricality: The Specificity of Theatrical Language.' *Substance* 31 (2002): 94–108.

Freud, Sigmund. *Beyond the Pleasure Principle,* trans. James Strachey. New York: Norton, 1961.

Gallop, Jane. 'Feminist Criticism and the Pleasure of the Text.' *North Dakota Quarterly* 54 (spring 1986): 119–32.

Garvin, Paul L., ed. *A Prague School Reader on Esthetics, Literary Structure and Style*. Washington, DC: Georgetown University Press, 1964.

Honzl, Jindřich. 'Dynamics of the Sign in the Theater.' In *Semiotics of Art: Prague School Contributions*, eds. Ladislav Matejka and Irwin R. Titunik, 74–93. Cambridge: MIT Press, 1976.

Johnson, Barbara. 'Bringing Out D.A. Miller.' *Narrative* 10:1 (2002): 3–8.

Kleist, Heinrich von. 'On the Marionette Theater.' 1810. Trans. Roman Paska. In *Zone 3: Fragments for a History of the Human Body, Part One*, ed. Michel Feher, Ramona Nadaff, and Nadia Tazi, 415–20. Cambridge: MIT Press, 1989.

Knight, Diana. *Barthes and Utopia: Space, Travel, Writing*. New York: Oxford University Press, 1997.

– 'The Woman without a Shadow. In *Writing the Image after Roland Barthes*, ed. Jean-Michel Rabaté, 132–43. Philadelphia: University of Pennsylvania Press, 1997.

Kristeva, Julia. 'Modern Theater Does Not Take (a) Place.' In *Mimesis, Masochism, and Mime: The Politics of Theatricality in Contemporary French Thought*, ed. Timothy Murray, 277–81. Ann Arbor: University of Michigan Press, 1997.

– *Revolution in Poetic Language*, trans. Margaret Waller. New York: Columbia University Press, 1984.

– 'The Subject in Process.' In *The Tel Quel Reader*, ed. Patrick ffrench and Roland-François Lack, 133–78. London and New York: Routledge, 1998.

Kruger, Loren. *The National Stage: Theatre and Cultural Legitimation in England, France, and America*. Chicago: University of Chicago Press, 1992.

Lacan, Jacques. *Ecrits*, trans. Alan Sheridan. New York: Norton, 1977.

Lavers, Annette. *Roland Barthes: Structuralism and After*. Cambridge, MA: Harvard University Press, 1982.

Leclerc, Guy. *Le TNP de Jean Vilar*. Paris: 10/18, 1971.

Marx-Scouras, Danielle. *The Cultural Politics of Tel Quel: Literature and the Left in the Wake of Engagement*. University Park: Pennsylvania State University Press, 1996.

Matejka, Ladislav, and Irwin R. Titunik, eds. *Semiotics of Art: Prague School Contributions*. Cambridge: MIT Press, 1976.

Miller, D.A. *Bringing Out Roland Barthes*. Berkeley: University of California Press, 1992.

– 'Foutre! Bougre! Ecriture!' *Yale Journal of Criticism* 14 (2001): 503–11.

Moriarty, Michael. 'Barthes's Theatrical Aesthetic.' *Nottingham French Studies* 36, no. 1 (Spring 1997): 3–13.

– *Roland Barthes*. Stanford, CA: Stanford University Press, 1991.

Murray, Timothy, ed. *Mimesis, Masochism, and Mime: The Politics of Theatricality in Contemporary French Thought*. Ann Arbor: University of Michigan Press, 1997.

Pavis, Patrice. *Problèmes de sémiologie théâtrale*. Montreal: Presses de l'Université du Québec, 1976.

Phelan, Peggy. *Unmarked: The Politics of Performance*. New York: Routledge, 1993.

Pratt, Murray. 'From 'Incident' to 'Texte': Homosexuality and Autobiography in Barthes's Later Writing.' *French Forum* 22 (May 1997): 217–33.

Quinn, Michael. *The Semiotic Stage: Prague School Theater Theory.* New York: Peter Lang, 1995.

Rabaté, Jean-Michel, ed. *Writing the Image after Roland Barthes.* Philadelphia: University of Pennsylvania Press, 1997.

Reinelt, Janelle. 'The Politics of Discourse: Performance Meets Theatricality.' *Substance* 31 (2002): 201–15.

Roger, Philippe. 'Barthes with Marx.' In *Writing the Image after Roland Barthes,* ed. Jean-Michel Rabaté, 174–86. Philadelphia: University of Pennsylvania Press, 1997.

– *Roland Barthes, roman.* Paris: Bernard Grasset, 1986.

Rokem, Freddie. 'A chair is a Chair is a CHAIR: The Object as Sign in the Theatrical Performance.' In *The Prague School and Its Legacy,* ed. Yishai Tobin, 275–88. *Linguistic and Literary Studies in Eastern Europe* 27. Amsterdam and Philadelphia: John Benjamins Publishing Company, 1988.

Ross, Kristin. *Fast Cars, Clean Bodies: Decolonization and the Reordering of French Culture.* Cambridge, MA: MIT Press, 1995.

Rylance, Rick. *Roland Barthes.* Hemel Hempstead: Harvester Wheatsheaf, 1994.

Saint-Amand, Pierre. 'The Secretive Body: Roland Barthes's Gay Erotics.' *Yale French Studies* 90 (1996): 153–71.

Sarrazac, Jean-Pierre. 'The Invention of "Theatricality": Rereading Bernard Dort and Roland Barthes. *Substance* 31 (2002): 57–72.

Sartre, Jean-Paul. *Sartre on Theater,* ed. Michel Contat and Michel Rybalka, trans. Frank Jellinek. New York: Pantheon, 1976.

Schehr, Lawrence. 'Roland Barthes's Semioerotics.' *Canadian Review of Comparative Literature/Revue canadienne de littérature comparée* (March–June 1994): 65–77.

– *The Shock of Men: Homosexual Hermeneutics in French Writing.* Stanford, CA: Stanford University Press, 1995.

Scheie, Timothy. 'Body Trouble: Corporeal "Presence" and Performative Identity in Cixous's and Mnouchkine's *L'Indiade ou l'Inde de leurs rêves.*' *Theatre Journal* 46 (March 1994): 31–44.

– '"Questionable Terms": Shylock, Céline's *L'Eglise,* and the Performative.' *Text and Performance Quarterly* 17 (April 1997): 153–69.

Schor, Naomi. 'Dreaming Dissymmetry: Barthes, Foucault, and Sexual Difference.' In *Men in Feminism,* ed. Alice Jardine and Paul Smith, 98–110. New York: Methuen, 1987.

Shawcross, Nancy M. *Roland Barthes on Photography: The Critical Tradition in Perspective.* Gainesville: University Press of Florida, 1997.

Shookman, Ellis. 'Barthes's Semiological Myth of Brecht's Epic Theater.'
   Monatshefte 18, no. 4 (1989).

Silverman, Kaja. *The Acoustic Mirror: The Female Voice in Psychoanalysis and
   Cinema*. Bloomington: Indiana University Press, 1988.

Sontag, Susan. *On Photography*. New York: Farrar, Strauss & Giroux, 1977.

Stafford, Andy. 'Constructing a Radical Popular Theatre: Roland Barthes,
   Brecht, and *Théâtre populaire*.' *French Cultural Studies* 7 (1996): 33–48.

– *Roland Barthes: Phenomenon and Myth*. Edinburgh: Edinburgh University
   Press, 1998.

Stewart, Phillip. 'What Barthes Couldn't Say: On the Curious Occultation of
   Homoeroticism in *S/Z*.' *Paragraph* 24 (2002): 1–16.

Thody, Philip. *Roland Barthes: A Conservative Estimate*. London: Macmillan,
   1977.

Ubersfeld, Ann. *L'école du spectateur: Lire le théâtre II*. Paris: Editions Sociales,
   1977.

Ungar, Steven. *Roland Barthes: The Professor of Desire*. Lincoln: University of
   Nebraska Press, 1983

Veltruský, Jiří. 'Man and Object in Theater.' In *A Prague School Reader on
   Esthetics, Literary Structure and Style,* ed. and trans. Paul L. Garvin, 83–91.
   Washington: Georgetown University Press, 1964.

– 'Puppetry and Acting.' *Semiotica* 47 (1983). Quoted in Michael Quinn. *The
   Semiotic Stage: Prague School Theater Theory*. Peter Lang: New York, 1995.

Vilar, Jean. *De la tradition théâtrale*. Paris: Gallimard, 1955.

– *Jean Vilar par lui-même*. Avignon: Maison Jean Vilar, 1991.

– *Le théâtre: service public*. Paris: Gallimard, 1975.

Index